Law of Arbitration

The daring publisher, Universal Law Publishing Company, among the foremost in the law publishing field and progressive in venturing to bring out rare legal literature of avant garde *character has rightly enriched the* corpus juris *of India*

Justice V R Krishna Iyer
Random Reflections, page 14

Law of Arbitration

P.K. Basu Majumdar

B.Tech., LL.B., FICA
Senior Consultant, Fox Mandal Little
Former Executive Director and Principal Law Officer
Steel Authority of India Ltd.

Foreword by

Dr. Justice Arijit Pasayat

Judge, Supreme Court of India

&

Jagdeep Dhankhar

Senior Advocate, Supreme Court of India
Formerly Member, ICC International Council of Arbitration, Paris

Universal
Law Publishing Co. Pvt. Ltd.
NEW DELHI - INDIA

2011 Edition

ISBN: 978-93-5035-021-8

Published by
UNIVERSAL LAW PUBLISHING CO. PVT. LTD.
C-FF-1A, Dilkhush Industrial Estate,
(Near Azadpur Metro Station) G.T. Karnal Road,
Delhi-110 033
Tel.: 011-27438103, 27215334, 42381334
Fax : 011-27458529
E-mail *(For sales inquiries)* : sales@unilawbooks.com
E-mail *(For editorial inquiries)* : edit@unilawbooks.com
Website : www.unilawbooks.com

Recommended citation: P.K. Basu Majumdar, *Law of Arbitration,* (New Delhi: Universal Law Publishing Co. Pvt. Ltd., 2011)

Computer Typeset at Aesthetic and *Printed* at Mudrak, New Delhi

Dr. Justice Arijit Pasayat
Judge,
Supreme Court of India (Retd.)

Banglow No. 84, New Moti Bagh,
New Delhi-110023
Tel.: 24105683, 24105684 (Res.)

FOREWORD

Arbitration is a well recognized mode for resolving disputes arising out of commercial transactions. This is equally true for international commercial transactions.

The Arbitration Act, 1940 (in short the '1940 Act') consolidated and amended the law relating to arbitration as contained in the Indian Arbitration Act, 1899 and the Second Schedule to the Code of Civil Procedure, 1908. It was also largely based on the English Arbitration Act, 1934.

The successor Act is Arbitration and Conciliation Act, 1996. The object of the said statute is to consolidate and amend the law relating to domestic arbitration international commercial arbitration, and the enforcement of foreign arbitral awards. The said Act repealed the three earlier Acts, namely 1937 Act, 1940 Act and 1961 Act.

Arbitration is no longer an Alternate Dispute Resolution ('ADR') mechanism. It is the forum of choice for resolving disputes arising out of international and domestic commercial contracts. It gives an opportunity to the parties to resolve conflict of laws and select substantive and procedural laws and rules in keeping with the spirit of the contractual provisions, and parties' perception of the strengths of various legal sub-systems.

The ADR movement has led to growth of arbitral institutions in India including some specialized sector specific arbitral institutions like those for the construction industry, shipping industry, etc.

The Author, who worked as Executive Director and General Counsel of one the largest Public Sector Undertaking in India has used his professional expertise to pen this Book. He has highlighted the positive as well as weak aspects of the law relating to Arbitration. According to him, the parties together, with assistance from the Arbitral Tribunal, can make the process less time consuming and more transparent. This will also lay to rest the trend that has developed in India to challenge every arbitral award.

Institutional arbitrations obviously are better than *'ad-hoc'* ones. In institutional arbitration, a neutral institution oversees the process, thus lending it credibility through fair and impartial conduct. The institution can fast track the process to see that it is quickly and efficiently carried forward, and exercises great influence on the parties and the arbitrator. It can also find out ways of keeping the costs down.

It is widely assumed that many parties select arbitration to resolve their disputes at least in part because an arbitral award offers an effective and early end to the dispute in a way that a court judgment does not. Increased finality, so the argument goes, brings with it corresponding advantages in speed and cost savings. However, speed and finality come at a price: "The sacrifice that arbitration entails in terms of legal precision is recognized", (*see* Sobel *v.* Hertz, Warner & Co. 469 F.2d.1211). As a result, however desirable it may seem at first, finality can be a universally positive quality in dispute resolution only if one of two basic assumptions is true. First finality would always be an asset if arbitrators, unlike distinguished judges, never make mistakes. Even the most avid proponent of arbitration is unlikely to make such a claim (per William H. Knull III and Noah D. Rubins).

There are many credible arbitral institutions in India, and author has taken a look at the rules followed by them. The efficacy of these institutions can be accessed from their actual performance, but obviously there is much more to be done by them. Also the mindset of the parties must evolve from that of adversarial litigants to co-operative commercial partners.

The book has been very well written keeping in view the priorities of the users of this dispute resolution mechanism. The areas where the law gives freedom to the parties to lay down their own procedure have been clearly identified, and the parties can examine the bye-laws of the different institutions to see whether these are helpful in creating a fair and credible process.

I am sure this book will be an invaluable companion to the users of the process as well as to arbitrators and practitioners.

(DR. JUSTICE ARIJIT PASAYAT)

JAGDEEP DHANKHAR
Senior Advocate

FOREWORD

The author has bestowed deserving commendable focus on vital aspects of arbitral process.

He has highlighted areas of party autonomy in the arbitral process under the current Indian law, and how to effectively employ the same to have a good arbitration agreement. The need to contain judicial intervention and secure finality to the outcome has rightly been stressed.

India's fast growing economy eminently renders it as an important centre of dispute resolution as well. Arbitral institutions ensure better control of the arbitral process apart from being quick and cost effective. They generate greater sense of responsibility and transparency.

There are many arbitral institutions functioning in India. However the need for emergence of a credible institution that can occupy the space cannot be over emphasized. I am sure that the book is bound to contribute to strengthening these institutions, and growth of institutional arbitration in the country.

The book contains micro analysis of all vital aspects of the arbitral process. It would be invaluable asset to all concerned including lawyers, arbitrators and users of the arbitral process.

Jagdeep Dhankhar

Jagdeep Dhankhar
Sr. Advocate Supreme Court of India
Formerly Member ICC International Court of Arbitration, Paris

8A, Sagar Apartments, 6 Tilak Marg, India Gate, New Delhi-110001
Tel. : 91-11-23388903, Fax : 91-11-23383246 # E-mail : jdhankhar@hotmail.com

PREFACE

It is ideal if every commercial transaction concluded with a settlement of accounts. But it does not always happen that way, and disputes have to be resolved between the parties. The preferred way is through the arbitral process. It is also a neat solution to the conflict of laws, because a well drafted arbitration agreement can take care of these issues.

As the General Counsel of Steel Authority of India Ltd. ('SAIL'), it was very important for me to understand the process, and the statutes and regulations associated with the process. Even within the structure and ambit of the present laws, much can be done to make arbitration a credible method of dispute resolution.

I discovered that there are many publications which give the rules and procedures guiding the process of arbitration. But I needed to filter the information and understand the actual working of this very important machinery for dispute resolution, from the point of view of a user of the process.

I was fortunate to have a very good guide in Mr. Jagdeep Dhankhar, a Senior Advocate of the Supreme Court, who had been a member of the International Court of Arbitration. He has had significant achievements in representing different parties in a number of very high stake international arbitrations. And during my many discussions with him, he lucidly dissected the way party autonomy, even under the present statute, can be used to structure an effective arbitral process. I acknowledge unhesitatingly his great contribution to this book.

After years of working with the process, I have tried to capture the statutory framework of the arbitral process, as well as key concepts relating to damages for breach of contract, which is really the subject matter of the arbitral process, so that readers can make the best use of the process.

The users of the process are primarily concerned with speed of the process, and cost. The process of challenge to the award, which often delays execution of the award, is a frustrating sequel to the arbitral process. Much of the problems connected with challenge to an arbitral award have their genesis in rendition of an award which is either beyond the jurisdiction of the arbitrator, or one which is not well reasoned. This is often the case in ad-hoc arbitration, but not negligible in an institutional arbitration.

In this book, I have tried to clarify the legal issues so that the reader, who is a party to the arbitral process, is able to assist the arbitrator to get the best results. The ultimate goal is not the award, but the execution of the award, and hence the parties should have a proper understanding about the status of the arbitral award in the jurisdiction in which the award will have to be executed.

I have not attempted a very lengthy tome, but a very practical book, and I am sure readers will find the book very useful for a proper understanding and effective use of the arbitral process for resolution of commercial disputes.

New Delhi, 2011 **P.K. BASU MAJUMDAR**

CONTENTS

THE ARBITRATION AGREEMENT

AMICABLE DISPUTE RESOLUTION

APPOINTING THE ARBITRATOR

INTERIM MEASURES

PROCEEDINGS BEFORE ARBITRAL TRIBUNAL

COURT INTERVENTION IN ARBITRATION

INSTITUTIONAL ARBITRATION

DAMAGES FOR BREACH OF CONTRACT

MITIGATION OF LOSS

JURISDICTION OF ARBITRATOR

THE ARBITRAL AWARD

CHALLENGE TO AWARD

ENFORCEMENT OF AWARD

TABLE OF CASES

D

E

F

G

H

I

J

K

L

M

S

U

V

INTRODUCTION

Arbitration is the process of resolution of a dispute. In this book, we shall primarily look at arbitration as a process of resolution of commercial disputes. The process pre-supposes existence of legally enforceable right(s) arising out of a commercial relationship, mainly a commercial contract.

An act of omission or commission by a party that is in breach of the contract, would lead to a demand for adherence to the contract by the other party, or a claim for payment of damages. Refusal or constructive refusal by the party in breach to acknowledge any breach and/or to remedy the situation to the satisfaction of the other party lead, would lead to a dispute.

There are various methods resolving such disputes—through intervention of a court of law, or by a tribunal of choice of the parties, *i.e.*, through arbitration. The parties can either agree in advance to refer such disputes, as and when they arise, to an arbitral tribunal, or agree to make such reference after the dispute arises. Such an agreement could also be part of the contract agreement, but as we shall see later, it is independent of it, and can survive even after the contract agreement has been terminated.

To make the decision of the arbitral tribunal legally binding on the parties, and legally enforceable, the agreement would have to be within the parameters laid down in the arbitration law. In India, the current governing law is the Arbitration and Conciliation Act, 1996. Therefore, the arbitration agreement must follow the law, and where the law allows the parties to decide procedures, governing law, place, etc., the parties can supplement the law while drawing up the arbitration agreement.

In the following Chapters of this book, I shall deal with the following:—

(i) The arbitration agreement.

(ii) Amicable Dispute Resolution.

(iii) Appointing the Arbitrator.

(iv) Interim measure of protection.

(v) The arbitration process.

(vi) Damages for Breach of Contract.

(vii) Jurisdiction of arbitrator

(viii) The arbitration award.

(ix) Challenge to award.

(x) Enforcement of the arbitration award.

THE ARBITRATION AGREEMENT

SYNOPSIS

1. Form of Arbitration Agreement

The arbitration agreement is the framework which guides the constitution of the arbitration forum or tribunal. It also lays down the types of disputes that may be referred to arbitration, either by laying down an exhaustive list of items, or an inclusive list, or by excluding certain types of disputes from the purview of the arbitral forum.

The Arbitration and Conciliation Act, 1996 defines an 'arbitration agreement' as under:

> "7. *Arbitration agreement.*—(1) In this Part, "arbitration agreement" means an agreement by the parties to submit to arbitration all or certain disputes which have arisen or which may arise between them in respect of a defined legal relationship, whether contractual or not.
>
> (2) An arbitration agreement may be in the form of an arbitration clause in a contract or in the form of a separate agreement.
>
> (3) An arbitration agreement shall be in writing.

(4) An arbitration agreement is in writing if it is contained in—

(a) a document signed by the parties; or

(b) an exchange of letters, telex, telegrams or other means of telecommunication which provide a record of the agreement; or

(c) an exchange of statements of claim and defence in which the existence of the agreement is alleged by one party and not denied by the other.

(5) The reference in a contract to a document containing an arbitration clause constitutes an arbitration agreement if the contract is in writing and the reference is such as to make that arbitration clause part of the contract.".

The first requirement therefore is that the agreement must be in writing. In *Bihar State Mineral Development Corporation* v. *Encon Builders (I) (P) Ltd.*[1], the Apex Court has said that the essential elements that comprise an arbitration agreement are as follows:

(a) There must be a present or a future difference in connection with some contemplated affair/contract.

(b) There must be the intention of the parties to settle such difference by a private tribunal.

(c) The parties must agree in writing to be bound by the decision of such tribunal.

(d) The parties must be *ad idem*.

1.1 Arbitration Agreement to be in Writing

In the *Punjab State* v. *Dina Nath*[2], the parties entered into a contract for the work of dowel drain and wire crate at RD No. 9,400 to 10,400 km in the State of Punjab. In clause 4 of Work Order No. 114, dated 16-5-1985 it was provided that:

"Any dispute arising between the department and the contractor/society shall be referred to the Superintending Engineer, Anandpur Sahib, Hydel Circle No. 1, Chandigarh for orders and his decision will be final and acceptable/binding on both the parties."

The question before the Hon'ble Supreme Court was whether the above provision constituted an arbitration agreement.

As seen earlier, the law requires the arbitration agreement to be 'in writing'. It may, therefore, be in the form of an arbitration clause in a contract, or in the form of a separate agreement. A reference in a written agreement to the standard 'General Conditions of Contract' containing the arbitration clause would make the arbitration clause part of the contract.

In the above *Punjab State* case, the Court had referred to its earlier decision, and reiterated the essentials of an 'arbitration agreement' in the following manner:

1. AIR 2003 SC 3688: (2003) 3 BLJR 1907: (2003) 6 Supreme 1: (2003) 6 SCALE 592: (2003) 3 Arb LR 135: (2003) 7 SCC 418.
2. (2007) 5 SCC 28: AIR 2007 SC 2157: (2007) 7 SCALE 443: (2007) 5 Supreme 502.

(i) The parties are in a 'legal relationship', including a contractual one.
(ii) The parties agree to refer any dispute arising out of such relationship for decision by a 'tribunal'.
(iii) The parties undertake to abide by the decision of the 'tribunal'.
(iv) Such 'agreement' is reduced to writing.

The question as to how an arbitration agreement is to be reduced to writing has been answered by the Apex Court in *Shakti Bhog Foods Ltd.* v. *Kola Shipping Ltd.*[1]. It has been held that 'an arbitration is considered to be in writing if it is contained in a document signed by the parties or in an exchange of letters, telex, telegrams or other means of telecommunication which provide a record of the agreement, or an exchange of statement of claim and defence in which the existence of an agreement is alleged by one party and not denied by the other'.

1.2 Intention of Parties

It was noted that the definition of arbitration agreement in the Act would clearly show that an arbitration agreement is required to be in writing[2], but it is not required to be in any particular form[3]. What is required to be ascertained is whether the parties have agreed that if any dispute arises between them in respect of the subject-matter of the contract, such dispute shall be referred to arbitration. It was noted that it had been held by the Court in an earlier decision[4] that:

> "What is required to be ascertained is whether the parties have agreed that if disputes arise between them in respect of the subject-matter of contract such dispute shall be referred to arbitration, then such an arrangement would spell out an arbitration agreement."

Even the term 'arbitration' is not required to be specifically mentioned such 'agreement'[5]. However, in the above *Bihar State Mineral Development Corpn.* case, it was observed that to interpret the agreement as an 'arbitration agreement' one has to ascertain the intention of the parties, and the parties should have agreed to treat the decision of the authority as final:

> "If the parties had desired and intended that a dispute must be referred to arbitration for decision and they would undertake to abide by that decision, there cannot be any difficulty to hold that the intention of the parties was to have an arbitration agreement, that is to say, an arbitration agreement immediately comes into existence."

The Hon'ble Court had therefore concluded that clause 4 of the Work Order between the parties can be interpreted to be an arbitration agreement even though the term 'arbitration' is not expressly mentioned in the agreement.

---

1. (2009) 2 SCC 134: AIR 2009 SC 12: (2008) 71 AIC 254: (2008) 12 SCALE 822: (2008) 4 Arb LR 1.
2. *See* Section 7(3) of the Act.
3. *See* Section 7(2) of the Act.
4. *Rukmanibai Gupta* v. *Collector, Jabalpur,* AIR 1981 SC 479: 1981 LLR 107: 1980 UJ (SC) 988: (1980) 4 SCC 556.
5. *Bihar State Mineral Development Corpn.* v. *Encon Builders (I) (P) Ltd.,* (2003) 7 SCC 418: AIR 2003 SC 3688: (2003) 3 BLJR 1907: (2003) 6 Supreme 1: (2003) 6 SCALE 592: (2003) 3 Arb LR 133.

2. Party Autonomy in Arbitration Agreement

Arbitration is resolution of dispute through a tribunal of choice of the parties. The law, however, recognises such a process, and allows the execution of awards made by the 'arbitral tribunal'. The 'tribunal' is a creature of the arbitration agreement. The agreement sets out the composition of the tribunal, the procedure for appointment of members of the tribunal, the procedure to be followed by the tribunal in conducting the arbitration proceeding, time limits, contents of award, etc.

The Party autonomy is of two kinds:

(i) The parties are free to agree upon a procedure; but the arbitral tribunal decides in case the parties cannot agree upon a procedure;

(ii) The parties are free to agree upon a procedure; failing which the default procedure given in the statutes must prevail.

The areas of autonomy enjoyed by the parties under the Arbitration and Conciliation Act, 1996 are set out below:

Area of Party Autonomy	Section	Autonomy of Parties
Number of arbitrators	10(1)	Any number of arbitrators, provided that such number is not an even number.
Nationality of arbitrators	11(1)	Any nationality agreed to by parties.
Procedure for appointment of arbitrator(s)	11(2)	Any procedure agreed to by parties.
Order of interim measure of protection by Arbitral tribunal	17(1)	Parties may agree otherwise.
Procedure to be followed by arbitral tribunal while conducting arbitration	19(2)	Any procedure for conducting arbitral proceedings.
Place of arbitration	20(1)	Any place agreed to by parties.
Language of written statement by a party, any hearing and any arbitral award, decision or other communication by the arbitral tribunal	22(1)	Any language agreed to by parties.
Time-limit for submission of facts in support of claim, etc., and statement of defence	23(1)	(a) Parties can decide on time period. (b) Parties can decide on required elements in the statements.
Party amending or supplementing statement of claim, etc., and statement of defence	23(3)	Parties can agree otherwise.
Arbitral tribunal can decide whether to hold oral hearings for evidence and arguments	24	Parties can agree otherwise.

Arbitral tribunal can appoint 'expert'	26(1)	Parties can agree otherwise.
Cross-examination of expert after submission of 'report' at the request of party	26(2)	Parties can agree otherwise.
Expert to make available source material for report	26(3)	Parties may agree otherwise.
Substantive law in the case of international commercial law	28	Parties can designate substantive law.
Decisions of panel of arbitrators —normally by majority	29(1)	Parties can agree to other formulation.
Arbitral award to be reasoned	31(3)	Parties may agree otherwise.
Arbitral tribunal can award interest *pendente lite*	31(7)	Parties can decide otherwise.
Arbitrator can decide on— (i) fees and expenses of the arbitrators and witnesses, (ii) legal fees and expenses, (iii) any other expenses incurred in connection with the arbitral proceedings and the arbitral award	31(8)	Parties may agree to other scale of 'costs'.
Applicability of institutional rules to arbitration	2(6) & 6	Parties can opt for institutional arbitration; institutional rules will apply but substantive law for 'domestic' arbitration will be relevant Indian laws.

It may be mentioned that section 2(6) provides that 'where this Part, except section 28, leaves the parties free to determine a certain issue, that freedom shall include the right of the parties to authorise any person including an institution, to determine that issue'. This forms the statutory bedrock of the rules of the different arbitral institutions.

3. Excepted Matters

The arbitration agreement must clearly spell out the 'excluded issues' or 'excepted matters', which are to be decided by some other authority, and are not to be referred to arbitration.

3.1 Excepted Matters to be Specifically Mentioned

In *Food Corpn. of India* v. *Sreekanth Transport*[1], it was noted that in the usual governmental contracts, there is exclusion of some matters from the purview of arbitration and a senior officer of the department usually is given the authority and power to adjudicate the same. The clause itself records that the decision of the senior officer, being the adjudicator, shall be final and binding between the parties —this is usually known as 'excepted matters' in the contract.

1. (1999) 4 SCC 491: AIR 1999 SC 2184: JT 1999 (3) SC 649: (1999) 3 SCALE 690: (1999) 5 Supreme 541: (1999) 2 Arb LR 531.

If a clause is inserted in a contract agreement for the purpose of prevention of dispute, it will not be an arbitration agreement[1]. The contract may confer power on an Officer to take a decision in relation to certain specified matters for operational reasons. It was held in *Food Corpn. of India* v. *Sreekanth Transport*[2], that for such matters, 'the agreement itself provides a named adjudicator—concurrence to the same obviously is presumed by reason of the unequivocal acceptance of the terms of the contract by the parties and this is where the courts have been found out lacking in their jurisdiction to entertain an application for reference to arbitration as regards the disputes arising therefrom'.

It was noted that these exceptions were questions of fact, and usually mentioned in the contract documents and form part of the agreement, and as such there is no ambiguity in the matter of adjudication of these specialised matters and termed in the agreement as the 'excepted matters'.

3.2 Categories of 'Excepted Matters'

In *G.M.N. Rly.* v. *Sarvesh Chopra*[3], the Hon'ble Supreme Court observed that in the particular *(railway)* contract, there were two categories of 'excepted matters'—

(i) **Claim not admissible:** In one category, the relevant clauses of 'Special Conditions' provided for such claims being not capable of being raised or adjudged by employing such phraseology as 'shall not be payable', 'no claim whatsoever will be entertained by the Railways', or 'no claim will/shall be entertained'. These could be termed as 'no claim', 'no damage', or 'no liability' clauses. This category is an 'excepted matter', because the claim as per the terms and conditions of the contract is simply not entertainable.

(ii) **Claim to be decided by named authority only:** The other category of claims was where the dispute or difference has to be determined by an authority of the Railways as provided in the relevant clause. This second category of claims falls within 'excepted matters' because the claim is liable to be adjudicated upon by an authority of the Railways whose decision the parties have, under the contract, agreed to treat as final and binding, and hence not arbitrable.

In either case therefore, the claim falls within the broad category of 'excepted matter'.

4. Law Governing Arbitration Proceedings

The UNCITRAL Model Law on International Commercial Arbitration has been around since 1985. Around 1996, when India decided to align its arbitration law with the UNCITRAL Model Law, some other countries like England and Germany also decided to do the same. India went in for a composite legislation applicable to both domestic and international commercial arbitration, and covers both conciliation and arbitration.

1. Refer *Mallikarjun* v. *Gulbarga University*, (2004) 1 SCC 372: 2003 AIR SCW 6384: (2003) 3 Arb LR 579: JT 2005 (6) SC 402: 2003 (7) SLT 139: 2003 (9) SCALE 596: 2003 (8) Supreme 255.
2. AIR 1999 SC 2184: (1999) 4 SCC 491: JT 1999 (3) SC 649: (1999) 3 SCALE 690: (1999) 5 Supreme 541: (1999) 2 Arb LR 531.
3. AIR 2002 SC 1272: (2002) 4 SCC 45: JT 2002 (2) SC 445: (2002) 2 SCALE 394: (2002) 2 Supreme 170: (2002) 1 Arb LR 506.

As provided in section 28(1)(a) of the 1996 Act, in a 'domestic' arbitration, the arbitral tribunal is to 'decide the dispute submitted to arbitration in accordance with the substantive law for the time being in force in India'. However, in 'international commercial arbitration' the parties can designate the rules of law as applicable to the substance of the dispute.

In either case, the arbitral tribunal is to decide on the dispute in accordance with the terms of the contract, and can take into account the usages of the trade applicable to the transaction. The tribunal cannot make an award *de hors* the contract agreement.

The Apex Court had occasion to consider the applicability of Indian laws to international commercial arbitrations which take place in India. It has held in *Bhatia International* v. *Bulk Trading S.A.*[1] that the provisions of Part I are compulsorily applicable to an arbitration, including an international commercial arbitration, which takes place in India. Parties cannot, by agreement, override or exclude the non-derogable provisions of Part I in such arbitrations. In respect of arbitrations held outside India, it was observed by the Apex Court that:

> "... by not specifically providing that the provisions of Part I apply to international commercial arbitrations held out of India, the intention of the legislature appears to be to allow parties to provide by agreement that Part I or any provision therein will not apply...."

Thus, in cases of international commercial arbitrations held outside India, any or all the provisions of Part I could be excluded by agreement, express or implied. In that case the laws or rules chosen by the parties would prevail. Any provision in Part I which is contrary to or excluded by that law or rules will not apply.

In *Shreejee Traco (I) (P) Ltd.* v. *Paperline International Inc.*[2], the Hon'ble Supreme Court of India has opined that in a case of conflict of laws, the selection of the place of arbitration would have significance, if choice of place for submission for the arbitration is supported by the rest of the contract and surrounding circumstances, which indicate the intention of the parties.

The parties have the freedom to choose the law governing an international commercial arbitration agreement. However, if there is no express choice of the law governing the contract as a whole, or the arbitration agreement in particular, there is a presumption that the parties have intended that the proper law of the contract, as well as the law governing the arbitration agreement to be the law of the country in which the arbitration is agreed to be held.

5. Contents of an Arbitration Agreement

Following *Russel*, the Hon'ble Supreme Court, in *Visa International Ltd.* v. *Continental Resources (USA) Ltd.*[3], had noted the following elements of an arbitration agreement:

---

1. AIR 2002 SC 1432: JT 2002 (3) SC 150: (2003) 1 Jab LJ 264: (2002) 2 SCALE 612: (2002) 2 Supreme 395: (2002) 1 Arb LR 675: (2002) 4 SCC 105.
2. (2003) 9 SCC 79.
3. (2009) 2 SCC 55: AIR 2009 SC 1366: (2008) 15 SCALE 497: (2008) 4 Arb LR 539.

1. Proper identification of the parties.
2. Clear reference to arbitration in accordance with the provisions of Arbitration and Conciliation Act, 1996.
3. Disputes that had arisen between the parties which could not be amicably settled are to be referred to arbitration.
4. The seat of the arbitration is to be in terms of sections 20(1) and 20(2).
5. The substance of the dispute is to be determined in accordance with the provisions of sections 19, 23, 24, 25, 26, 27 and other provisions of the Arbitration and Conciliation Act, 1996.

Arbitral institutions like the Indian Council of Arbitration (ICA), or the International Chamber of Commerce (ICC), or different commercial organisations, have developed their own standard arbitration agreements.

However, if the arbitration proposed is an *'ad hoc'* one, the arbitration agreement has to be worded so as to avail of the flexibility allowed by the arbitration law to the parties in determining the contours of the agreement. An arbitral agreement may, therefore, have certain 'necessary elements' and 'recommended elements', as well as 'optional elements'. These are suggested below, but the list is illustrative, and not exhaustive, and based on experience, the parties may include other elements where the law does not have specific mandate. Merely because some elements are missing, but the intention of the parties to go for arbitration is clear, the arbitration agreement cannot be said to be unenforceable.

5.1 Necessary Elements

(a) Disputes or Nature of Disputes to be Referred to Arbitration

In the arbitration agreement, expressions such as 'arising out of', or 'in respect of', or 'in connection with', or 'in relation to', or 'in consequence of', or 'concerning', or 'relating to', are of the widest amplitude and content[1]. They include questions as to the existence, validity, and scope of the arbitration agreement. However, certain contracts, even if they can be traced to an original contract, operate as independent contracts. The arbitration clause of the original contract will not operate in such cases. An example would be a dispute on dishonoured cheque, when there is no dispute on quality of goods sold, or quantum of sale consideration. The arbitration clause in the contract of sale will not cover such a dispute[2].

The Arbitration and Conciliation Act, 1996 is a general Act. So far recovery of debts to banks is concerned, the Recovery of Debts due to Banks and Financial Institutions Act, 1993 is a special statute enacted for a specific object which provides exclusive jurisdiction with regard to claims by banks. This Act overrides the provisions of the Arbitration and Conciliation Act, 1996, and it has been observed in a catena of decisions that no consent of the other side is necessary for a bank to invoke its remedy under this statute and to seek dispute redressal by the

1. *Renusagar Power Co. Ltd.* v. *General Electric Co.,* (1984) 4 SCC 679: AIR 1985 SC 1156: (1985) 1 SCR 432: (1984) 3 Comp LJ 110.
2. *Vasanji Navji & Co.* v. *K.P.C. Spinners,* AIR 1983 Mad 31: (1982) 2 Mad LJ 216: ILR (1983) 1 Mad 221: 1982 TLNJ 121.

Debt Recovery Tribunal. Hence it is clear that while noting the nature of disputes to be referred to arbitration, the parties should have regard to statutes which have created special Tribunals, or other means of redress.

(b) Number of Arbitrators Comprising the Arbitral Tribunal

The procedure to be followed when appointing the arbitrator(s) would the one laid down in the 'arbitration agreement'. The number of arbitrators can be decided in advance, but must be an odd number. However, the law provides that if there is no agreement regarding number of arbitrators, under section 10 of the 1996 Act, 'the arbitral tribunal shall consist of a sole arbitrator'.

In *Sime Darby Engineering SDN. BHD.* v. *Engineering India Ltd.*[1], the Hon'ble Supreme Court noted that clause 12.2 of the concerned arbitration agreement provided that 'if any dispute or difference, which cannot be mutually resolved by the parties, the same shall be referred to arbitration in accordance with the provisions contained in the Indian Arbitration and Conciliation Act, 1996 which is generally in accordance with the UNCITRAL Rules.'

In that context, the Hon'ble Court compared the Indian law and the UNCITRAL Rules. Under section 2(1)(d) of the Arbitration and Conciliation Act, 1996 the term arbitral tribunal means 'a sole arbitrator or a panel of arbitrators'. Section 10(2) makes it very clear where the number of arbitrators is not determined, the arbitral tribunal shall consist of a sole arbitrator. The UNCITRAL Model Law on international commercial arbitration also accepts the same definition of arbitral tribunal in article 2(b). Article 10 of those Rules is almost identical with section 10 of the said Act.

> "*Article 2. Definition and rules of interpretation.*—For the purposes of this law:
>
> * * *
>
> (b) 'arbitral tribunal' means a sole arbitrator or a panel of arbitrators.
>
> "*Article 10. Number of arbitrators.*—(1) The parties are free to determine the number of arbitrators.
>
> (2) Failing such determination, the number of arbitrators shall be three."

Therefore, it was held that the definition of arbitral tribunal in section 2(1)(d) of the said Act is *verbatim* the same as in article 2(b). Article 10 of the UNCITRAL Model Law has close similarity with section 10 of the said Act, but deviates from article 10 of the UNCITRAL Model Law only in the sense that section 10(1) of the Act provides that despite the freedom given to the parties to determine the number of arbitrators such numbers shall not be even number. But in default of determination of the number, section 10(2) of the Act provides that the Tribunal is to consist of a sole arbitrator.

In the light of the above, it was held that:

> "In the instant case, the arbitration clause 12.2 is silent as to the number of arbitrators. The said clause read with section 10(2) of the Act makes it very clear that the arbitral tribunal in the instant case would be consisting of a sole arbitrator."

1. (2009) 7 SCC 545: AIR 2009 SC 3158: (2009) 80 AIC 14: (2009) 4 CLJ 274.

Thus, if the arbitration agreement does not specify a number, the reference of the dispute shall be to a sole arbitrator. Arbitral institutions, however, have their own rules, and the number is generally *one* or *three*, depending on the claim amount. These rules are recognised in law to the extent that they do not derogate from the settled legal propositions.

(c) Procedure for Appointing Arbitrator(s)

There is a tendency in India to have retired judges as arbitrators. They are not necessarily the only persons suited for this job, and the parties can opt to have a commercial person or an engineer as the arbitrator. The arbitration agreement may also provide that a member of the tribunal must possess a certain qualification.

Under section 11 of the 1996 Act, the parties are free to agree upon a process of appointing arbitrator(s), who may be of any nationality. The arbitration agreement itself could designate a person *(persona designata)* who would act as the arbitrator, or who would appoint the arbitrator. If parties consent to appointment of the arbitrator by the Managing Director of one of the parties, and that he can even nominate a serving or ex-employee of the company, appointment will not be made by Court, even if the other party alleges apprehension of partiality on the part of such nominated arbitrator.

In *You One Engineering & Construction Co. Ltd.* v. *National Highways Authority of India (NHAI)*[1], the Hon'ble Supreme Court held that:

> "... The arbitration agreement clearly envisages the appointment of the presiding arbitrator by IRC. There is no qualification that the arbitrator has to be a different person depending on the nature of the dispute. If the parties have entered into such an agreement with open eyes, it is not open to ignore it and invoke exercise of powers in section 11(6)."

If the appointed arbitrator resigns, the process of appointment has again to be initiated, in accordance with the terms of the arbitration agreement. In *National Highways Authority of India* v. *Bumihiway DDB Ltd. (JV)*[2], the presiding arbitrator, Mr. Justice Y. Bhaskar Rao had resigned. The Hon'ble Supreme Court held that:

> "On the vacancy created by the resignation of Mr Justice Y. Bhaskar Rao, the process of appointment of the presiding arbitrator started afresh in accordance with the agreed terms of the contract."

If the arbitral tribunal is to consist of three arbitrators, if there is no agreed procedure for appointment of all three arbitrators, under section 10(3) of the Arbitration and Conciliation Act, 1996 'each party shall appoint one arbitrator, and the two appointed arbitrators shall appoint the third arbitrator who shall act as the presiding arbitrator'.

Section 2(6) of the Arbitration and Conciliation Act, 1996 also allows the parties to opt for institutional arbitration. The name of the institute should be specified, in which case the arbitral tribunal will be constituted from among the panel of the institution, in accordance with the rules of the institution. In some cases, institutional arbitration could prove to be quicker and cheaper.

---

1. (2006) 4 SCC 372: AIR 2006 SC 3453: (2006) 41 AIC 113: (2006) 2 Arb LR 68: (2006) 3 SCALE 219.
2. (2006) 10 SCC 763: 2006 AIR SCW 4968: (2006) 9 SCALE 564.

In the case of *Nandan Biomatrix Ltd.* v. *D 1 Oils Ltd.*[1], the 'arbitration agreement' was contained in clause 15.1 of the supply agreement:

"15.1. Any dispute that arises between the parties shall be resolved by submitting the same to the institutional arbitration in India under the provisions of the Arbitration and Conciliation Act, 1996."

It was held by the Hon'ble Supreme Court that:

"... the parties unequivocally agreed for resolution of the disputes through institutional arbitration and not through an *ad hoc* arbitration. Therefore, in my view, there exists a valid arbitration agreement between the parties *vide* clause 15.1 in the supply agreement dated 10-8-2004."

The agreement should also provide for the means of securing appointment of arbitrator, if the *persona designata* fails to appoint the arbitrator as per procedure[2].

(d) Damages and Interest Pendente Lite

The arbitration agreement should clearly provide that the arbitrator can only award compensatory damages in case of breach of the contract, and not punitive damages. It must also provide for a ceiling rate of interest *pendente lite.*

It had been clarified by the majority judgment of the Constitutional Bench of the Hon'ble Supreme Court in *Executive Engineer, Dhenkanal Minor Irrigation Division, Orissa* v. *N.C. Budharaj*[3] that—

"As long as there is nothing in the arbitration agreement to exclude the jurisdiction of the arbitrator to entertain a claim for interest on the amounts due under the contract, or any prohibition to claim interest on the amounts due and become payable under the contract, the jurisdiction of the arbitrator to consider and award interest in respect of all periods subject only to section 29 of the Arbitration Act, 1940 and that too the powers of the court thereunder, has to be upheld."

It has again been held by the Hon'ble Supreme Court in *Bhagawati Oxygen Ltd.* v. *Hindustan Copper Ltd.*[4], that 'an arbitrator has power and jurisdiction to grant interest for all the three stages[5] provided the rate of interest is reasonable'. So far as interest for pre-reference period is concerned, it has been held that an arbitrator has power to grant interest, provided there is no prohibition in the arbitration agreement excluding his jurisdiction to grant interest.

Therefore, the inclusion/exclusion of this element in the contract and in the arbitration agreement would be significant.

As to the rate of interest, it is left to the discretion of the arbitrator. It was observed by the Apex Court in *Numaligarh Refinery Ltd.* v. *Daelim Industrial Co. Ltd.*[6] that:

1. (2009) 4 SCC 495.
2. Section 11(6)(c) of Arbitration and Conciliation Act, 1996.
3. (2001) 2 SCC 721: AIR 2001 SC 626: JT 2001 (1) SC 486: (2001) 1 Arb LR 346: (2001) 1 Supreme 205.
4. (2005) 6 SCC 462: AIR 2005 SC 2071: (2005) 1 Arb LR 608: JT 2005 (4) SC 73: (2005) 4 Cal HN 88.
5. Three stages referred to are—pre-reference period, *pendente lite* and post-award period.
6. (2007) 8 SCC 466: (2007) 10 SCALE 577.

"The majority of the arbitrators have granted interest on the amount at the rate of 12 per cent. *pendente lite* and post *pendente lite* at the rate of 18 per cent. but the minority arbitrator, Justice M.M. Dutt has granted 10 per cent. interest uniformly. The grant of interest is discretionary and the majority of the arbitrators have rightly granted interest at the rate of 12 per cent. *pendente lite* and at the rate of 18 per cent. post *pendente lite.*"

In the view of the author, the contract agreement should clarify the rate of interest that is payable, or whether any interest is payable at all.

5.2 Recommended Elements

(a) Exclusivity of the Arbitration Process

The law does not envisage continuation of other judicial proceedings, when a dispute is under reference before an arbitral tribunal. Under section 8 of the 1996 Act, if a party applies before a judicial authority before which an action is brought, before submitting his first written statement, then the parties are to be referred to arbitration. The following suits are barred:

(a) Suit to challenge or enforce an arbitration agreement, except by way of approach to Court to appoint an arbitrator[1].

(b) Suit to affirm an arbitration agreement, *i.e.*, a suit either for a declaration that a valid arbitration agreement is in existence, or that the arbitration agreement does not exist[2].

(c) The High Court cannot issue prerogative writ to interfere with arbitration[3].

(b) Substantive Law to be Followed

In 'international commercial arbitration' the parties may specify the substantive law to be followed. It would be sufficient to designate the law or legal system of a country to be followed. This would imply the laws of that country that define rights and duties, *e.g.*, contract law, criminal law, tort law, etc., would apply.

The proper law of the arbitration agreement is the substantive law governing the contract itself. If it is a foreign law, in a case before an Indian court to decide on the validity of the arbitration agreement, the legal propositions under foreign law may have to be proved on the basis of affidavits as in the case of facts in a trial[4].

This question of choice of law has been decided by the judgment of the Hon'ble Supreme Court in *National Thermal Power Corpn.* v. *Singer Co.*[5] where it was observed:

---

1. *Government of India* v. *Jaraunadhar Rungta,* AIR 1960 Pat 19: 1959 BLJR 527.
2. *Jawahar Lal Burman* v. *Union of India,* AIR 1962 SC 378: (1962) 3 SCR 769: (1962) 1 SCJ 654: (1962) 1 MLJ (SC) 269.
3. *Rukmani Bai Gupta* v. *Collector,* AIR 1981 SC 479: (1980) 4 SCC 556: 1981 Land LR 107: 1980 UJ (SC) 988.
4. *Shin-Etsu Chemical Co. Ltd.* v. *Aksh Optifibre Ltd.,* (2005) 7 SCC 234: AIR 2005 SC 3766: (2005) 3 Arbi LR 1: JT 2005 (7) SC 426: (2005) 6 Supreme 15
5. (1992) 3 SCC 551: AIR 1993 SC 998: (1992) 2 Arb LR 154: JT 1992 (3) SC 198: (1992) 3 SCR 106.

"The proper law of the arbitration agreement is normally the same as the proper law of the contract. It is only in exceptional cases that it is not so even where the proper law of the contract is expressly chosen by the parties. Where, however, there is no express choice of the law governing the contract as a whole, or the arbitration agreement as such, a presumption may arise that the law of the country where the arbitration is agreed to be held is the proper law of the arbitration agreement. But that is only a rebuttable presumption."

If the seat of arbitration is in India, the Arbitration and Conciliation Act, 1996 provides that 'the arbitral tribunal is required to decide the dispute submitted to arbitration in accordance with the substantive law for the time being in force in India'[1]. This is the position in most countries. Hence, there should generally be a correspondence between the seat of arbitration and the substantive law to be followed by the arbitral tribunal.

(c) Procedure to be Followed in Arbitration

The Code of Civil Procedure and the Indian Evidence Act do not bind the arbitral tribunal. It is not bound by the technical rules of procedure that the courts must follow. However, the rules of procedure can be specified either in an institutional arbitration, or even in an *ad hoc* arbitration. If the rules of procedure are not specified, the arbitrator nevertheless has to follow the principles of natural justice, and give a fair hearing to both the parties[2]. In such case, it is advisable for the arbitrator to specify the procedure to be followed at the commencement of the arbitration proceedings.

The rules of the Indian Council of Arbitration[3] have provision for 'Fast Track Arbitration'. The Parties may request the arbitral tribunal, before the commencement of the arbitration proceedings, to decide the reference in a fixed time frame of 3 to 6 months, according to the Fast Track Arbitration procedure, as under:

"(1) The arbitral tribunal will be authorised to decide the dispute on the written pleadings, documents and written submissions filed by the Parties without any oral hearings.

(2) The arbitral tribunal shall have power to call for any further information/clarification from the parties in addition to the pleading and documents filed by them.

(3) An oral hearing may be held if both the parties make a joint request or if the Arbitration Tribunal considers an oral hearing necessary in any particular case.

(4) If an oral hearing is held, the arbitral tribunal may dispense with any technical formalities and adopt such procedure as it deems appropriate and necessary for economic and expeditious disposal of the case."

---

1. *Centrotrade Minerals & Metals Inc.* v. *Hindustan Copper Ltd.*, (2006) 11 SCC 245: 2006 AIR SCW 3172: JT 2006 (5) SC 507: (2006) 3 Arb LR 201.
2. *President of India* v. *Kesar Singh*, AIR 1966 J&K 113: 1966 Kash LJ 287.
3. Rule 44 of Rules of Arbitration of ICA.

In international commercial contracts, unless the parties agree that the arbitrator can decide the dispute *ex æequo et bono,* or as *amiable compositeur, i.e.,* in equity, the arbitrator has to decide the dispute in terms of the contract, and the substantive law applicable.

(d) Place of Arbitration

For 'domestic' arbitration, the place of arbitration should be in India. Unfortunately, the clause 'where the arbitration is situate in India' placed at the beginning of section 28(1) may give the impression that even in 'domestic' arbitration the place of arbitration could be outside India.

Remember to choose a place of arbitration, keeping in mind the relative convenience of the parties, the expense on travel and stay of arbitrator(s), counsel, witnesses, outstation fees of counsel, and other relevant factors. If the parties agree on a 'place'[1] of arbitration, the arbitrator does not have the liberty to change it. In *Jagson Airlines Ltd.* v. *Bannari Amman Exports (P) Ltd.,*[2] the Hon'ble Delhi High clearly held that:

> "Once parties agree in writing as to the venue of arbitration, the same cannot be changed by the Arbitrator until and unless the parties subsequently change the venue."

But, if the parties do not designate the seat of the arbitral tribunal, section 20(1) of the Arbitration and Conciliation Act, 1996 gives the tribunal the authority to designate the seat of the tribunal. In the same judgment, the Hon'ble High Court clarified that:

> "Section 20 of the Act provides place of arbitration subject to limitations. It is only in case of failure of any such agreement that place of arbitration will be determined by the Arbitral Tribunal having regard to all the facts and circumstances including the convenience of the parties. Wherever there is a written agreement on the place of arbitration, sub-section (2) of section 20 becomes non-applicable."

Even if the parties agree to institutional arbitration, the parties can still designate the place of arbitration. The institution can only take a decision in respect of the 'place', if the parties have not sealed the matter. In the case of *Sanshin Chemicals Industry* v. *Oriental Carbons and Chemicals Ltd.*[3], it was held by the Hon'ble Supreme Court that:

> "Section 20 is the provision which sees that the parties are free to agree on the place of arbitration and failing upon any agreement, then under sub-section (2) it has to be determined depending upon the circumstances of the case and convenience of the parties. ... section 20 therefore leads to a conclusion that in the event, parties do not agree with regard to the place of arbitration, though they were free to determine the same then they had the right to authorise any person including an institution ... for deciding

1. 'Place' is not the same as 'venue'.
2. 2003 (2) Arb LR 315 (Del).
3. AIR 2001 SC 1219: (2001) 3 SCC 341: (2001) 1 Arb LR 521: JT 2001 (2) SC 602: (2001) 90 DLT 28.

the venue of arbitration and such decision ... will not partake the character of adjudication of a dispute arising out of the agreement..."

Another factor to be considered is the preferred forum (court) for enforcing the award. This also depends on where the assets of the party against whom an award has been rendered are located. The arbitration award will have to be enforced, and if the party does not pay, it can only be enforced by executing it as against the assets of the party. Hence, it is wise to keep in mind enforceability of an award, when deciding on such matters as procedure, place of arbitration, etc.

(e) Fees of the Arbitrator(s)

If fees are not decided in advance, under section 31(8) the tribunal can specify the fees and expenses incurred in connection with the arbitral proceedings, and the arbitral award. This is a judicial power, which must be exercised with independence and a proper regard for the interests not only of those who will receive the costs, but also of those who will have to pay them[1].

The arbitration agreement too, can specify the fees of the arbitrator(s). In case of institutional arbitration, the costs are generally governed by the rules of the institution.

(f) Language to be Used in Arbitral Proceedings

This could prove tricky, if not specified, especially in international arbitration! If a document is in a language different from the one agreed to by the parties, then the same will be taken on record only if an authentic translated copy of the same is given in such language. All communications also must be made in such language.

5.3 Optional Elements

(a) Qualifications of Arbitrator

The parties may desire the arbitrator to be a qualified expert, so that he can bring his expertise in understanding the facts and interpreting the contract. The agreement could therefore, specify the qualification and experience that an arbitrator must possess.

The Hon'ble Supreme Court has held that *'an agreed procedure for appointing the arbitrators has been placed on high pedestal and has to be given preference to any other mode for securing appointment of an arbitrator.... In clause (a) of sub-section (8) of section 11 of the Act it is specifically provided that the Chief Justice or the person or institution designated by him, in appointing an arbitrator, shall have due regard to any qualifications required of the arbitrator by the agreement of the parties.'*[2]

Under section 12(3) of the 1996 Act, a party can challenge the appointment of an arbitrator if he does not possess the requisite qualification and experience. However, if knowingly the parties do not raise objection during the course arbitral proceedings, the parties would be deemed to have waived the objection.

---

1. *Rolimpex Centrala Handlu Zagranicznego* v. *Haji E. Dossa & Sons Ltd.*, [1971] Vol. 1 Lloyd's Law Rep 380.
2. *Iron & Steel Co. Ltd.* v. *Tiwari Road Lines*, (2007) 5 SCC 703: AIR 2007 SC 2064: (2007) 2 Arb LR 270: (2007) 5 MLJ 599: (2007) 56 AIC 214.

(b) Time Limits

The arbitration agreement between the parties may:

(a) impose a time limit for commencement of arbitration proceedings;

(b) provide that a claim may not be enforced through arbitration, after the lapse of a period mentioned in the arbitration agreement[1].

The time-limits for various activities set by the Arbitration and Conciliation Act, 1996 are separately tabulated and given below:

TIME LIMITS UNDER THE 1996 ACT

Activity	Section	Max. Time Limit
1. Party appointing arbitrator	11(4)(a)	30 days after receiving request from other party.
2. Two arbitrators appointing third arbitrator	11(4)(b)	30 days from date of appointment of other two arbitrators.
3. Party appointing arbitrator in terms of arbitration agreement, when such agreement does not provide any time limit	11(6)	Within 30 days of receiving request from other party, and before other party files application before CJ to appoint arbitrator.
4. Party challenging constitution of arbitral tribunal	13(2)	15 days after becoming aware of circumstances being grounds of challenge under section 12(3).
5. Filing of 'Statement of Claim'	23(1)	Time agreed upon, or as determined by the arbitral tribunal.
6. Filing of 'Statement of Defence'	23(1)	- do -
7. Correction of error of computation, clerical or typographical by arbitral tribunal *suo motu*	33(3)	30 days after making award.
8. Request to arbitral tribunal by a party for correction or interpretation of award	33(1)	30 days after making award.
9. Correction or interpretation of award by arbitral tribunal	33(2)	30 days after receiving request from party.
10. Request to arbitral tribunal by any party to make additional award on claims omitted from arbitral award	33(4)	30 days after receiving award.
11. Arbitral Tribunal additional award after receiving request from party as in 9 above	33(5)	60 days after receiving request.

1. This must be in consonance with section 28 of the Indian Contract Act.

If the parties settle for institutional arbitration, many of the above areas will be covered in the rules of the institution, and the same will be followed in respect of the institutional arbitration.

A very important criticism of the arbitration process is that though it is faster than court proceedings, it is still very time consuming and costly. It will be noticed that no time limits have been fixed for certain very important activities connected with the arbitral process, which could have contributed to speeding up the arbitral process.

The rules of arbitration of institutions have tried to plug this gap by making provisions for—

* Number of hours the arbitral tribunal will sit every day.
* Number of days to be allotted to claimant and respondent for oral evidence and arguments.
* Whether 'examination-in-chief' can be done through sworn affidavit of witness.
* 'Fast track' arbitration.

The Law Commission has identified the absence of time-limits at this stage of arbitration as a major lacuna of the Arbitration and Conciliation Act, 1996. An amending Bill was moved in 2004, but it did not become law. It provided, *inter alia,* for speeding up pending was well as future arbitrations by providing for a time-limit within which proceedings will have to be concluded.

AMICABLE DISPUTE RESOLUTION

SYNOPSIS

1. From ADR to ADR

Dispute resolution process like arbitration, which falls outside of the State administered judicial process, is known as Alternative Dispute Resolution ("ADR"). Arbitration has gained widespread acceptance among both the general public and the legal profession in recent years.

However, this is still an adversarial process. Commercial organisations are happier with a dispute resolution mechanism that will not leave the parties with a bitter after-taste in their mouths. They would still be ready to do business with each other.

Over the years therefore, mediation and conciliation have come to be accepted as alternate to arbitration or "ADR", as it was known. None of the above processes is adversarial, and therefore these processes are referred to as 'Amicable Dispute Resolution' (strangely, with the same acronym—"ADR"). The new "ADR" is being recognised as more wholesome alternative to the older "ADR". The wheel has turned full circle, and now the alternative to the old adversarial dispute resolution mechanism is for the parties to essentially resolves their own differences, with a little nudging from a mutually acceptable 'neutral'[1]—the 'amicable dispute resolution' process.

2. Mediation/Conciliation

Amicable Dispute Resolution, embracing mediation or conciliation, is being included in agreements for dispute resolution, as essential first steps in resolving commercial disputes.

---

1. Under the ADR Rules of the International Chamber of Commerce, the 'mediator' or 'conciliator' or facilitator, as variously described, is called a 'neutral'. But under the Arbitration and Conciliation Act of 1996, reference is to 'conciliator'.

'Mediation' finds mention only in section 30 of the 1996 Act:

> "30. *Settlement.*—(1) It is not incompatible with an arbitration agreement for an arbitral tribunal to encourage settlement of the dispute and, with the agreement of the parties, the arbitral tribunal may use *mediation*, conciliation or other procedures at any time during the arbitral proceedings to encourage settlement ...."

The process may be used by the arbitrator, and leads to an award by the arbitrator 'on agreed terms' as provided in sub-sections (3) and (4). It is an arbitrator driven process, rather than a mechanism separate from arbitration.

On the other hand, the entire Part III (sections 61 to 81) is devoted to 'conciliation'. The concepts of 'mediation' and 'conciliation' are used interchangeably in the Indian context, and only 'conciliation' has sanction as a separate dispute resolution mechanism in the 1996 Act, and leads to a legally enforceable 'agreement'/'award'. The status of such a 'settlement agreement' is defined in section 74 of the Act:

> "74. *Status and effect of settlement agreement.*—The settlement agreement shall have the same status and effect as if it is an arbitral award on agreed terms on the substance of the dispute rendered by an arbitral tribunal under section 30."

3. Agreement for Conciliation

Section 62 of the Arbitration and Conciliation Act, 1996 gives the procedure for commencing conciliation proceedings:

> "62. *Commencement of conciliation proceedings.*—(1) The party initiating conciliation shall send to the other party a written invitation to conciliate under this Part, briefly identifying the subject of the dispute.
>
> (2) Conciliation proceedings shall commence when the other party accepts in writing the invitation to conciliate.
>
> (3) If the other party rejects the invitation, there will be no conciliation proceedings.
>
> (4) If the party initiating conciliation does not receive a reply within thirty days from the date on which he sends the invitation, or within such other period of time as specified in the invitation, be may elect to treat this as a rejection of the invitation to conciliate and if he so elects, he shall inform in writing the other party accordingly."

The above section 62 says that the party initiating conciliation shall send to the other party a written invitation to conciliate under Part III, briefly identifying the subject of the dispute. The conciliation proceedings shall commence when the other party accepts in writing the invitation of conciliation. If the other party rejects the invitation, there will be no conciliation proceedings.

Interestingly, it has been held in *Visa International Ltd.* v. *Continental Resources (USA) Ltd.*[1] that—

1. (2009) 2 SCC 55: AIR 2009 SC 1366: (2008) 15 SCALE 497: (2008) 4 Arb LR 539.

"Part III of the Act does not envisage any agreement for conciliation of future disputes. It only provides for an agreement to refer the disputes to conciliation after the disputes had arisen....."

In fact, section 62 does indicate that the dispute has already arisen before any of the parties propose conciliation. It is an *ad hoc* agreement entered into after the dispute has arisen.

Section 28 of the Indian Contract Act, 1872 deals with the question of restraint on legal proceedings 'in the ordinary tribunals'. Such agreement in restraint of proceedings is void:

"28. *Agreements in restrain of legal proceedings void.*—Every agreement, by which any party thereto is restricted absolutely from enforcing his rights under or in respect of any contract, by the usual legal proceedings in the ordinary tribunals, or which limits the time within which he may thus enforce his rights, is void to the extent.

However, two exceptions have been carved out in respect of agreements to refer to Arbitral Tribunal:

(a) future disputes, or

(b) disputes 'already arisen'.

An arbitration agreement is thus saved:

"*Exception 1: Saving of contract to refer to arbitration dispute that may arise.*— This section shall not render illegal contract, by which two or more persons agree that any dispute which may arise between them in respect of any subject or class of subject shall be referred to arbitration, and that only and amount awarded in such arbitration shall be recoverable in respect of the dispute so referred.

"*Exception 2: Saving of contract to refer question that have already arisen.*— Nor shall this section render illegal any contract in writing, by which two or more persons agree to refer to arbitration any question between them which has already arisen, or affect any provision of any law in force for the time being as to reference to arbitration."

It would appear that an agreement entered into for reference of future dispute to conciliation is not enforceable in view of section 28 of the Indian Contract Act, 1872. The *Exceptions* to that section only save arbitration agreements.

But after the enactment of the Arbitration and Conciliation Act, 1996, there can be no objection to the parties to enter into a settlement agreement through conciliation, since the Act treats the conciliation settlement agreement authenticated by the conciliator on par with award on agreed terms which in turn is treated on par with any arbitral award. [See sections 74 and 30 of Arbitration and Conciliation Act, 1996].

In the case of *Municipal Corpn.* v. *Rajesh Construction Co.*[1], the fact was that clause 29 of the contract specifically stipulated that if any dispute arises between

1. (2007) 5 SCC 344: AIR 2007 SC 2069: (2007) 2 Arb LR 65: (2007) 4 MPLJ 26.

the parties, the party seeking invocation of the arbitration clause, shall first approach the Chief Engineer and on his failure to arbitrate the dispute, the party aggrieved may file an appeal to MPL Com, failing which, the Corporation shall constitute an Arbitration Board to resolve the disputes in the manner indicated in clause 29. However, before doing so, the party invoking arbitration clause was required to furnish security of a sum to be determined by the Corporation.

In that case admittedly, the security had not been furnished by the respondent to the Corporation. The Hon'ble Court observed that to invoke the jurisdiction of the Chief Justice under section 11, the condition precedent must be satisfied—

> "... we hold that the obligation of the Corporation to constitute an Arbitration Board to resolve disputes between the parties could not arise because of failure of the respondent to furnish security as envisaged in clause 29(d) of the contract. Therefore, we are of the opinion, that on account of non-furnishing of security by the respondent, the question of constituting an Arbitration Board by the Corporation could not arise at all."

Thus, the above ratio requires that all conditions precedent to invoking arbitration should first be satisfied before the jurisdiction of the Chief Justice can be invoked. It is the author's view that this ratio would extend to a stipulation in the arbitration agreement regarding conciliation as a condition precedent to invoking arbitration.

4. Preparing for Conciliation

Experience shows that parties (clients) and advocates have to work together closely for bringing about a realistic appreciation of the claim, and the factual and legal matrix of the strengths and weaknesses of the brief, so as to draw up an effective strategy for dealing with dispute resolution. From his experience, the author suggests that, the following steps should be taken as prelude to conciliation—

(i) **Sift through relevant facts**

Only this will lead to correct factual appreciation of the nature of the dispute. Counsel should examine all facts and documents—both those favouring the client, as well as those that may be used against the client. At this stage the 'excluded items' should also be listed, wherever they occur in the contract agreement, and the standard or generally accepted methods of computing 'damages'.

(ii) **Formulate legal propositions**

The legal propositions should include admissible damages and exclude 'remote damages', mitigation of losses incurred as a result of the breach, legal limits of liability for loss, liquidated damages, etc.

Keeping the above in view, a Table has been prepared that indicates the limits within which it may be possible for the claimant to accept an offer of the second party, and reach an agreement in course of conciliation:

Table showing process of Settlement through Conciliation

POSSIBLE OUTCOME OF ARBITRATION	POSSIBLE OUTCOME OF CONCILIATION	RESULT OF CONCILIATION
BEST POSSIBLE OUTCOME	DESIRABLE OUTCOME	HAVE A SETTLEMENT
↕		
PROBABLE OUTCOME	FLOOR LEVEL	
WORST POSSIBLE OUTCOME		WALK AWAY

The above gives indicia about the leeway available to the negotiators in a negotiation process.

5. The Conciliation Process

As indicated above, client and counsel will have to work together to make out a negotiating brief. Realistically, this may also require vetting and approval at different levels of the client's organisation, before making it available to the negotiators.

5.1 Choosing the Conciliator

Section 63 of the Arbitration and Conciliation Act, 1996 mentions nomination of a sole conciliator, unless the parties agree to two or three conciliators. If the number is more than one, the conciliators are to work jointly. The author's own experience is that if the parties are unable to agree to a single conciliator, and each must have its own 'spokesperson' on the conciliation board, the process of conciliation is bound to fail.

Of utmost importance is the choice of the 'conciliator'. Besides being 'independent' and 'impartial', he must be suitably qualified to be able to appreciate the issues in dispute, and should have sufficient stature so that he can inspire confidence in the parties to seriously consider suggestions of the 'conciliator' towards resolution of the dispute. The Indian law allows appointment of conciliator(s) of any nationality as agreed by the parties, or as per the institutional rules, if parties go for institutional conciliation.

The Arbitration and Conciliation Act, 1996 allows the parties to take the assistance of an institution for the purpose of appointment of a conciliator:

> "64. (2) Parties may enlist the assistance of a suitable institution or person in connection with the appointment of conciliators and in particular—

(a) a party may request such an institution or person to recommend the names of suitable individuals to act as conciliator; or

(b) the parties may agree that the appointment of one or more conciliators be made directly by such an institution or person:

Provided that in recommending or appointing individuals to act as conciliator, the institution or person shall have regard to such considerations as are likely to secure the appointment of an independent and impartial conciliator and, with respect to a sole or third conciliator, shall take into account the advisability of appointing a conciliator of a nationality other than the nationalities of the parties."

5.2 Submission of Statements to Conciliator

By virtue of section 65, the conciliator may request each party to submit to him a brief written statement describing the general nature of the dispute and the points at issue.

It is a good idea to first brief the conciliator about the technology and the business/trade practices involved. If this can be done by both the parties in an agreed manner, it would help the conciliator to get down to the main job quickly.

The conciliator can ask each party to submit further statements/information. Since conciliation can only succeed in an atmosphere of transparency, the law enjoins that each party shall send copies of all statements to the other party.

5.3 Statement of the Issues by the Parties

At the commencement of the first meeting, parties should assist the conciliator to define the procedure to be followed, and draw up an agreed time-frame for the process. After the opening statement of the conciliator, the parties should narrate the events and the disputed issues from their own point of view. These statements would give the parties an opportunity to frame the core issues in their own mind, and the conciliator would be able to get to the crux of the problem. The process is directed towards assisting the parties to identify the contours of a possible agreed award. The objective is that—

(i) All the parties get into a 'conciliatory' mood.

(ii) The parties get a clear idea about the countours of any possible solution.

(iii) The parties can discover the common view points on some of the issues.

5.4 The Conciliation Meeting

The conciliation process works best if the parties speak for themselves, instead of counsels acing as their spokespersons. They may, however, confer with their attorneys, if they so like on the sidelines. The Indian law is silent on this aspect. But if parties opt for institutional assistance, institutions will insist that the process be pursued within the framework of the institutional rules in the matter:

"*68. Administrative assistance.*—In order to facilitate the conduct of the conciliation proceedings, the parties, or the conciliator with the consent of the parties, may arrange for administrative assistance by a suitable institution or person."

The process of conciliation typically includes joint or separate meetings. The conciliator may ask the parties to *caucus*[1] – the conciliator talks with each party, proposing solutions and tries to get commitment to a settlement by both parties. The conciliator goes back and forth between the parties during this time, clearing up misunderstandings, and carrying information, proposals, and points of agreement.

5.5 *Settlement Agreement*

Sections 61 to 81 of the Act make fascinating reading. It is a primer for conduct of conciliation proceedings. The author's own view is that that the conciliation process should be de-regulated. Otherwise there is danger that procedural wrangling will become the killing fields of conciliation. These provisions of the Arbitration and Conciliation Act, 1996 could come to be treated as conditions precedent to according legal status to the settlement agreement. The parties and the conciliator should be allowed to innovate procedures to reach a final settlement agreement.

The settlement agreement may be drawn up by the parties themselves, or the parties can give their suggestions separately to the conciliator, who would then formulate a possible settlement. The best course is to treat the provisions of sections 72 and 73 as mere recommendations for arriving at a settlement, and not mandatory provisions. The settlement agreement should be signed by the parties and 'authenticated' by the conciliator.

As in any settlement, the agreement should clearly indicate the issues in dispute, and the terms of settlement, so that any issue figuring as a dispute, but not finding mention in the terms of settlement would, by necessary implication, be considered to have been dropped.

Section 74 provides that 'the settlement agreement shall have the same status and effect as if it is an arbitral award on agreed terms on the substance of the dispute rendered by an arbitral tribunal under section 30.'

6. Termination of the Conciliation Process

One way for the conciliation process to end is to have a settlement agreement. But it may also end in failure. In that event, section 76 lays down the guidelines for declaring the conciliation process is at an end. It is deemed to end when a declaration is made in any of the following ways:

(i) After consultation with the parties, the conciliator makes a written declaration that further efforts at conciliation are no longer justified; or

(ii) Parties make a written declaration addressed to the conciliator that the conciliation proceedings are terminated; or

(iii) One party makes a written declaration to the other party and the conciliator (if appointed) that the conciliation proceedings are terminated.

---

1. In a conciliation process, 'to *caucus*' is to hold a confidential meeting of negotiators of one side of a dispute, usually with the conciliator, to discuss options and attempt to find a resolution.

7. Exclusive Nature of Conciliation Proceedings

Section 77 stipulates that during the conciliation proceedings, the parties shall not initiate any arbitral or judicial proceedings in respect of a dispute that is the subject-matter of the conciliation proceedings. However, a party may initiate arbitral or judicial proceedings, where such proceedings are necessary for preserving the party's rights.

APPOINTING THE ARBITRATOR

SYNOPSIS

1. **When Does a 'Dispute' Arise?**
2. **Does Arbitration Agreement Survive Breach of Contract Agreement?**
3. **Court Reference to Arbitration**
4. **Conditions Precedent to Invoking Arbitration**
5. **Appointment of Arbitrator in Terms of Agreement**
6. **Independence or Impartiality of Arbitrator**
7. **Challenge to Appointment of Arbitrator**
8. **Appointment of Arbitrator by Chief Justice**
9. **Appointment of Substitute Arbitrator**

1. When Does a 'Dispute' Arise?

The essence of arbitration is the resolution of a 'dispute'. Obviously therefore, there must be a 'dispute'. There can only be a dispute when a claim is asserted by one party and denied by the other on whatever grounds.

Dispute, in common parlance, entails an active element—an assertion of denying the claim, not merely inaction by not responding to the claim or request. However, it has been held by the Hon'ble Supreme Court in *McDermott International Inc.* v. *Burn Standard Co. Ltd.*[1], that 'the aforementioned principle ... would not mean that in every case the claim must be followed by a denial':

> "If a matter is referred to any arbitrator within a reasonable time, the party invoking the arbitration clause may proceed on the basis that the other party to the contract has denied or disputed his claim or is not otherwise interested in referring the dispute to the arbitrator."

Thus, there need not always be an act of denying the claim. By not responding in time, there is deemed to be constructive denial of the claim of the claimant. It is, however, suggested that the claimant should clarify in his notice that absence of response within a reasonable period[2] would also be construed as denial of the claim.

2. Does Arbitration Agreement Survive Breach of Contract Agreement?

The Hon'ble Supreme Court has dealt with the question as to whether the arbitration agreement, which is a clause in the contract agreement, survives after the contract stands terminated/repudiated. In *Magma Leasing & Finance Ltd.* v. *Potluri Madhavilata*[3], the Hon'ble Supreme Court drew attention to *National Agricultural Co-op. Marketing Federation India Ltd.* v. *Gains Trading Ltd.*,[4] and reiterated that:

1. (2006) 11 SCC 181: 2006 AIR SCW 3276.
2. You can specify the period.
3. AIR 2010 SC 488: (2009) 10 SCC 103.
4. (2007) 5 SCC 692: AIR 2007 SC 2327: (2007) 2 Arb LR 339: (2007) 5 MLJ 585.

"...Even if the performance of the contract comes to an end on account of repudiation, frustration or breach of contract, the arbitration agreement would survive for the purpose of resolution of disputes arising under or in connection with the contract.... This position is now statutorily recognised."

"Sub-section (1) of section 16 of the Act makes it clear that while considering any objection with respect to the existence or validity of the arbitration agreement, an arbitration clause which forms part of the contract, has to be treated as an agreement independent of the other terms of the contract; and a decision that the contract is *null* and *void* shall not entail *ipso jure* the invalidity of the arbitration clause."

Thus, the statement of law expounded by Viscount Simon, L.C. in *Heyman* as noticed above, equally applies to the situation where the contract is terminated by one party on account of the breach committed by the other particularly in a case where the clause is framed in wide and general terms.[1]

Merely because the contract has come to an end by its termination due to breach, the arbitration clause does not perish nor is rendered inoperative; rather it survives for resolution of disputes arising "in respect of" or "with regard to" or "under" the contract. This is in line with the earlier decisions of the Apex Court, particularly as laid down in *Kishorilal Gupta*[2].

3. Court Reference to Arbitration

Where there is an arbitration agreement, sub-sections (1) and (2) of section 8 of the Arbitration and Conciliation Act, 1996, grants power to the court to refer a dispute to arbitration. It provides as under:

"*8. Power to refer parties to arbitration where there is an arbitration agreement.*—(1) A judicial authority before which an action is brought in a matter which is the subject of an arbitration agreement shall, if a party so applies not later than when submitting his first statement on the substance of the dispute, refer the parties to arbitration.

(2) The application referred to in sub-section (1) shall not be entertained unless it is accompanied by the original arbitration agreement or a duly certified copy thereof."

Thus, the conditions which are required to be satisfied under sub-sections (1) and (2) of section 8 before the court can exercise its powers are:

(1) There must be an arbitration agreement [the agreement is to be submitted to court].

(2) A party to the agreement brings an action in the court against the other party.

(3) The subject-matter of the action is the same as the subject-matter of the arbitration agreement.

(4) The other party moves the court for referring the parties to arbitration, before it submits its first statement on the substance of the dispute.

1. *Magma Leasing & Finance Ltd.* v. *Potluri Madhavilata*, AIR 2010 SC 488: (2009) 10 SCC 103.
2. *Union of India* v. *Kishorilal Gupta and Bros.*, AIR 1959 SC 1362: (1960) 1 SCR 493: 1960 SCJ 1101: 1961 Andh LT 20.

Although this section implies that the respondent would have to invoke the arbitration agreement before submitting his 'statement on the substance of the dispute', the timing is not rigidly applied by the courts. If the party, who wants the matter to be referred to arbitration, applies to the court after submission of his statement and the party who has brought the action does not object, there is no bar on the court referring the parties to arbitration.[1]

4. Conditions Precedent to Invoking Arbitration

The provision for invoking the jurisdiction of the Hon'ble Chief Justice for appointment of arbitrator is contained in section 11 of the Arbitration and Conciliation Act, 1996—

11. * * *

(6) Where, under an appointment procedure agreed upon by the parties,—

(a) a party fails to act as required under that procedure; or

(b) the parties, or the two appointed arbitrators, fail to reach an agreement expected of them under that procedure; or

(c) a person, including an institution, fails to perform any function entrusted to him or it under that procedure,

a party may request the Chief Justice or any person or institution designated by him to take the necessary measure, unless the agreement on the appointment procedure provides other means for securing the appointment.

Thus, section 11(6)(c) implies that in case one of the parties to the arbitration agreement fails to perform any function entrusted to it, the other party shall have the right to approach the appropriate forum to take necessary measures in that regard. However, it is also implicit in the above provision that in a situation where the arbitration agreement provides for other measures for securing the appointment of an arbitrator, the same must be followed.

5. Appointment of Arbitrator in Terms of Agreement

The Arbitration Agreement should contain the name of the authority that has been designated by the parties to act as the arbitrator in the dispute which is the subject-matter of the agreement. In *ad hoc* arbitration, the arbitrator is to be appointed in the manner provided in the agreement.

The impartiality and/or independence of an arbitrator are essential features of this *quasi*-judicial process. In this context, we may look at the decision of the Hon'ble Supreme Court in *Indian Oil Corpn. Ltd.* v. *Raja Transport (P) Ltd.*[2]:

"If a party, with open eyes and full knowledge and comprehension of the said provision enters into a contract with a Government/statutory corporation/public sector undertaking containing an arbitration agreement providing that one of its Secretaries/Directors shall be the arbitrator, he cannot subsequently turn around and contend that he is agreeable for

1. *P. Anand Gajapathi Raju* v. *P.V.G. Raju,* (2000) 4 SCC 539: AIR 2000 SC 1886: (2000) 2 Arb LR 204: JT 2000 (4) SC 590: (2000) 3 MLJ 69.
2. (2009) 8 SCC 520.

settlement of the disputes by arbitration, but not by the named arbitrator who is an employee of the other party."

In a situation where the parties have agreed that the arbitrator could be an employee of one of the parties, there cannot be a challenge to the appointment of the arbitrator on the ground that the arbitrator is not 'impartial or independent' merely because he is an employee with one of the parties, if such appointment is permitted by the arbitration agreement. It has been held that—

> "Unless there is allegation against the named arbitrator either against his honesty or capacity or *mala fides* or interest in the subject-matter or reasonable apprehension of the bias, a named and agreed arbitrator cannot and should not be removed in exercise of a discretion vested in the Court under section 5 of the Act."[1]

There cannot be any automatic presumption of bias. But in a recent case before the Apex Court[2], it was noted that 'a provision for serving officers of one party being appointed as arbitrator(s) brings out considerable resistance from the other party, when disputes arise'. The Hon'ble Court observed that—

> "Having regard to the emphasis on independence and impartiality in the new Act, Government, statutory authorities and government companies should think of phasing out arbitration clauses providing for serving officers and encourage professionalism in arbitration."

The above observation should be treated as an *obiter,* and does not affect the legality of appointment serving or retired officials as arbitrators, if so permitted in the arbitration agreement.

6. Independence or Impartiality of Arbitrator

Section 12 provides that when a person is approached in connection with his possible appointment as an arbitrator, he shall disclose in writing any circumstances likely to give rise to justifiable doubts as to his independence or impartiality. This is a statutory requirement, and hence does not fall within the domain of 'party autonomy'. Throughout the arbitral proceedings, he is required disclose to the parties in writing, without delay, any change in circumstances which may reflect on his independence or impartiality.

It is interesting to note that the ICC Rules refer to the 'independence' of an arbitrator, while the 1996 UK Arbitration Act refers to 'impartiality' of an arbitrator. The LCIA Rules, on the other hand, use both the conjunctive and the disjunctive in relating 'independence' and 'impartiality'. It would thus appear that the expressions are intimately related.

As to what comprises 'independence' or 'impartiality', the International Bar Association ("IBA" for short) has laid down guidelines for the arbitrator to assess situations of conflict of interest. These have been included in ANNEXURE–E. Incidentally, there is now a proposal to formally introduce these 'guidelines' into the Arbitration law as standards of 'independence' and 'impartiality'.

---

1. *Indian Oil Corpn. Ltd.* v. *Raja Transport (P) Ltd.,* (2009) 8 SCC 520.
2. *Union of India* v. *Singh Builders Syndicate,* (2009) 4 SCC 523: (2009) 2 Arb LR 1.

The IBA has drawn up four lists depicting situations to help the arbitrator in deciding whether he/she is obligated to make a disclosure, and whether the arbitrator is obligated to withdraw from arbitration:

1. NON-WAIVABLE RED LIST—These are situations which give rise to justifiable doubts about independence and impartiality of arbitrator. The list includes situations deriving from the overriding principle that no person can be his or her own judge. Disclosure by arbitrator of such a situation cannot cure the conflict of interest situation. .
2. WAIVABLE RED LIST—These are situations which may give rise to doubts about independence and impartiality of arbitrator. The arbitrator is obligated to make full disclosure of such situations. These should be considered waivable only if the parties expressly state their willingness to have such a person act as arbitrator.
3. ORANGE LIST—These are potential conflict of interest situations. The arbitrator has a duty to disclose such situations. In all these situations, the parties are deemed to have accepted the arbitrator if, after disclosure, no timely objection is made.
4. GREEN LIST—In these situations, conflict of interest does not exist. The arbitrator has no duty to disclose situations falling within the Green List.

The lists should not be considered exhaustive. The IBA guidelines are annexed as Annexure E.

It is interesting to note that although a Bill to amend the 1996 Act was introduced in the Rajya Sabha in 2004, this has been withdrawn because of the huge amount of modifications/amendments suggested to the Bill. The government has now submitted a consultation paper on the subject, with proposals for amendment, which, *inter alia,* recognises the IBA guidelines.

What is important to note is that the appointment of a party nominated arbitrator can also be challenged by the other party, if there is doubt on the independence or impartiality of the a party appointed arbitrator.

7. Challenge to Appointment of Arbitrator

Section 12 casts on the arbitrator the duty to disclose any disqualification he may have—

(a) when he is approached in connection with his possible appointment as an arbitrator; and

(b) at any time throughout the arbitral proceedings, whenever such circumstance arises.

The above section, in sub-section (3) also sets out the grounds of challenge to the person appointed as arbitrator.

> "12(3) An arbitrator may be challenged only if—
>
> (a) circumstances exist that give rise to justifiable doubts as to his independence or impartiality, or
>
> (b) he does not possess the qualifications agreed to by the parties."

Section 13 lays down the procedure for such a challenge to appointment of an arbitrator. It has been held in *S.B.P. & Co.* v. *Patel Engineering Ltd.*[1] that:

> "A person aggrieved by the rejection of his objection by the Tribunal on its jurisdiction or the other matters referred to in that section, has to wait until the award is made to challenge that decision in an appeal against the arbitral award itself in accordance with section 34 of the Act. But an acceptance of the objection to jurisdiction or authority, could be challenged then and there, under section 37 of the Act. No second appeal is contemplated, but the right to approach the Supreme Court is saved."

8. Appointment of Arbitrator by Chief Justice

Section 11(8) of the Arbitration and Conciliation Act provides as under:

> "11(8) The Chief Justice or the person or institution designated by him, in appointing an arbitrator, shall have due regard to—
>
> (a) any qualifications required of the arbitrator by the agreement of the parties, and
>
> (b) other considerations as are likely to secure the appointment of an independent and impartial arbitrator."

On a plain understanding of the above provisions of the Act, it is seen that in a case where there is an arbitration agreement, a dispute has arisen and one of the parties has invoked the agreed procedure for appointment of an arbitrator and the other party has not co-operated, the party seeking arbitration, could approach the Chief Justice of the High Court if it is a 'domestic' arbitration, or of the Supreme Court if it is an 'international arbitration' to have an arbitrator or arbitral tribunal appointed. In *S.B.P. & Co.* v. *Patel Engg. Ltd.*,[1] the Hon'ble Supreme Court has held that:

> "The Chief Justice, when so requested, could appoint an arbitrator or arbitral tribunal depending on the nature of the agreement between the parties and after satisfying himself that the conditions for appointment of an arbitrator under sub-section (6) of section 11 do exist. The Chief Justice could designate another person or institution to take the necessary measures. The Chief Justice has also to have the qualification of the arbitrator in mind before choosing the arbitrator."

As to whether this was judicial or administrative function performed by the Hon'ble Chief Justice, it was observed the Hon'ble Chief Justice having been conferred with a power to act under the statute, he had the jurisdiction to satisfy himself that the conditions for the exercise of that power existed and that the case calls for the exercise of that power. It was held that before appointing the arbitrator, the Chief Justice has to adjudicate on issues which might have been raised, *e.g.*—

(i) the jurisdiction of the Chief Justice; or

(ii) whether the arbitration agreement, or any clause thereof is *null* or *void*; or

---

1. (2005) 8 SCC 618: AIR 2006 SC 450: (2005) 3 Arb LR 285: JT 2005 (9) SC 219: (2005) 7 Supreme 610.

(iii) whether there is a dispute subsisting which was capable of being arbitrated upon; or

(iv) whether conditions for exercise of power under section 11(6) of the Act exist; or

(v) the qualifications contemplated for the arbitrator by the parties.

Ordinarily, an arbitral tribunal has the right to decide whether it has jurisdiction to proceed with the arbitration, whether there was any agreement between the parties and the other matters referred to therein. However, the Hon'ble Supreme Court observed that in the above situation, it would be difficult to say that in spite of the finality conferred by sub-section (7) of section 11 of the Act to a decision of the Chief Justice on the issues of jurisdiction, existence of arbitral tribunal, etc., the arbitral tribunal can still go behind that decision and rule on its own jurisdiction, or on the existence of an arbitration clause. 'It would be incongruous to say' that after the Chief Justice had appointed an arbitral tribunal, the arbitral tribunal—the very creature brought into existence by the exercise of power by its creator, the Chief Justice – can turn round and say that the Chief Justice had no jurisdiction or authority to appoint the Tribunal. The Apex Court therefore held that section 16 has full play only when an arbitral tribunal is constituted without intervention under section 11(6) of the Act.

> "We are inclined to the view that the decision of the Chief Justice on the issue of jurisdiction and the existence of a valid arbitration agreement would be binding on the parties when the matter goes to the arbitral tribunal and at subsequent stages of the proceeding except in an appeal in the Supreme Court in the case of the decision being by the Chief Justice of the High Court or by a Judge of the High Court designated by him."

The decision in *Konkan Rly. Corporation Ltd.* v. *Rani Construction (P) Ltd.*[1] thus stood overruled.

The Hon'ble Court also dealt with other relevant aspects of exercise of powers under section 11 of the Act. The conclusions in the above case are summarised as follows:

(i) The power exercised by the Chief Justice of the High Court or the Chief Justice of India under section 11(6) of the Act is not an administrative power. It is a judicial power.

(ii) The power under section 11(6) of the Act, in its entirety, could be delegated, by the Chief Justice of the High Court only to another Judge of that Court, and by the Chief Justice of India to another Judge of the Supreme Court.

(iii) In case of designation of a Judge of the High Court or of the Supreme Court, the power that is exercised by the designated Judge would be that of the Chief Justice as conferred by the statute.

(iv) The Chief Justice or the designated Judge will have the right to decide the preliminary aspects like his own jurisdiction to entertain the request, the

1. (2002) 2 SCC 388: AIR 2002 SC 778: (2002) 1 Arb LR 326: JT 2002 (1) SC 587: (2002) 2 Bom LR 354.

existence of a valid arbitration agreement, the existence or otherwise of a live claim, the existence of the condition for the exercise of his power and on the qualifications of the arbitrator or arbitrators.

(v) The Chief Justice or the designated Judge would be entitled to seek the opinion of an institution in the matter of nominating an arbitrator qualified in terms of sub-section (8) of section 11 of the Act if the need arises, but the order appointing the arbitrator could only be that of the Chief Justice or the designated Judge.

(vi) Designation of a District Judge as the authority under section 11(6) of the Act by the Chief Justice of the High Court is not warranted in the scheme of the Act.

(vii) Once the matter reaches the arbitral tribunal or the sole arbitrator, the High Court would not interfere with the orders passed by the arbitrator or the arbitral tribunal during the course of the arbitration proceedings and the parties could approach the Court only in terms of section 37 of the Act or in terms of section 34 of the Act.

(viii) Since an order passed by the Chief Justice of the High Court or by the designated Judge of that Court is a judicial order, an appeal will lie against that order only under article 136 of the Constitution to the Supreme Court.

(ix) There can be no appeal against an order of the Chief Justice of India or a Judge of the Supreme Court designated by him while entertaining an application under section 11(6) of the Act.

(x) In a case where an arbitral tribunal has been constituted by the parties without having recourse to section 11(6) of the Act, the arbitral tribunal will have the jurisdiction to decide all matters as contemplated by section 16 of the Act.

A *Scott Avery clause* in the contract/arbitration agreement would make it mandatory to first approach the arbitral tribunal, before approaching the court. But if it is held by an adjudicator that the arbitration agreement has no force of application, then the *Scott Avery clause* will not apply, and parties can agitate the dispute in court. Similarly, a dispute at the very outset, not covered by the terms of the arbitration agreement, would also be beyond the jurisdiction of the arbitral tribunal, and the matter can be taken to court.

9. Appointment of Substitute Arbitrator

In *Yashwith Constructions (P) Ltd.* v. *Simplex Concrete Piles India Ltd.*,[1] a dispute had arisen in respect of a contract between the parties. The Managing Director of the respondent Company appointed an arbitrator in terms of the arbitration clause. The arbitrator thereafter withdrew for health reasons. Thereupon, the Managing Director of the respondent Company, in view of the mandate in the arbitration agreement promptly appointed a substitute arbitrator. The petitioner claimed that in the arbitration agreement there was no specific provision authorising the

1. (2006) 6 SCC 204: AIR 2006 SC 2798: (2006) 3 Arb LR 55: (2006) 4 Mad LJ 945: (2006) 5 Supreme 461.

Managing Director to appoint a substitute arbitrator, if the original appointment terminates or if the originally appointed arbitrator withdraws from the arbitration. He, therefore, prayed to the Hon'ble Chief Justice to appoint the substitute arbitrator. The Hon'ble Chief Justice declined, holding that the substitute arbitrator had been validly appointed, and therefore, there was no occasion for him to appoint an arbitrator. The Hon'ble Supreme Court examined this question, and held that:

> "... this so-called omission in the arbitration agreement is made up by the specific provision contained in section 15(2) of the Act. The withdrawal of an arbitrator from the office for any reason is within the purview of section 15(1)(a) of the Act. Obviously, therefore, section 15(2) would be attracted and a substitute arbitrator has to be appointed according to the rules that are applicable for the appointment of the arbitrator to be replaced. Therefore, what section 15(2) contemplates is an appointment of the substituted arbitrator or the replacing of the arbitrator by another according to the rules that were applicable to the appointment of the original arbitrator who was being replaced. The term "rules" in section 15(2) obviously referred to the provision for appointment contained in the arbitration agreement or any rules of any institution under which the disputes were referred to arbitration."

In the case in hand, it was held that there was no failure on the part of the party concerned as per the arbitration agreement, to fulfil his obligation in terms of section 11 of the Act. Hence, the jurisdiction of the Chief Justice could not be invoked under section 11(6) of the Act for appointing a substitute arbitrator. It was observed that:

> "When section 15(2) says that a substitute arbitrator can be appointed according to the rules that were applicable for the appointment of the arbitrator originally, it is not confined to an appointment under any statutory rule or rule framed under the Act or under the scheme. It only means that the appointment of the substitute arbitrator must be done according to the original agreement or provision applicable to the appointment of the arbitrator at the initial stage."

But in *S.B.P. & Co. (2)* v. *Patel Engg. Ltd.*[1], the situation was that the arbitrator appointed by respondent 1 declined to accept the appointment/arbitrate in the matter on the ground that in his capacity as Superintending Engineer and Chief Engineer, he was associated with Koyna Hydel Project, implying thereby that he may not be able to objectively examine the claims of the parties or the other party may question his impartiality. He did not enter upon the arbitration; there was no question of his withdrawing from the office of arbitrator so as to enable respondent 1 to appoint a substitute arbitrator. The arbitration agreement did provide for appointment of another arbitrator in the event originally appointed arbitrator was to resign. It was noticed by the Hon'ble Supreme Court that 'there was no plausible reason for the Court to presume that there is an omission in the agreement on the issue of appointment of a substitute arbitrator'. It was also

1. (2009) 10 SCC 293.

observed that 'section 15(2) of the Act does not *per se* apply to a case where an arbitrator appointed by a party to the agreement declines to accept the appointment or refuses to arbitrate in the matter'.

Distinguishing this case from the *Yashwith Constructions* case, the Hon'ble Supreme Court held that:

> "... in the absence of a clear stipulation to that effect in the agreements, respondent-1 could not have appointed a substitute arbitrator and the learned Designated Judge gravely erred in appointing the third arbitrator by presuming that the appointment of Shri S.L. Jain was in accordance with law."

It was held that the judgment in the *Yashwith Constructions* case 'cannot be read as laying down a proposition of law that in the absence of a specific provision in the arbitration clause, either party to the agreement can appoint a substitute arbitrator in the event of the originally appointed arbitrator refusing to act'.

INTERIM MEASURES

SYNOPSIS

1. Interim Measures by Court

Any party, even before committing the dispute to arbitration, can approach the court of competent jurisdiction for interim measure of protection[1] in respect of the following:

(a) the preservation, interim custody or sale of any goods which are the subject-matter of the arbitration agreement;

(b) securing the amount in dispute in the arbitration;

(c) the detention, preservation or inspection of any property or thing which is the subject-matter of the dispute in arbitration, or as to which any question may arise therein and authorising for any of the aforesaid purposes any person to enter upon any land or building in the possession of any party or authorising any samples to be taken or any observation to be made, or experiment to be tried, which may be necessary or expedient for the purpose of obtaining full information or evidence;

(d) interim injunction or the appointment of a receiver.

It is to be noted that only parties to the arbitration agreement have the *locus standi* to approach the competent court for 'interim measure of protection'. This again presupposes a valid arbitration agreement in respect of the matter in dispute. It has been clarified in *Sundaram Finance Ltd.* v. *NEPC India Ltd.*[2] 'that the court is not debarred from dealing with an application under section 9 merely because no notice has been issued under section 21 of the Arbitration and Conciliation Act, 1996'.

A piquant situation arises when a party avails of the remedy/order under section 9 of the Arbitration and Conciliation Act, 1996, but thereafter does not take any step to set the arbitral process in motion. It has therefore been observed by the Apex Court in *Sundaram Finance Ltd.* v. *NEPC India Ltd.*,[2] that while passing an

1. Section 9 of the Arbitration and Conciliation Act, 1996.
2. (1999) 2 SCC 479: AIR 1999 SC 565: (199) 1 Arb LR 305: JT 1999 (1) SC 49: (1999) 2 MLJ 53.

order under section 9, in order to ensure that effective steps are taken to commence the arbitral proceedings, the court 'can pass a conditional order to put the applicant to such terms as it may deem fit with a view to see that effective steps are taken by the applicant for commencing the arbitral proceedings'. Taking a cue from the above, some courts are putting conditions like a time-frame for taking steps for reference to arbitration, etc. The position has been clearly put by the Apex Court in *Firm Ashok Traders* v. *Gurumukh Das Saluja*[1]:

> "The court may also while passing an order under section 9 put the party on terms and may recall the order if the party commits breach of the terms."

Therefore, it is suggested that when dealing with a petition under section 9, the respondent should insist that the petitioner be directed to initiate steps to refer the 'dispute' to arbitration within a reasonable time-frame.

But the Apex Court has observed that 'it would not be correct to say that the power under section 9 of the Act is totally independent of the well-known principles governing the grant of an interim injunction that generally govern the courts in this connection'[2]. Similarly, whether the attempted termination of the contract could be restrained would also be a question that had to be considered in the context of well-settled principles for the grant of an injunction. In the above *Adhunik Steels* matter, the Apex Court has held that while the power to grant injunction is embodied in section 9, the normal rules that govern the court in the grant of interim orders should be followed:

> "The grant of an interim prohibitory injunction or an interim mandatory injunction are governed by well-known rules and it is difficult to imagine that the legislature while enacting section 9 of the Act intended to make a provision which was *de hors* the accepted principles that governed the grant of an interim injunction. Same is the position regarding the appointment of a receiver since the section itself brings in the concept of "just and convenient" while speaking of passing any interim measure of protection. The concluding words of the section, "and the court shall have the same power for making orders as it has for the purpose and in relation to any proceedings before it" also suggest that the normal rules that govern the court in the grant of interim orders is not sought to be jettisoned by the provision."

Therefore, the competent court will deal with any such application before it by applying the principles of *prima facie* case, balance of convenience and irreparable injury. Basing upon its assessment with respect to these factors, it will only pass an order if it feels that it is just and convenient to pass an interim order, including an order of injunction. An injunction would not be granted if award of damages is an adequate compensation.

---

1. (2004) 3 SCC 155: AIR 2004 SC 1433: (2004) 1 Arb LR 141: JT 2004 (2) SC 352: (2004) 3 MPLJ 266: 2004 AIR SCW 366: 2004 (2) SRJ 565: (2004) 1 SCALE 297: 2004 (1) Supreme 754.
2. *Adhunik Steels Ltd.* v. *Orissa Manganese and Minerals (P) Ltd.*, (2007) 7 SCC 125: AIR 2007 SC 2563: (2007) 3 Arb LR 65: (2007) 6 MLJ 80: 2007 AIR SCW 4558: (2007) 9 SCALE 126.

In *Mohit Bhargava* v. *Bharat Bhushan Bhargava*[1], in respect of the power of court to issue interim orders in the nature of injunction, the Hon'ble Supreme Court has discussed two orders passed by the executing court. The court had passed an injunction on a third party not to hand over possession of the building in question to the judgment-debtor, and when that party surrendered the title deeds to the court, an order was passed for safekeeping of title deed documents. It was observed that:

> "...These two orders are certainly within the jurisdiction of the court which passed the decree since they are only orders of restraint being issued to a person from handing over a property in his possession to the judgment-debtor along with the documents concerned and keeping the documents in safe custody. They are in the nature of a "freezing order" or a "Mareva injunction" and an order akin to an Anton Piller order, orders that can be issued even if the property or the person concerned is outside the jurisdiction of the court. In the circumstances, especially since the judgment-debtor never bothered to question those orders as and when they were passed, we are of the view that the High Court was not in error in refusing to interfere with those orders...."

Although the above two types of orders are slightly different from each other, they have been spoken of by the Hon'ble Court in the same breath, in the above judgment. These orders can also be issued by the competent court while dealing with an application under section 9 of the Act. The nature of the above two orders is discussed below.

1.1 The Mareva Injunction

The 'Mareva Injunction' (also known as a 'freezing order' or 'Mareva order'), is a court order which freezes assets so that a defendant to an action cannot dissipate the assets from beyond the jurisdiction of a court so as to frustrate a judgment. It is variously construed as part of a court's inherent jurisdiction to restrain breaches of its process. It is named after *Mareva Compania Naviera SA* v. *International Bulkcarriers SA*[2], decided in 1975. [*See* Annexure G].

In the above cited case, Lord Denning, the celebrated Master of Rolls observed that 'if it appears that the debt is due and owing, and there is danger that the debtor may dispose of his assets so as to defeat it before judgment, the court has jurisdiction in a proper case to grant an interlocutory judgment so as to prevent him from disposing of those assets'.

There are thus the following essential pre-conditions for making such an order:

(i) There must be strong *prima facie* evidence in favour of the claimant that the claim is due;

(ii) There is real possibility that the defendants might dispose of the assets before a judicially enforceable order is pronounced.

---

1. (2007) 4 SCC 795: AIR 2007 SC 1717: (2007) 55 AIC 89: (2007) 2 Jab LJ 383: (2007) 3 MPLJ 419: (2007) 3 Supreme 828: 2007 AIR SCW 2707: (2007) 6 SCALE 38.
2. [1975] 2 Lloyd's Rep 509.

However, in the concurring judgment Lord Justice Roskill cautioned:

> "This court should not, therefore, on an *ex parte* interlocutory application be too ready to disturb the practice of the past save for good reasons."

Therefore, the courts would not be inclined to pass an order of Mareva injunction unless it is necessary to prevent a grave injustice.

1.2 The Anton Piller Order

An 'Anton Piller order' is an order allowing for an applicant, without notice to a respondent, to enter the respondent's premises and inspect or seize documents or other items. For getting an Anton Piller order from a Court, it is necessary to demonstrate to the Court through substantial evidence that this legally binding order is both vital and necessary to preserve evidence.

An 'Anton Piller order' can include the following four conditions:

- a requirement that the respondent disclose the whereabouts of specified documents;
- an inventory of seized items to be prepared and that the defendant have an opportunity to check it and sign it before documents are removed;
- an order not to use documents or items seized for any purpose other than for the purpose under which the order was originally granted;
- an offer of explanation to the persons served with the order in plain language as to the meaning and effect of the order and the person's right to obtain legal advice before compliance with it.

It is named after the celebrated case of *Anton Piller KG* v. *Manufacturing Processes Ltd.*[1], before the Court of Appeal. [*See* Annexure H].

Although its origin lay in an equitable discretionary remedy, in effect it is like a search warrant. As the celebrated Lord Denning observed:

> "Under these orders, the plaintiff and his solicitors are authorised to enter the defendant's premises so as to inspect papers, provided the defendant gives permission."

In the *Anton* case, Lord Denning has himself observed that 'such an order can only be justified in the most exceptional circumstances'. He observed such orders would be given in the extreme case when there would grave danger of the property being spirited away, or evidence being destroyed. It is trite law that the plaintiff must show the nature of evidence in possession of the defendant, and also show a strong *prima facie* case that evidence is likely to be destroyed.

There are four essential pre-conditions for making such an order:

(i) there must be extremely strong *prima facie* case;

(ii) the damage, potential or actual, must be very serious for the applicant;

(iii) there must be clear evidence that defendants have in their possession incriminating documents or things; and

(iv) there is real possibility that the defendants might destroy such material before application *inter partes* can be made.

1. [1976] Ch 55.

In enforcing such orders, Lord Denning has suggested circumspection:

> "On the service of it, the plaintiffs should be attended by their solicitor, who is an officer of the court. They should give the defendants an opportunity of considering it and of consulting their own solicitor. If the defendants wish to apply to discharge the order as having been improperly obtained, they must be allowed to do so. If the defendants refuse permission to enter or to inspect, the plaintiffs must not force their way in. They must accept the refusal, and bring it to the notice of the court afterwards, if need be on an application to commit."

The catch, however, is that the court orders the defendant to give the necessary permission. The defendant can only refuse permission on pain of either committing contempt, or the adjudicator may also draw adverse inference.

2. Pre-conditions for Order of Interim Measure from Court

Although there is no need for the party approaching the court under section 9 to first send a notice invoking arbitration, it has been held by the Apex Court in *Firm Ashok Traders* v. *Gurumukh Das Saluja*[1], that 'if arbitral proceedings are not commenced within a reasonable time of an order under section 9, the relationship between the order under section 9 and the arbitral proceedings would stand snapped and the relief allowed to the party shall cease to be an order made "before", *i.e.*, in contemplation of arbitral proceedings'. Hence, it was decided that:

> "The court, approached by a party with an application under section 9, is justified in asking the party and being told how and when the party approaching the court proposes to commence the arbitral proceedings. Rather, the scheme in which section 9 is placed obligates the court to do so. The court may also while passing an order under section 9 put the party on terms and may recall the order if the party commits breach of the terms."

If no steps are taken by the beneficiary of the interim order to refer the dispute to arbitration within a reasonable time, it is open to the other party to approach the court to have the order set aside.

The term "party" occurring in section 9 of the Act has been defined in section 2(h) of the 1996 Act:

> '2(h) "party" means a party to an arbitration agreement'.

3. Interim Measure after Publication of Award

As mentioned earlier, section 9 permits a party to 'apply to the court for interim measures... after the making of the arbitral award but before it is enforced in accordance with section 36'. Such order in the nature of attachment of assets, or appointment of receiver, or even a Mareva injunction, may be necessary to ensure that execution of the award is not frustrated before the commencement of execution proceedings after the period of limitation for filing appeal.

The power of the court to impart interim measures before publication of the award cannot be taken to be on the same premise as after its publication. Interim

1. (2004) 3 SCC 155: AIR 2004 SC 1433: (2004) 1 Arb LR 141: JT 2004 (2) SC 352: (2004) 3 MPLJ 592: 2004 AIR SCW 366: (2004) 1 SCALE 297: 2004 (1) Supreme 754.

measures ordered by the court after publication of the award need to be in conformity and consonance of the award as such judicial intervention would be in anticipation of enforcement of the award of the arbitral tribunal in accordance with section 36.

It would be beyond the purview of the court under section 9 after publication of the award to accord interim measures that are in excess of the award or in conflict with it. Judicial intervention under section 9 after publication of the award can at best be in aid of enforcement of the award.

4. Interim Measure of Protection by Arbitral Tribunal

Under section 17 of the Arbitration and Conciliation Act, 1996, the arbitral tribunal may, at the request of a party, order a party to take any interim measure of protection as the arbitral tribunal may consider necessary in respect of the subject-matter of the dispute:

> "17. *Interim measures ordered by arbitral tribunal.*—(1) Unless otherwise agreed by the parties, the arbitral tribunal may, at the request of a party, order a party to take any interim measure of protection as the arbitral tribunal may consider necessary in respect of the subject-matter of the dispute.
>
> (2) The arbitral tribunal may require a party to provide appropriate security in connection with a measure ordered under sub-section (1).

The powers of the court under section 9 are very wide. Section 17 clothes the arbitral tribunal with somewhat similar powers, but these powers are limited. The table below would make this clear:

Interim Measures under section 9	Interim Measures under section 17
(i) Appointment of a guardian for a minor or person of unsound mind; (ii) Preservation, interim custody or sale of any goods which are 'the subject-matter of the arbitration agreement; (iii) Detention, preservation or inspection of any property or thing which is the subject-matter of the dispute in arbitration; (iv) Samples to be taken or any observation to be made, or experiment to be tried, which may be necessary or expedient for the purpose of obtaining full information or evidence; (iv) Interim injunction or the appointment of a receiver.	The arbitral tribunal may, at the request of a party, order a party to take any interim measure of protection as the arbitral tribunal may consider necessary in respect of the subject-matter of the dispute.
Securing the amount in dispute in the arbitration	The arbitral tribunal may require a party to provide appropriate security in connection with a measure ordered under sub-section 1.

In the first part of section 9, the powers of the court are considerable, while those given to the arbitral tribunal under section 17 are nebulous. While the powers under section 9 can lead to a Mareva injunction or an Anton Piller order, it is clear that the powers of arbitral tribunal under section 17 are not so specific.

The provisions of section 9 are applicable to arbitrations which are held in India between Indian nationals, and to international commercial arbitrations held in India[1]. But section 17 can operate only during the existence of the arbitral tribunal and its being functional. 'During that period, the power conferred on the arbitral tribunal under section 17 and the power conferred on the court under section 9 may overlap to some extent'[2].

As seen above, in the 1996 Act, the arbitral tribunal is empowered by section 17 of the Act to make orders amounting to interim measures. But under section 17 of the 1996 Act the arbitrator cannot issue any direction which would go beyond the reference or the arbitration agreement.

It has been observed by the Supreme Court in *MD, Army Welfare Housing Organisation* v. *Sumangal Services (P) Ltd.*[3] that:

> "Even under section 17 of the 1996 Act, an interim order must relate to the protection of the subject-matter of dispute and the order may be addressed only to a party to the arbitration. It cannot be addressed to other parties. Even under section 17 of the 1996 Act, no power is conferred upon the Arbitral Tribunal to enforce its order nor does it provide for judicial enforcement thereof."

The above inherent weakness of an order under section 17 makes it more tempting to invoke the power of the judiciary under section 9. It should also be noticed that recourse to arbitrator can only be had after he has been appointed, and till he has rendered the award.

An order of the arbitral tribunal granting or refusing to grant an interim measure under section 17 is an appealable order.[4] Since an award/order of the arbitral tribunal has the force of a decree, the appeal has to be to a court having the jurisdiction to hear appeal from an original decree. No second appeal lies, but parties are free to approach the Hon'ble Supreme Court. Similarly, court assistance may be taken for enforcement in the same manner as in the case of decree.

---

1. *Bhatia International* v. *Bulk Trading S.A.,* (2002) 4 SCC 105: AIR 2002 SC 1432: (2002) 1 Arb LR 675: JT 2002 (3) SC 150: (2003) 1 Jab LJ 264: 2002 AIR SCW 1285: 2002 (2) SCJ 420: (2002) 2 SCALE 612: 2002 (2) Supreme 395.
2. *Firm Ashok Traders* v. *Gurumukh Das Saluja,* (2004) 3 SCC 155: AIR 2004 SC 1433: (2004) 1 Arb LR 141: JT 2004 (2) SC 352: (2004) 3 MPLJ 592: 2004 AIR SCW 366: (2004) 1 SCALE 297: 2004 (1) Supreme 754.
3. (2004) 9 SCC 619: AIR 2004 SC 1344.
4. Refer section 37(2)(b) of the Arbitration and Conciliation Act, 1996.

PROCEEDINGS BEFORE ARBITRAL TRIBUNAL

SYNOPSIS

1. Statements of Claim and Defence

Section 23 of the Arbitration and Conciliation Act, 1996 has the following provisions regarding statement of claim and defence:

> "23. *Statements of claim and defence.*—(1) Within the period of time agreed upon by the parties or determined by the arbitral tribunal, the claimant shall state the facts supporting his claim, the points at issue and the relief or remedy sought, and the respondent shall state his defence in respect of these particulars, unless the parties have otherwise agreed as to the required elements of those statements.
>
> (2) The parties may submit with their statements all documents they consider to be relevant or may add a reference to the documents or other evidence they will submit.
>
> (3) Unless otherwise agreed by the parties, either party may amend or supplement his claim or defence during the course of the arbitral proceedings, unless the arbitral tribunal considers it inappropriate to allow the amendment or supplement having regard to the delay in making it."

1.1 Statement of Claim

The above provisions imply that the parties are free to frame their own rules, or adopt institutional rules on the subject.

The International Chamber of Commerce has a detailed description of what the Statement of Claim should contain. Drawing upon its provisions, the author suggests that even in *ad hoc* arbitration, the contents should include:

(a) the name in full, description and address of each of the parties;

(b) a description of the nature and circumstances of the dispute giving rise to the claim(s);

(c) a statement of the relief sought, including, to the extent possible, an indication of any amount(s) claimed; and

(d) the relevant contract agreement and, in particular, the arbitration agreement.

It would be pertinent to give at this stage any comments as to the place of arbitration, the applicable rules of law and the language of the arbitration.

1.2 Statement of Defence

Again drawing on the ICC Rules, the respondent may be required to file a reply within the time allotted by the arbitration agreement, the arbitral rules of the institution, or by the arbitral tribunal. Such a reply is variously described as 'Statement of Defence', 'Answer', etc. It should, *inter alia,* contain the following information:

(a) the name in full, description and address of the respondent;

(b) its comments as to the nature and circumstances of the dispute giving rise to the claim(s); and

(c) its response to the relief sought.

The respondent can also file any counter-claim(s) made by the respondent along with the Statement of Defence. This should provide for the following:

(a) a description of the nature and circumstances of the dispute giving rise to the counter-claim(s); and

(b) a statement of the relief sought, including, to the extent possible, an indication of any amount(s) counter-claimed.

The claimant may file a reply to any counter-claim within the time allotted.

2. Evidence Before the Arbitral Tribunal

The arbitral tribunal will be guided by the arbitration agreement or by the institutional rules on the subject. However, for *ad hoc* arbitration, in line with the IBA Rules of Evidence [Annexure – F], some guidelines have been attempted, which can be considered by the parties/arbitrator.

2.1 Documents

Each Party may be required to submit to the arbitral tribunal and to the other Parties all documents available to it on which it relies, including public documents and those in the public domain, except for any documents that have already been submitted by another Party.

Within the time ordered by the arbitral tribunal, any Party may submit to the other Party and to the arbitral tribunal a request to produce containing;

(a) a description of a requested document sufficient to identify it, and reasonably believed to exist;

(b) a description of how the documents requested are relevant and material to the outcome of the case; and

(c) a statement that the documents requested are not in the possession, custody or control of the requesting Party, and of the reason why that

Party assumes the documents requested to be in the possession, custody or control of the other Party.

Within the time ordered by the arbitral tribunal, the Party to whom the Request to Produce is addressed shall produce to the arbitral tribunal and to the other Parties all the documents requested in its possession, custody or control as to which no objection is made.

If the Party to whom the Request to Produce is addressed has objections to some or all of the documents requested, it shall state them in writing to the arbitral tribunal within the time ordered by the arbitral tribunal.

The arbitral tribunal shall, in consultation with the Parties consider the Request to Produce and the objections. The arbitral tribunal may order the Party to whom such request is addressed to produce to the arbitral tribunal and to the other Party those that it considers relevant.

If a Party wishes to obtain the production of documents from a person or organisation who is not a Party to the arbitration and from whom the Party cannot obtain the documents on its own, the Party may take recourse to an Anton Piller order from the competent court.

If copies are submitted or produced, they must conform fully to the originals. At the request of the arbitral tribunal, any original must be presented for inspection.

2.2 *Witnesses of Fact*

Evidence of witness may be through 'Witness Statement' in the form of an affidavit. Each Witness Statement shall contain:

(a) the full name and address of the witness, his or her present and past relationship (if any) with any of the Parties, and a description of his or her background, qualifications, training and experience, if such a description may be relevant and material to the dispute or to the contents of the statement;

(b) a full and detailed description of the facts, and the source of the witness's information as to those facts, sufficient to serve as that witness's evidence in the matter in dispute;

(c) an affirmation of the truth of the statement; and

(d) the signature of the witness and its date and place.

Parties may also be allowed to submit revised or additional Witness Statements, including statements from persons not previously named as witnesses, in response to matters contained in another Party's Witness Statement or Expert Report.

Each witness who has submitted a Witness Statement may be asked to appear for testimony at an Evidentiary Hearing, unless the Parties agree otherwise. If a witness does not appear without a valid reason at Evidentiary Hearing, the arbitral tribunal may disregard that Witness Statement.

Under section 27 of the Arbitration and Conciliation Act, 1996 assistance of court may be taken in the matter of taking evidence. The procedure given in section 27 will have to be followed.

2.3 *Party-Appointed Expert*

A Party can rely on a 'Party-Appointed Expert' as a means of evidence on specific issues. The arbitral tribunal may be approached by the Party for time for the Party-Appointed Expert to submit an Expert Report. The Expert Report shall contain:

(a) the full name and address of the Party-Appointed Expert, his or her present and past relationship (if any) with any of the Parties, and a description of his or her background, qualifications, training and experience;

(b) a statement of the facts on which he or she is basing his or her expert opinions and conclusions;

(c) his or her expert opinions and conclusions, including a description of the method, evidence and information used in arriving at the conclusions;

(d) an affirmation of the truth of the Expert Report (an Affidavit); and

(e) the signature of the Party-Appointed Expert with date and place.

The Party-Appointed Expert should be prepared to appear for testimony at an Evidentiary Hearing. If a Party-Appointed Expert does not appear without a valid reason for testimony at an Evidentiary Hearing, the Arbitral Tribunal can disregard his or her Expert.

2.4 *Tribunal-Appointed Experts*

The Arbitral Tribunal may also appoint one or more independent Tribunal-Appointed Experts to report to it on specific issues designated by the arbitral tribunal.

The Apex Court noted in *Sime Darby Engg. SDN. BHD.* v. *Engineering India Ltd.*[1], that 'it is clearly provided in the said Act[2] that an Arbitral Tribunal can, if necessary, take the help of experts in terms of section 27 of the said Act. If the sole arbitrator requires the assistance of an expert he can always take such assistance.'

Section 6 of Arbitration and Conciliation Act, 1996 provides as under:

"26. *Expert appointed by arbitral tribunal.*—(1) Unless otherwise agreed by the parties, the arbitral tribunal may—

(a) appoint one or more experts to report to it on specific issues to be determined by the arbitral tribunal, and

(b) require a Party to give the expert any relevant information or to produce, or to provide access to, any relevant documents, goods or other property for his inspection.

"(2) Unless otherwise agreed by the Parties, if a Party so requests or if the arbitral tribunal considers it necessary, the expert shall, after delivery of his written or oral report, participate on an oral hearing where the Parties

---

1. (2009) 7 SCC 545: AIR 2009 SC 3158: (2009) 80 AIC 14: (2009) 9 SCALE 740: 2009 AIR SCW 5063.
2. The Arbitration and Conciliation Act, 1996.

have the opportunity to put questions to him and to present expert witnesses in order to testify on the points at issue.

"(3) Unless otherwise agreed by the Parties, the expert shall, on the request of a Party, make available to that Party for examination all documents, goods or other property in the possession of the expert with which he was provided in order to prepare his report.

The clause 'unless otherwise agreed by the parties' at the beginning of each sub-para would mean that the Parties are free to agree otherwise, or that the arbitral tribunal could be guided by institutional rules on the subject.

The Tribunal-Appointed Expert may be required to submit to the arbitral tribunal and to the Parties a statement of his or her independence from the Parties and the arbitral tribunal. Within the time ordered by the arbitral tribunal, the Parties shall inform the arbitral tribunal whether they have any objections to the Tribunal-Appointed Expert's independence. The arbitral tribunal may decide promptly whether to accept any such objection.

The Tribunal-Appointed Expert may report in writing to the arbitral tribunal. The Tribunal-Appointed Expert shall describe in the report the method, evidence and information used in arriving at the conclusions. The arbitral tribunal may send a copy of such Expert Report to the Parties. The Parties may examine any document that the Tribunal-Appointed Expert has examined and any correspondence between the arbitral tribunal and the Tribunal, Appointed Expert.

The Parties have to be given the opportunity to respond to the report. At the request of a Party or of the arbitral tribunal, the Tribunal-Appointed Expert may be present at an Evidentiary Hearing.

2.5 Role and Duties of 'Expert Witnesses' Generally

Whether the expert is appointed by a Party, or by the arbitral tribunal, the expert's duty is to the arbitral tribunal and not to the instructing Party.

Experts have the responsibility and duty to exercise reasonable skill and care to those instructing them, and to comply with any relevant code of ethics of their profession. However, when they are instructed to give or prepare evidence for the purpose of arbitration, they should have an overriding duty to help the arbitral tribunal on matters within their expertise. This duty overrides any obligation to the person instructing or paying them. Experts must not serve the exclusive interest of those who retain them.

Experts are expected to give opinions which are 'independent'. One way for the expert to test this independence is to ensure that evidence/opinion is such that it would have been the same if given the same instructions by an opposing Party. Experts are not expected to promote the point of view of the Party instructing them.

Experts should confine their opinions to matters which are material to the disputes between the Parties, and provide opinions only in relation to matters which lie within their expertise. Experts should indicate if particular questions or issues fall outside their expertise.

Experts should take into account all material facts placed before them. Their reports should set out those facts and any 'authority' on which they have relied in forming their opinions. They should indicate if any further information is required for forming a 'final' opinion.

Experts should inform those instructing them without delay of any change in their opinions on any material matter and the reason for it.

2.6 Evidentiary Hearing

The arbitral tribunal may limit or exclude any question to, answer by or appearance of a witness, if it considers such question, answer or appearance to be irrelevant, immaterial, burdensome, and duplicative.

Questions to a witness during direct and redirect testimony should not be unreasonably leading.

The claimant may ordinarily be required to first present the testimony of its witnesses, followed by the respondent presenting testimony of its witnesses, and then by the presentation by claimant of rebuttal witnesses, if any. Following direct testimony, any other Party may question such witness, in an order to be determined by the arbitral tribunal. The Party who initially presented the witness may subsequently have the opportunity to ask additional questions on the matters raised in the other Party's questioning. The arbitral tribunal, upon request of a Party or on its own motion, may vary this order of proceeding, including the arrangement of testimony by particular issues or in such a manner that witnesses presented by different Parties be questioned at the same time and in confrontation with each other. The arbitral tribunal may ask questions to a witness at any time.

Any witness providing testimony may be required to first affirm, in an appropriate manner, that he or she is telling the truth. If the witness has submitted a Witness Statement or an Expert Report, the witness would be required to confirm it. The Parties may agree or the arbitral tribunal may order that the Witness Statement or Expert Report shall serve as that witness's direct testimony.

The arbitral tribunal may also request any person to give oral or written evidence on any issue that the arbitral tribunal considers to be relevant and material. Any witness called and questioned by the arbitral tribunal may also be questioned by the Parties.

2.7 Admissibility and Assessment of Evidence

The arbitral tribunal has to determine the admissibility, relevance, materiality and weight of evidence. The arbitral tribunal may, at the request of a Party or on its own motion, exclude from evidence or production any document, statement, oral testimony or inspection for reasons like:

(a) lack of sufficient relevance or materiality;

(b) legal impediment or privilege under the legal or ethical rules determined by the arbitral tribunal to be applicable;

(c) unreasonable burden to produce the requested evidence;

(d) loss or destruction of the document that has been reasonably shown to have occurred;

(e) grounds of commercial or technical confidentiality that the arbitral tribunal determines to be compelling;

(f) grounds of special political or institutional sensitivity (including evidence that has been classified as secret by a government or a public international institution) that the arbitral tribunal determines to be compelling; or

(g) considerations of fairness or equality of the Parties that the arbitral tribunal determines to be compelling.

The arbitral tribunal may also make necessary arrangements to permit evidence to be considered subject to suitable confidentiality protection.

The arbitral tribunal may draw adverse inference, if a Party fails without satisfactory explanation to make available any other relevant evidence, including testimony, sought by one Party to which the Party to whom the request was addressed has not objected in due time, or fails to make available any evidence, including testimony, ordered by the arbitral tribunal to be produced.

COURT INTERVENTION IN ARBITRATION

SYNOPSIS

1. **Intervention by Court**
2. **Termination of Mandate of Arbitrator**
3. **Court Assistance in Ensuring Attendance of Witnesses**

1. Intervention by Court

The Arbitration and Conciliation Act, 1996 provides for taking assistance of court in four types of situations, during the arbitral process:

(i) Interim measures by court, prior to appointment of arbitrator [Section 9];

(ii) Assistance of Chief Justice (of High Court)/Chief Justice of India in the matter of appointment of arbitrator(s) [Section 11];

(iii) Termination of mandate of arbitrator, who has *de jure* or *de facto* become unable to perform his functions [Section 14]; and

(iv) Court assistance in ensuring attendance of witnesses [Section 27].

The first two situations have been exhaustively dealt with earlier. Here we will look at court assistance in termination of mandate of arbitrator, and ensuring attendance of witnesses.

2. Termination of Mandate of Arbitrator

Section 14(2) of the Act provides for taking assistance of court for termination of mandate of arbitrator. 'Sub-section (1) of section 14 lays down that the mandate of an arbitrator shall terminate if he becomes *de jure* or *de facto* unable to perform his functions or for other reasons fails to act without undue delay and he withdraws from his office or the Parties agree to terminate his mandate. Sub-section (2) lays down that if there is any controversy between the Parties in relation to any of the grounds referred to in clause (a) of sub-section (1) and there is no other provision in the agreement between the parties, either Party can apply to the Court for termination of the mandate of an arbitrator ....'[1]

On the termination of mandate of the arbitrator, section 15(2) requires that such an appointment shall be made according to the rules which were applicable to the appointment of an original arbitrator. The term "rules" is not confined to statutory rules or the rules framed by the competent authority in exercise of the power of delegated legislation, but it also includes the terms of the arbitration agreement entered into between the Parties.[1] For example, on the termination of the

1. *S.B.P. & Co. (2)* v. *Patel Engg. Ltd.*, (2009) 10 SCC 293.

mandate of the presiding arbitrator, in accordance with section 15(2) of the Act, the two nominated arbitrators were first required to reach a consensus.[1]

In *Ashalata S. Lahoti* v. *Hiralal L. Tiladhar*[2] it has been held that if the Tribunal is constituted contrary to section 10 of the Act, the arbitrators will *de jure* not be able to perform those functions. In that event the parties can move the Court to decide whether the mandate stood terminated.

In *N.B.C.C. Ltd.* v. *J.G. Engineering Pvt. Ltd.*[3], the Hon'ble Supreme Court has observed that 'apparently there is no provision under the Act for the Court to fix a time-limit for the conclusion of an arbitration proceeding, but the Court can opt to do so in the exercise of its inherent power on the application of either party. Where, however, the arbitration agreement itself provides the procedure for enlargement of time and the parties have taken recourse to it, and consented to the enlargement of time by the arbitrator, the Court cannot exercise its inherent power in extending the time fixed by the parties in the absence of the consent of either of them.'

In the case in hand, the arbitration agreement provided that the arbitrator had the power to enlarge the time to make and publish the award only by mutual consent of the Parties. The respondent in that case had not given any consent for extension of time of the arbitrator. Thus, the arbitrator had no power to further enlarge the time to make and publish the award, and, therefore, his mandate had automatically terminated after the expiry of the time fixed by the Parties to conclude the proceedings.

It was held that the mandate of the arbitrator stood automatically terminated only because of the fact that the arbitrator having failed to conclude his proceedings within time did not warrant to be continued as an arbitrator in the absence of the consent of both the Parties.

3. Court Assistance in Ensuring Attendance of Witnesses

Section 27 of the Arbitration and Conciliation Act, 1996 makes a provision for rendering assistance to the Parties in ensuring attendance of witnesses:

> "27. *Court assistance in taking evidence.*—(1) The arbitral tribunal, or a Party with the approval of the arbitral tribunal, may apply to the Court for assistance in taking evidence.
>
> *　　*　　*
>
> "(4) The Court may, while making an order under sub-section (3), issue the same processes to witnesses as it may issue in suits tried before it.
>
> (5) Persons failing to attend in accordance with such process, or making any other fault, or refusing to give their evidence, or guilty of any contempt to the arbitral tribunal during the conduct of arbitral proceedings, shall be subject to the like disadvantages, penalties and punishments by order of the

---

1. *National Highways Authority of India* v. *Bumihiway DDB Ltd. (JV)*, (2006) 10 SCC 763: 2006 AIR SCW 4968: (2006) 9 SCALE 564.
2. 1999 (2) RAJ 384 (Bom).
3. AIR 2010 SC 640.

Court on the representation of the arbitral tribunal as they would incur for the like offences is suits tried before the Court."

The above provisions are quite clear. The process may be initiated either by the arbitral tribunal or by any of the Parties with the approval of the arbitral tribunal. The above provisions may be used for ensuring attendance of witness and/or production of documents.

INSTITUTIONAL ARBITRATION

SYNOPSIS

1. Taking Assistance of an Institution

The Arbitration and Conciliation Act, 1996 provides for taking assistance of institutions in the arbitration process. Section 2(1)(a) defines "arbitration" as meaning any arbitration whether or not administered by a permanent arbitral institution. Thus, this definition recognises that the arbitration could be under a body like the Indian Chamber of Commerce or the International Chamber of Commerce[1].

Again, section 6 of the Act specifically provides as under:

"6. *Administrative assistance.*—In order to facilitate the conduct of the arbitral proceedings, the parties, or the arbitral tribunal with the consent of

1. *Bhatia International* v. *Bulk Trading S.A.*, (2002) 4 SCC 105: AIR 2002 SC 1432: (2002) 1 Arb LR 675: JT 2002 (3) SC 150: (2003) 1 Jab LJ 264: 2002 AIR SCW 1285: 2002 (2) SCJ 420: (2002) 2 SCALE 612: 2002 (2) Supreme 395.

the Parties, may arrange for administrative assistance by a suitable institution or person."

Some specialised institutions have grown up which provide physical facilities and secretarial and other facilities to Parties for the arbitration proceedings. The provisions of the above section would indicate that even in *ad hoc* arbitration, the parties or the arbitrator can take the assistance of such an institution.

Of more importance is the use of institutions for having institution administered arbitrations. The rules of these institutes typically deal with areas of party autonomy. By submitting to such institutional arbitration, the Parties agree to be bound by their rules, and the arbitrators from their panels also agree to be bound by their rules. The Arbitration and Conciliation Act, 1996 permits this:

> "2(6) Where this Part, except section 28, leaves the Parties free to determine a certain issue, that freedom shall include the right of the Parties to authorise any person including an institution, to determine that issue."

These institutes may or may not have physical structures to facilitate arbitration, but these are available for hire in any case.

2. The UNCITRAL Model

The UNCITRAL Arbitration Rules are a comprehensive, internationally accepted, set of rules which parties can adopt for an arbitration arising under their contract. These rules, however, are designed essentially for a non-institutional form of arbitration. The UNCITRAL does not play any role in the administration of the arbitration. Lack of institutional support often means delays and frustrations in arbitration according to these rules.

Parties need to make special provision if they are to enjoy the benefit of institutional support in the conduct of a UNCITRAL rules arbitration. The two main areas to be considered are:

(a) appointment of the arbitrator(s); and

(b) institutional support for the progress of the arbitration.

*2.1 **Appointment of Arbitrator(s): Appointing Authority***

The Model Arbitration clause, footnoted to the UNCITRAL Arbitration Rules, in fact, advises parties to consider designating an appointing authority. If the parties fail to do so, then they have to ask the Permanent Court of Arbitration in The Hague to designate an appointing authority. The appointing authority designated by the Permanent Court then appoints the arbitrator. This process takes time, and can result in substantial and sometimes serious delays to the whole process.

*2.2 **Administration of the Arbitration***

The UNCITRAL Arbitration Rules do not provide for the management of the financial and other practical aspects of the arbitration. This is left entirely to the arbitral tribunal and the parties. The tribunal fixes its own fees, determines the amount of deposits towards its fees, collects the deposits from the parties, and pays itself at the end of the arbitration from the deposits. The parties and the tribunal also try to manage other administrative chores in the proceedings. In an *ad hoc* arbitration, if the fees are not fixed in advance by the parties, they generally go along with the fees fixed by the arbitral tribunal.

3. Arbitral Institutions

Arbitral institutions try to take care of the routine administration involved in the arbitral process, and give a framework to regulate aspects like time management, expenses, etc. Some of the well-known arbitral institutions are:

India	The Indian Council of Arbitration (New Delhi)
International	The International Chamber of Commerce (Paris) The London Court of International Arbitration (London) The Singapore International Arbitration Centre (Singapore)

Besides, the chambers of commerce also have their own regulations to assist their members to have chamber administered arbitration for resolving differences among members *inter se*.

We can look into the rules of the above institutes and see how they have covered the areas of party autonomy.

4. The Indian Council of Arbitration (New Delhi)

Principally the Indian Council of Arbitration (New Delhi), or the 'ICA', deals with domestic arbitrations. It also handles maritime arbitrations and international arbitrations. It has 'tie-in' arrangements with the International Chamber of Commerce (Paris), commonly known as the 'ICC'.

4.1 Appointment of Arbitrators

The ICA maintains a panel of arbitrators consisting of Retired Judges, Advocates, Shipping Experts, Chartered Accountants, Chartered Engineers, Businessmen, Foreign Nationals and Executives for acting as arbitrators.

Under the rules of arbitration of the ICA, either a sole arbitrator or three arbitrators may be appointed. The sole arbitrator is appointed by consent of the parties and, failing such consent, the Council appoints the sole arbitrator. Where three arbitrators have to be appointed, each of the parties appoints one arbitrator and the Council appoints the third arbitrator who acts as the Presiding Arbitrator of the arbitral tribunal.

The rules provide that before accepting his nomination the prospective arbitrator shall disclose any circumstances such as financial or personal interest in the outcome of the award, likely to disqualify him as an impartial arbitrator. Upon receipt of such information, the Registrar shall disclose it to the parties, who if willing to proceed under the circumstances disclosed, shall advise the Registrar accordingly. Otherwise, the arbitrator shall stand disqualified. Going by the rules, a party can even object to appointment of the nominee arbitrator of the other party.

4.2 Jurisdiction of Tribunal

The arbitration commences with filing by the claimant of a 'Statement of Claim' with the ICA. The claim must have full details, supported by documents. The rules of the ICA provide that the respondent may make a counter-claim against the claimant, provided the counter-claim arises under the same transaction as the original claim. The respondent must submit the counter-claim with full details supported by all documents and information as in the case of the claim.

The jurisdiction of the arbitral tribunal appointed to adjudicate upon the original claim also extends to the counter-claim, and there is no change in the number of members of arbitral tribunal already constituted on the basis of the original claim.

4.3 Time Taken in the Arbitral Process

Rule 44 of the ICA arbitration rules provides for 'Fast Track Arbitration' to decide the reference in a fixed time frame of 3 to 6 months, or any other time agreed between the parties, according to the Fast Track Arbitration Procedure. The arbitral tribunal will be authorised to decide the dispute on the written pleadings, documents and written submissions filed by the parties without any oral hearings. The tribunal shall have power to call for any further information/clarification from the parties in addition to the pleading and documents filed by them. However, an oral hearing may be held if both the parties make a joint request or if the tribunal considers an oral hearing necessary in any particular case.

The arbitration sessions will go on as far as possible on a day-to-day basis from 10.30 a.m. to 4.30 p.m. once the hearing begins after completion of all the formalities. The arbitral tribunal would not ordinarily adjourn a hearing at the request of any party, and if the tribunal agrees for adjournment, it may impose costs.

The Rules of Arbitration of the ICA are annexed at Annexure A.

5. The International Chamber of Commerce (Paris)

If parties agree, disputes and difference in relation to the contract can be settled through arbitration in accordance with the rules of arbitration of the International Chamber of Commerce ("ICC" for short).

5.1 Number of Arbitrators

The parties are free to agree on whether there should be a sole arbitrator or three. Failing an agreement, the Court will decide. When three arbitrators are required, the parties can chose one arbitrator each. The parties also have the right to decide how the presiding or the sole arbitrator should be appointed. Often the task of choosing the presiding arbitrator is given to the two arbitrators the parties have already selected.

5.2 The Arbitrators

The party can pick its arbitrator of his or her nationality, language or expertise—someone who understands the culture or line of business. The Court checks all arbitrators for their independence and availability. It will step in to appoint a chair or a sole arbitrator if there is no agreement, or even choose the arbitrators if the parties so desire.

5.3 Place of Arbitration

The ICC claims that it has a worldwide network of 'national committees', and is, therefore, able to cast its net wide in choosing the arbitrator. ICC arbitrations can, therefore, be held anywhere in the world. The parties can choose the best place for getting the arbitration handled, keeping in view the convenience in getting the award enforced, if necessary. This choice of seat of arbitration may have effect on the law applicable to the arbitral procedure.

5.4 Rules of Law Governing the Arbitration

The parties can agree on the substantive law to be applied to the arbitration process.

5.5 Language of Arbitration

Arbitrations can take place in any language. Parties may agree on the language either at the time of entering into the contract, or even before commencement of arbitration.

5.6 Deadlines

Parties can indicate a deadline for completing the arbitration, and include it in the arbitration agreement. Every effort is made by the ICC to meet the deadline.

5.7 Protection

Parties may apply to the arbitrators for interim measures—for example an injunction not to sell assets or transfer funds—pending an award. This is provided in section 17 of the Arbitration and Conciliation Act, 1996.

5.8 Parameters of the Case

Parties can decide on how to proceed with the arbitration. They can decide whether the arbitral tribunal should proceed with the matter solely on the basis of documents, or also rely on oral evidence. They can decide whether the case warrants an expert opinion.

The Rules of Arbitration of the ICC are annexed at Annexure B.

6. The London Court of International Arbitration (London)

The London Court of International Arbitration ("LCIA" for short), is a very old institution, but it came into its own when the Arbitration Court was established in 1985. Based in London, the LCIA claims to provide flexible and impartial administration of arbitration.

6.1 Place of Arbitration

Parties adopting the LCIA's recommended clauses can specify the seat of arbitration in the arbitration agreement.

6.2 Appointment of Arbitrators

The parties can nominate their respective nominee arbitrators. But the LCIA Court may refuse to appoint the party-nominated arbitrator if it determines that the nominee is not independent or impartial or is not suitable. The LCIA claims that it ensures arbitrators are suitably qualified and without conflict, and have an immediately clear diary.

6.3 Coverage of LCIA Rules

The LCIA rules take care of many areas of party autonomy:

(i) mechanism and time-frame for appointment of the tribunal;

(ii) challenges to arbitrators;

(iii) seat and language of arbitration;

(iv) interim measures of protection; and control of costs of arbitration.

The Rules of Arbitration of the LCIA are annexed at Annexure C.

7. The Singapore International Arbitration Centre (Singapore)

With its substantial experience in the appointment of arbitrators and its wide network of arbitrators in the region and beyond, the Singapore International Arbitration Centre ('SIAC') claims to be in a commendable position to act as an appointing authority.

Where SIAC is simply designated as the appointing authority in the arbitration agreement, the rules of SIAC on appointment of arbitrators, arbitrators' fees and financial management will apply.

7.1 Administration of the Arbitration

SIAC, as an institution that regularly administers arbitrations, can provide support to the Tribunal and the parties in the management of practical matters. Parties would have to make provision in their contract for the administration of their arbitration cases by SIAC.

7.2 Appointment of Arbitrators

Unless the parties agree otherwise, the number of arbitrators is at the discretion of the Registrar. Normally, a sole arbitrator is appointed.

The candidates nominated by the parties, or by any third person(s) including the arbitrators already appointed, are subject to confirmation by the Chairman of SIAC.

The Chairman will have due regard to any qualifications required of the arbitrator by the agreement of the parties, and will ensure appointment of an independent and impartial arbitrator.

7.3 Time taken in the Arbitration

The SIAC rules fix a time-table for the various steps in the arbitral process:

Statement of the case by claimant	30 days
Statement of defence/counter-claim	30 days
Further written statements as decided by tribunal	45 days
Framing of issues by tribunal	45 days
Publishing award after close of proceedings	45 days

However, there is no time-limit on the arbitration proceedings, though the SIAC claims to monitor the progress, and is the 'gentle persuader'.

7.4 Seat of Arbitration

The infrastructure of SIAC is best suited to having the arbitration in Singapore, though it has tie-up arrangements for other places as well.

The Rules of Arbitration of the SIAC are annexed at Annexure D.

DAMAGES FOR BREACH OF CONTRACT

SYNOPSIS

1. **Breach of Contract**
2. **Damages for Breach**
3. **Computation of Damage under CISG**
4. **Liquidated Damage**
5. **Penalty**
   - **5.1 Forfeiture of Security Deposit**
   - **5.2 Forfeiture of Earnest Money Deposit**
   - **5.3 Withdrawal of Concession**
6. **Liquidated Damages and Penalty under UK Law**
7. **Unliquidated Damage**

1. Breach of Contract

The process of commercial arbitration has the objective of resolving a dispute that arises out of performance or non-performance of contractual obligations by a party to the contract. Hence, it is essential to have a fair idea about what claims are admissible under the Indian Contract Act, 1872 in relation to domestic arbitration, or a contract governed by the Indian law.

2. Damages for Breach

Most contracts will not leave it open for determination at a later date the compensation to be paid for breach of contract. The parties would either make a genuine pre-estimate of damages to be paid by the party in breach, or seek to put a cap on it. In the Indian law of contract, section 74 deals with liquidated damage, penalty, performance guarantee and mitigation of loss:

Damages for Breach of Contract

> *73. Compensation for loss or damage caused by breach of contract.*—When a contract has been broken, the party who suffers by such breach is entitled to receive, from the party who has broken the contract, compensation for any loss or damage caused to him thereby, which naturally arose in the usual course of things from such breach, or which the parties knew, when they made the contract, to be likely to result from the breach of it.

Remote or Indirect Loss

> Such compensation is not to be given for any remote and indirect loss or damage sustained by reason of the breach.

Failure to discharge Obligation

> *Compensation for failure to discharge obligation resembling those created by contract*—When an

obligation resembling those created by contract has been incurred and has not been discharged, any person injured by the failure to discharge it is entitled to receive the same compensation from the party in default, as if such person had contracted to discharge it and had broken his contract.

Mitigation

Explanation.—In estimating the loss or damage arising from a breach of contract, the means which existed of remedying the inconvenience caused by the non-performance of the contract must be taken into account.

Liquidated Damage

74. Compensation for breach of contract where penalty stipulated for.—When a contract has been broken, if a sum is named in the contract as the amount to be paid in case of such breach, or if the contract contains any other stipulation by way of penalty, the party complaining of the breach is entitled, whether or not actual damage or loss is proved to have been caused thereby, to receive from the party who has broken the contract, reasonable compensation not exceeding the amount so named or, as the case may be, the penalty stipulated for.

Penalty

Explanation.—A stipulation for increased interest from the date of default may be a stipulation by way of penalty.

Performance Guarantee

Exception.—When any person enters into any bail-bond, recognizance or other instrument of the same nature, or, under the provisions of any law, or under the orders of the Central Government or of any State Government, gives any bond for the performance of any public duty or act in which the public are interested, he shall be liable, upon breach of the condition of any such instrument, to pay the whole sum mentioned therein.

Explanation.—A person who enters into a contract with Government does not necessarily thereby undertake any public duty, or promise to do an act in which the public are interested.

The above sections of the Act dealing with damages or penalty applies when there is a breach of contract. It contemplates and provides against two classes of cases—

Class: I—If an amount is named in the contract to be paid in case of such breach; or

Class: II—If the contract contains any other stipulation by way of penalty.

In the *first class of cases*, the parties make a genuine pre-estimate of the amount of compensation that the defaulting party will pay to the suffering party on a breach. The sum is mentioned in the contract, and is not left for a competent court to determine.

In the *second class of cases*, the measure of damages is reasonable compensation if it realistically can be assessed, not exceeding the *'penalty'* stipulated. If the compensation agreed to be paid in the event of breach of contract is excessive and highly disproportionate to the likely loss, *viz.*, the amount is fixed *in terrorem*[1], with a view to discouraging breach of contract, it is known as *'penalty'*. Whether a stipulation was a penalty or liquidated damages, depended on the construction of the contract to be judged as at the time it is made, and a mere description as a penalty or liquidated damages, though relevant, is not decisive[2].

3. Computation of Damage under CISG

Under CISG[3], the formulation for compensation for breach of contract is contained in article 74 of CISG:

> *Article 74.*—Damages for breach of contract by one party consist of a sum equal to the loss, including loss of profit, suffered by the other party as a consequence of the breach. Such damages may not exceed the loss which the party in breach foresaw or ought to have foreseen at the time of the conclusion of the contract, in the light of the facts and matters of which he then knew or ought to have known, as a possible consequence of the breach of contract.

Since it deals with sale of goods, the formulation is slightly different from that of section 73 of the Indian Contract Act. The above rule not only indicates the amount which can be claimed, but also the circumstances in which damages can be claimed.

Taking a view of the legal propositions given above, we can lay down the criteria that need to be met, for losses to graduate to a claim in damages:

(i) Losses must have been suffered by the party not in breach, as a consequence of a breach of contract.

(ii) The consequences naturally arose in the usual course of things from such breach.

(iii) The consequences of the breach must have been foreseeable by the party in breach at the time of the conclusion of the contract.

(iv) Such compensation is not to be given for any remote and indirect loss or damage sustained by reason of the breach.

(v) The damages payable to the party not in breach cannot exceed the loss that the party foresaw (pre-estimate), or ought to have foreseen.

The ability to claim damages is capped by the foreseeability rule. The amount of damages that can be recovered by the party not in breach 'may not exceed the

1. As a threat.
2. *State of Orissa* v. *Calcutta Co. Ltd.*, AIR 1981 Ori 206.
3. United Nations Convention on International Sale of Goods (CISG).

loss which the party in breach foresaw or ought to have foreseen at the time of the conclusion of the contract, in the light of the facts and matters which he then knew or ought to have known, as a possible consequence of the breach of contract'.

4. Liquidated Damage

If the compensation to be paid is a genuine pre-estimate of the prospective damages, it is known as *liquidated damage*. The Hon'ble Supreme Court has laid down the law[1] relating to *liquidated damage:*

"(i) If the terms are clear and unambiguous stipulating the liquidated damages in case of the breach of the contract unless it is held that such estimate of damages/compensation is unreasonable or is by way of penalty, party who has committed the breach is required to pay such compensation and that is what is provided in section 73 of the Contract Act.

(ii) Section 74 is to be read along with section 73 and, therefore, in every case of breach of contract, the person aggrieved by the breach is not required to prove actual loss or damage suffered by him before he can claim a decree. The court is competent to award reasonable compensation in case of breach even if no actual damage is proved to have been suffered in consequence of the breach of a contract.

(iii) In some contracts, it would be impossible for the court to assess the compensation arising from breach and if the compensation contemplated is not by way of penalty or unreasonable, the court can award the same if it is genuine pre-estimate by the parties as the measure of reasonable compensation."

Section 74 thus provides that 'for breach of contract where penalty is stipulated for or a sum is named and lays down that when a contract has been broken, if a sum is named in the contract as the amount to be paid in case of such breach, or if the contract contains any other stipulation by way of penalty, the party complaining of the breach is entitled, whether or not actual damage or loss is proved to have been caused thereby, to receive from the party who has broken the contract reasonable compensation not exceeding the amount so named or, as the case may be, the penalty stipulated for'[2].

If the question whether a named sum is 'liquidated damage' goes before a court/arbitral tribunal, the authority will go into the facts of the case. In deciding whether the amount fixed is genuine pre-estimate or reasonable compensation or not, it would be a factor for consideration whether the sum named in the agreement is not disproportionate to the injury caused and whether the burden evenly and equitably falls on both parties to the contract. When parties have expressly agreed that recovery from the contractor for breach of the contract is pre-estimated genuine liquidated damages and is not by way of penalty duly agreed by the parties, there

1. *Oil & Natural Gas Corpn. Ltd.* v. *SAW Pipes Ltd.,* (2003) 5 SCC 705: AIR 2003 SC 2629: (2003) 2 Arb LR 5: JT 2003 (1) SC 171: 2003 AIR SCW 3041: (2003) 4 SCALE 92: 2003 (3) Supreme 449.
2. *Shiva Jute Baling Ltd.* v. *Hindley & Co. Ltd.,* AIR 1959 SC 1357: 1960 SCJ 35: (1960) 1 MLJ (SC) 1: (1960) 1 SCR 569.

would be no justifiable reason to arrive at a conclusion that still the purchaser should prove loss suffered by it because of delay in supply of goods[1].

It is possible for the parties to sign a contract that provides for liquidated damages for specific breaches only, leaving other types of breaches to be dealt with as unliquidated damages. The arbitrator has to determine which 'breaches' are covered by the provision for 'liquidated damages' in the contract agreement. It has been held by the Apex Court in *SAIL* v. *Gupta Brother Steel Tubes Ltd.*,[2] that—

> "We are not aware of any principle that once the provision of liquidated damages has been made in the contract, in the event of breach by one of the parties, such clause has to be read covering all types of breaches although parties may not have intended and provided for compensation in express terms for all types of breaches."

5. Penalty

As regard 'penalty', a Division Bench of the Rajasthan High Court[3] enunciated the principles by which the Courts are to be governed in holding whether a particular clause amounts to a penalty or not:

(i) Where a sum is named in the agreement as payable on breach thereof, the plaintiff cannot be entitled to the entire sum so named *'simpliciter'*.

(ii) The plaintiff will be entitled to a 'reasonable compensation', subject to the amount named therein being maximum.

(iii) What is 'reasonable compensation' would depend upon and must be determined by the circumstances of each case.

(iv) The effect of the Indian Law of Contract, as embodied in section 74 is to do away with the distinction between *'penalty'* and *'unliquidated damages'*.

(v) The plaintiff must prove the damages suffered by him, but such proof may be direct or circumstantial, and need not have arithmetical exactitude.

(vi) If the plaintiff succeeds in establishing that the sum named in the agreement is genuine pre-estimate of damages, or would otherwise be a reasonable compensation for the breach, the Court may grant the entire sum named in the agreement as compensation. If, on the other hand, the Court comes to the conclusion that the amount as fixed was *in terrorem*, or unconscionable, and extravagant, it would be open to it to award such sum as may appear to be reasonable.

Where the Court is unable to assess the compensation, the sum named by the parties, if it be regarded as a genuine pre-estimate, may be taken as the measure of reasonable compensation, but not if the sum named is regarded as being in the nature of penalty. Therefore, in Indian law, what is called a "penalty clause" in

1. *Oil & Natural Gas Corpn. Ltd.* v. *SAW Pipes Ltd.*, (2003) 5 SCC 705: AIR 2003 SC 2629: (2003) 2 Arb LR 5: JT 2003 (1) SC 171: 2003 AIR SCW 3041: (2003) 4 SCALE 92: 2003 (3) Supreme 449.
2. (2009) 10 SCC 63.
3. *Badhava Singh* v. *Charan Singh*, AIR 1955 Raj 87: ILR (1954) 4 Raj 755.

a contract is a mere *brutum fulmen*[1], an agreement that neither party has any intention of enforcing at all to any extent. Such a penalty clause merely fixes a maximum for damages, which would be difficult to estimate in terms of money, and any how does not deprive the aggrieved party of his right to damages that can be so estimated[2].

5.1 Forfeiture of Security Deposit

In ordinary course a security deposit is intended to be refunded and the amount in question is kept in deposit only for the purpose of securing the performance of the contract. The said amount is forfeited only when a breach of the contract occurs and results in a legal injury. The Hon'ble Supreme Court has held[3] that *'there is no ground for holding that the expression "contract contains any other stipulation by way of penalty" is limited to cases of stipulation in the nature of an agreement to pay money or deliver property on breach and does not comprehend covenants under which amounts paid or property delivered under the contract, which by the terms of the contract expressly or by clear implication are liable to be forfeited'*. It, therefore, applies to forfeiture of security deposit as provided in the contract.

From the mere fact that a contract was broken by the other side, and that the remaining part of the contract was required to be done departmentally or by giving a new contract, the Court cannot hold that a legal injury has occurred[4].

5.2 Forfeiture of Earnest Money Deposit

Earnest money is part of the purchase price when the transaction goes forward. It is forfeited when the transaction falls through by reasons of the fault or failure of the vendee[5]. What is strictly known as a deposit must possess a two-fold character. It must first be a part payment and next it must be of the nature of money 'staked'. Such a deposit is forfeitable upon default made by the depositor. It has been held by the Hon'ble Supreme Court[6] that *'forfeiture of reasonable amount paid as earnest money does not amount to imposing a penalty'*. Hence in such a case, section 74 will not apply.

5.3 Withdrawal of Concession

In a case before the Hon'ble Supreme Court, a beneficial right was bestowed on one of the defendants to acquire a property for an amount considerably lower than the market price. However, the said defendant was subjected to the condition that if he had to take the advantage of the bargain he was under a duty to pay the stipulated amount by the time mentioned in the agreement. On failure to do so within time, he was to be deprived of this special benefit. It was held by the Hon'ble Supreme Court[7] that:

---

1. A provision by which no rights are divested, and from which none can be obtained, and neither binds nor bars anyone—Black's Law Dictionary.
2. *State of Orissa* v. *Calcutta Co. Ltd.*, AIR 1981 Ori 206.
3. *Fateh Chand* v. *Balkishan Dass*, AIR 1963 SC 1405: (1964) 1 SCA 174: (1964) 1 MLJ (SC) 60: (1964) 1 SCJ 187: (1964) 1 SCR 515.
4. *Messrs. Variety Body Builders* v. *Union of India*, AIR 1973 Guj 256 (259).
5. *Chiranjit Singh* v. *Har Swarup*, AIR 1926 PC 1: 24 All LJ 248: 94 Ind Cas 782.
6. *Maula Bux* v. *Union of India*, (1969) 2 SCC 554: AIR 1970 SC 1955: (1970) 1 SCR 928: 1970 All LJ 783: (1970) 2 MLJ (SC) 61: 1970 (2) SCJ 249.
7. *Sova Ray* v. *Gostha Gopal Dey*, (1988) 2 SCC 134: AIR 1988 SC 981: JT 1988 (1) SC 583: (1988) 3 SCR 287.

"Such a clause cannot be considered to be a penalty clause. The expression 'penalty' is an elastic term with many different shades of meaning but it always involves an idea of punishment. The impugned clause in the present case does not involve infliction of any punishment; it merely deprives Defendant 9 of a special advantage in case of default".

6. Liquidated Damages and Penalty under UK Law

It is a decided principle under English law that the parties to a contract may set down a sum that would be paid by a party in the event of a breach of contract. The liquidated damages clause is enforceable. However, such liquidated damages clause may not be penal in nature. It has been decided[1] that a liquidated damages clause would be considered a penalty and unenforceable where the sum to be paid by the defendant was 'extravagant and unconscionable in amount in comparison with the greatest loss that could conceivably be provided to have followed from the breach'. The differences between such 'liquidated damages' and 'penalty' have been laid down as follows:

(i) Though the parties to a contract who use the words 'penalty' or 'liquidated damages' may *prima facie* be supposed to mean what they say, yet the expression used is not conclusive. The Court must find out whether the payment stipulated is in truth a penalty or liquidated damages. This doctrine may be said to be found passim in nearly every case.

(ii) The essence of a penalty is a payment of money stipulated as *in terrorem* of the offending party; the essence of liquidated damages is a genuine covenanted pre-estimate of damage.

(iii) The question whether a sum stipulated is penalty or liquidated damages is a question of construction to be decided upon the terms and inherent circumstances of each particular contract, judged of as at the time of the making of the contract, not as at the time of the breach.

(iv) To assist this task of construction various tests have been suggested, which if applicable to the case under consideration may prove helpful, or even conclusive. Such tests are:

(a) It will be held to be penalty if the sum stipulated for is extravagant and unconscionable in amount in comparison with the greatest loss that could conceivably be proved to have followed from the breach.

(b) It will be held to be a penalty if the breach consists only in not paying a sum of money, and the sum stipulated is a sum greater than the sum which ought to have been paid.

(c) There is a presumption that it is penalty when 'a single lump-sum is made payable by way of compensation, on the occurrence of one or more or all of several events, some of which may occasion serious and others but trifling damage'.

(d) It is no obstacle to the sum stipulated being a genuine pre-estimate of damage, that the consequences of the breach are such as to make

1. *Dunlop Pneumatic Tyre Co. Ltd.* v. *New Garage Co Ltd.*, [1915] AC 79 (House of Lords).

> precise pre-estimation almost impossible. On the contrary, that is just the situation when it is probable that pre-estimated damage was the true bargain between the parties.

Penalty clauses are not enforceable. The principle that penalty clauses are unenforceable apply equally to payments that a party to the contract would otherwise be entitled to withhold. That is to say, if a liquidated damages clause is in the form of a right to withhold payment, and meets the criterion of a penalty, the right to withhold the payment is unenforceable.

Where liquidated damages clause is characterised as a penalty, the claimant is still entitled to sue for damages and have them quantified by a court, and the measure of damage will be the actual loss proved.

7. Unliquidated Damage

The discussion on the consequences of breach of contract would not be complete without a discussion on 'unliquidated damage', although this is more relevant as a liability in tort. It is a sum of money not established in advance by the contracting parties as a compensation for a breach of contract, but determined by a judicial authority/arbitral tribunal after such breach occurs. In general, no interest will be allowed on unliquidated damages.

In calculating unliquidated damages, it must be borne in mind that 'damages must have some correlation with the loss suffered .... The authority imposing the penalty or damages must, therefore, apply its mind to this aspect of the matter'[1].

In 'works contract', loss of profit to the contractor resulting from breach of contract or illegal termination of contract by the other party is admissible in damages. The measure of the loss is to be judicially determined. It has been held in *A.T. Brij Paul Singh* v. *State of Gujarat*[2] that:

> "What must be the measure of profit and what proof should be tendered to sustain the claim are different matters. But the claim under this head is certainly admissible."

The concept of damages is restitutory. It is awarded only to compensate the party not in breach for the loss suffered by that party as a result of the breach. As seen above, it could include loss of profit. It has been observed by the Hon'ble Supreme Court in *McDermott International Inc.* v. *Burn Standard Co. Ltd.*,[3] that 'sections 55 and 73 of the Indian Contract Act do not lay down the mode and manner as to how and in what manner the computation of damages or compensation has to be made'.

> "As computation depends on circumstances and methods to compute damages, how the quantum thereof should be determined is a matter which would fall for the decision of the arbitrator."

Hence, the relevance of adjudication of a claim in damages.

---

1. *Organo Chemical Industries* v. *Union of India*, (1979) 4 SCC 573: AIR 1979 SC 1803: (1979) 2 Lab LJ 416: 1979 Lab IC 1261: (1979) 55 FJR 283.
2. (1984) 4 SCC 59: AIR 1984 SC 1703: 1984 UJ (SC) 915: 1984 SCC (Lab) 18.
3. (2006) 11 SCC 181: 2006 AIR SCW 3276: (2006) 6 SCALE 220: (2006) 2 (Supp) 2 SCR 409: JT 2006 (11) 376.

MITIGATION OF LOSS

SYNOPSIS

1. **Duty to Mitigate Loss under Indian Law**
2. **Duty to Mitigate under International Law**
3. **Recovery of Expenses Incurred in Mitigation**

1. Duty to Mitigate Loss under Indian Law

When deciding on a claim of damages for breach of contract for sale of goods, a question that is often posed to the claimant is whether he has done enough to mitigate the loss consequent on the breach. The two factors on the basis of which damages to the aggrieved party are calculated in case of breach by a party to the contract are well-settled[1]:

(i) As far as possible, he who has proved a breach of a bargain to supply what he contracted to get is to be placed in as good a situation as if the contract had been performed.

(ii) The injured party has the duty of taking all reasonable steps to mitigate the loss consequent on the breach, and therefore cannot claim any part of the damage which is attributable to his negligence in taking such steps.

Mitigation of loss is, therefore, a duty cast on the aggrieved party. In the Indian Law of Contract, this principle of mitigation of loss is embodied in the following '*Explanation*' to section 73 of the Contract Act:

> "*Explanation.*—In estimating the loss or damage arising from a breach of contract, the means which existed of remedying the inconvenience caused by the non-performance of the contract must be taken into account."

In terms of the above *Explanation* to section 73, 'the principle of mitigation of loss does not give any right to the party who is in breach of the contract but it is a concept that has to be borne in mind by the court while awarding damages'[2]. But the aggrieved party is under no obligation to injure himself or his commercial reputation in trying to reduce the damages payable by the party in breach, nor need he take steps which would injure other innocent persons.

2. Duty to Mitigate under International Law

International conventions, also clearly lay down the duty of the aggrieved party to take positive steps to reduce the damage caused by the breach of contract. The UN Convention on Contracts for the International Sale of Goods (CISG) has incorporated this doctrine of mitigation specifically in article 77.

---

1. *Organo Chemical Industries* v. *Union of India,* (1979) 4 SCC 573: AIR 1979 SC 1803: (1979) 2 Lab LJ 416: 1979 Lab IC 1261: (1979) 55 FJR 283.
2. (1984) 4 SCC 59: AIR 1984 SC 59: 1984 UJ (SC) 915.

"Article 77: A party who relies on a breach of contract must take such measures as are reasonable in the circumstances to mitigate the loss, including loss of profit, resulting from the breach. If he fails to take such measures, the party in breach may claim a reduction in the damages in the amount by which the loss should have been mitigated."

The idea behind the above article 77 is that the injured party cannot recover damages or losses which he should have avoided. It may be noticed that 'losses' include 'loss of profit'.

This principle is also accepted in the Principles of European Contract Law (PECL) in article 9:505:

"Article 9:505: Reduction of Loss: (1) The non-performing party is not liable for loss suffered by the aggrieved party to the extent that the aggrieved party could have reduced the loss by taking reasonable steps.

"(2) The aggrieved party is entitled to recover any expenses reasonably incurred in attempting to reduce the loss."

The above article of PECL allows recovery of expenses incurred in mitigating loss, but does not mention anything about loss of profit. However, article 9:502 mentions loss of profit as a measure of damage:

"Article 9:502: General Measure of Damages: The general measure of damages is such sum as will put the aggrieved party as nearly as possible into the position in which it would have been if the contract had been duly performed. Such damages cover the loss which the aggrieved party has suffered and the gain of which it has been deprived."

The concept of 'damages' in PECL is similar to that in the Indian Law of Contract. It is to be noticed that while in article 9:505, the word 'loss' is mentioned, in article 9:502, what is mentioned is 'damages'. Looking at the above provisions in CISG and PECL, it is possible to take a view that the term 'damages' is to be understood to expand on 'losses', and includes 'loss of profit'.

The CISG text provides that a party who relies on a breach of contract 'must' take measures to mitigate the 'loss'. This language is imperative, and it imposes a duty on the aggrieved party to mitigate the 'loss'. But PECL only suggests that the non-performing party is not liable for damages which the injured party could have reduced. The wording is not as strong as the one in the CISG.

The Indian law would seem to leave it to the court or tribunal to decide whether means 'existed of remedying the inconvenience caused by the non-performance of the contract'. It states that means of mitigating the breach 'must be taken into account' when deciding on a claim of damage. The inactivity or failure to take reasonable steps would be held against the claimant when the adjudicator assesses the claim of damages.

3. Recovery of Expenses Incurred in Mitigation

The UNIDROIT Principles (2004) attempt to state the law in clear terms:

"*Article 7.4.8* (Mitigation of harm)

(1) The non-performing party is not liable for harm suffered by the aggrieved party to the extent that the harm could have been reduced by the latter party's taking reasonable steps.

(2) The aggrieved party is entitled to recover any expenses reasonably incurred in attempting to reduce the harm."

The language is very lucid. But it adds a new dimension—reasonableness of expenses incurred in attempting to 'reduce the harm'. It would be open to determination by the court or tribunal as to what expense would be considered reasonable when steps are taken to mitigate the loss.

From the above discussions, therefore, the following principles emerge in regard to mitigation of losses, when the adjudicator decides on claim of damages:

(i) The aggrieved party/claimant is not entitled to recover damages for any part of the loss resulting from breach of contract that he could have avoided by taking reasonable steps.

(ii) The aggrieved party may recover 'reasonable' expenses incurred in taking 'reasonable steps' to mitigate the loss occasioned by breach of contract by the defendant.

(iii) Even if the injured party takes more than 'reasonable steps' to mitigate loss, the party cannot recover for the losses avoided by such extraordinary effort, nor recover anything more than 'reasonable expenses'.

In order to claim relief, the party in breach will have to prove that mitigation was possible, and also the extent to which the loss could have been reduced. On the other hand, the aggrieved party could set-up a defence that mitigation would not have been possible without putting himself out of the way.

JURISDICTION OF ARBITRATOR

SYNOPSIS

1. **Jurisdiction of Arbitral Tribunal**
2. **Error within the Jurisdiction**
3. **Error in Excess of Jurisdiction**

1. Jurisdiction of Arbitral Tribunal

The arbitral tribunal is a creature of the arbitration agreement, and deals only with matters referred to it for arbitration. If either of the parties feels that the tribunal has exceeded its 'jurisdiction' or the scope of its authority, it should raise the plea before the arbitral tribunal as soon as the matter alleged to be beyond the scope of its authority is raised during the arbitral proceedings. The tribunal will then proceed to decide on the matter. This has been provided in sub-section (5) and (6) of section 16 of the Arbitration and Conciliation Act, 1996:

> "16. (5) The arbitral tribunal shall decide on a plea referred to in sub-section (2) or sub-section (3) and, where the arbitral tribunal takes a decision rejecting the plea, continue with the arbitral proceedings and make an arbitral award.
>
> (6) A party aggrieved by such an arbitral award may make an application for setting aside such an arbitral award in accordance with section 34."

It has been held by the Apex Court that 'the Tribunal's authority under section 16 is not confined to the width of its jurisdiction but it goes to the very root of the jurisdiction'. The Hon'ble Court further said that 'all objections with regard to validity and existence of the arbitration agreement can be gone into by the arbitral tribunal under section 16 of the said Act, 1996'.[1]

It has further been held by the Apex Court in *National Thermal Power Corpn. Ltd.* v. *Siemens Atkeingesellschaft*,[2], that even 'any refusal to go into the merits of a claim may be in the realm of jurisdiction. Even the dismissal of the claim as barred by limitation may in a sense touch on the jurisdiction of the court or tribunal. When a claim is dismissed on the ground of it being barred by limitation, it will be, in a sense, a case of the court or tribunal refusing to exercise jurisdiction to go into the merits of the claim'. Even a plea of limitation or a plea of *res judicata* is a plea of law which concerns the jurisdiction of the court which tries the proceedings. A finding on these pleas in favour of the party raising them would oust the jurisdiction of the court.

---

1. *Ruchi Strips & Alloys Ltd.* v. *Tata South East Asia Ltd.*, (2004) 13 SCC 470.
2. (2007) 4 SCC 451: AIR 2007 SC 1491: (2007) 1 Arb LR 377: (2007) 138 DLT 435: (2007) 3 Mad LJ 613: 2007 AIR SCW 1985: (2007) 3 SCALE 657: 2007 (2) Supreme 987.

The law, however, provides that if a challenge to jurisdiction is rejected by the arbitrator, there can be no appeal against the decision of the arbitrator. This can only be agitated in an appeal under section 34 of the Act.

A caveat must, however, be added on the competence of the arbitrator to rule on its own jurisdiction. As mentioned earlier in this book, this power of the arbitrator can be exercised in a situation when the parties have gone to the arbitral tribunal without recourse to section 8 or section 11 of the 1996 Act. But where the jurisdictional issues are decided under these sections, before a reference is made, section 16 does not empower the arbitral tribunal to ignore the decision given by the judicial authority or the Chief Justice before the reference to it was made. 'Once it is held that there is an adjudicatory function entrusted to the Chief Justice by the Act, obviously, the right of the arbitral tribunal to go behind the order passed by the Chief Justice would take another hue and would be controlled by section 11(7) of the Act.'[1]

2. Error within the Jurisdiction

The Hon'ble Supreme Court has held in *Bharat Coking Coal Ltd.* v. *Annapurna Construction*[2] that:

> "... the role of the arbitrator is to arbitrate within the terms of the contract. He has no power apart from what the parties have given him under the contract. If he has travelled beyond the contract, he would be acting without jurisdiction, ..."

It has elsewhere been held in the same judgment that 'if he (arbitrator) has remained inside the parameters of the contract, his award cannot be questioned on the ground that it contains an error apparent on the face of the record'.

However, the Hon'ble Supreme Court in *DDA* v. *R.S. Sharma and Co.*[3] has held that 'the learned Single Judge is perfectly right in holding that there is an error apparent on the face of the award and the award is liable to be set aside'. What would be clear, by looking at the facts of different cases is that the courts would act if there is total disconnect between facts and conclusion. If the view taken by the arbitrator is a possible view though perhaps not the only correct view, the award cannot be examined by the court.

3. Error in Excess of Jurisdiction

'Error in excess of jurisdiction' can best be described in the words of the Apex Court in *W.B. State Warehousing Corpn.* v. *Sushil Kumar Kayan*[4]. The Hon'ble Court observed that 'in order to determine whether the arbitrator has acted in excess of his jurisdiction what has to be seen is whether the claimant can raise a particular claim before the arbitrator. If there is a specific term in the contract or the law

1. *SBP & Co.* v. *Patel Engg. Ltd.*, (2005) 8 SCC 618: AIR 2006 SC 450: (2005) 3 Arb LR 285: JT 2005 (9) SC 219: (2005) 7 Supreme 610: 2005 AIR SCW 5932: 2005 (7) SCJ 461: (2005) 9 SCALE 1.
2. (2003) 8 SCC 154: AIR 2003 SC 3660: (2003) 3 Arb LR 119: (2003) 3 MLJ 185: (2003) 6 Supreme 517: 2003 AIR SCW 4146: (2003) 7 SCALE 20.
3. (2008) 13 SCC 80.
4. (2002) 5 SCC 679: AIR 2002 SC 2185: (2002) 2 Arb LR 236: JT (Supp) 2002 (3) SC 235: (2002) 3 Supreme 662: 2002 AIR SCW 2280: (2002) 4 SCALE 389.

which does not permit the parties to raise a point before the arbitrator and if there is a specific bar in the contract to the raising of the point, then the award passed by the arbitrator in respect thereof would be in excess of his jurisdiction.'

The power of the court to intervene if the arbitrator acts in excess of jurisdiction had been examined by the Apex Court in *Numaligarh Refinery Ltd.* v. *Daelim Industrial Co. Ltd.*[1]. It was observed that 'in a case where it is found that the arbitrator has acted without jurisdiction and has put an interpretation on the clause of the agreement which is wholly contrary to law then in that case there is no prohibition for the courts to set things right'.

In *J.C. Budhraja* v. *Chairman, Orissa Mining Corpn. Ltd.*[2], the Apex Court noted that the Ld. Arbitrator had exceeded his jurisdiction on the following counts:

(i) By awarding more than what was claimed in the claim statement (by showing a lesser amount as having been paid by respondent, though claim statement showed a higher amount);

(ii) By awarding an escalation in excess of what was claimed.

On the above counts, the Hon'ble Supreme Court observed that the Ld. Arbitrator had committed legal misconduct. It is thus seen that the courts will intervene if arbitral award is challenged on the ground that the arbitrator has exceeded his jurisdiction.

---

1. (2007) 8 SCC 466: 2007 (9) SCR 724: JT 2007 (11) SC 73: (2007) 10 SCALE 577.
2. (2008) 2 SCC 444: AIR 2008 SC 1363: (2008) 1 Arb LR 238: JT 2008 (1) SC 514: (2008) 8 MLJ 179: (2008) 1 SCR 821: 2008 AIR SCW 800: (2008) 1 SCALE 597.

THE ARBITRAL AWARD

SYNOPSIS

1. Reasoned Award

The arbitrator is required to give reasons for the conclusions in the award, unless the parties specifically provide that the award need not be reasoned. Section 31(3) provides that "the arbitral award shall state the reasons upon which it is based, unless the parties have agreed that no reasons are to be given". The Hon'ble Supreme Court has also held in *Centrotrade Minerals & Metals Inc.* v. *Hindustan Copper Ltd.*[1] that—

> "In the 1996 Act, reasons are required to be stated unless agreed to otherwise by the parties. The court's intervention is sought to be minimised under the provisions of the 1996 Act not only having regard to the concerns expressed in the international community as regards delay in the arbitration proceedings but also in view of the fact that an award under the 1996 Act is to be a reasoned one."

The *raison d'être* for reducing intervention by the courts is that award, being reasoned, would address the concerns of the parties in an objective manner.

The arbitral tribunal is a *quasi*-judicial authority. Hence, the award, which is equivalent to an enforceable judicial determination, must satisfy the tests of *Wednesbury* reasonableness. These tests had been laid down in the celebrated case of *Associated Provincial Picture Houses Limited* v. *Wednesbury Corporation* [Court of Appeal (UK)][2]:

(i) The award must take into consideration the matters which the tribunal is bound to consider; and

(ii) The award must exclude from consideration matters which are irrelevant, or what is in the personal knowledge of the arbitrator(s).

As provided in section 31(8) of the Arbitration and Conciliation Act, 1996, the award should also provide for the following:

(i) the party entitled to costs,

(ii) the party who shall pay the costs,

(iii) the amount of costs or method of determining that amount, and

(iv) the manner in which the costs shall be paid.

---

1. (2006) 11 SCC 245: JT 2006 (5) SC 507: (2006) 2 (Supp) SCR 146: (2006) 5 SCALE 535.
2. (1947) 2 All ER 680: 63 TLR 623: [1948] 1 KB 223.

The term "costs" as used in the above section of the Act means reasonable costs relating to—

(i) the fees and expenses of the arbitrators and witnesses,

(ii) legal fees and expenses,

(iii) any administration fees of the institution supervising the arbitration, and

(iv) any other expenses incurred in connection with the arbitral proceedings and the arbitral award.

2. Award of Interest

Award of interest by the arbitrator is integral to an award, and is regulated by section 31(7) of the Arbitration and Conciliation Act, 1996. The Act provides as under:

Interest prior to claim and interest *pendente lite.*

> "*31(7)* (a) Unless otherwise agreed by the parties, where and insofar as an arbitral award is for the payment of money, the arbitral tribunal may include in the sum for which the award is made interest, at such rate as it deems reasonable, on the whole or any part of the money, for the whole or any part of the period between the date on which the cause of action arose and the date on which the award is made.

Interest after the award.

> (b) A sum directed to be paid by an arbitral award shall, unless the award otherwise directs, carry interest at the rate of *eighteen per centum per annum* from the date of the award to the date of payment."

Thus, interest may be awarded by the arbitrator for the period prior to the publication of 'Award', but it has to be a reasonable amount. In *McDermott International Inc.* v. *Burn Standard Co. Ltd.*[1], the Hon'ble Supreme Court has held that:

> "... Section 31(7)(a) provides that the arbitral tribunal may award interest, at such rate as it deems reasonable, on the whole or any part of the money, for the whole or any part of the period between the date on which the cause of action arose and the date on which award is made, *i.e.*, pre-award period. This, however, is subject to the agreement as regards the rate of interest on unpaid sums between the parties ... The arbitral tribunal in this behalf will have to exercise its discretion as regards (i) at what rate interest should be awarded; (ii) whether interest should be awarded on the whole or any part of the award money; and (iii) whether interest should be awarded for the whole or any part of the pre-award period."

If no particular rate of interest has been prescribed in the contract, or in the arbitration agreement, the arbitrator may apply the provisions of the Interest Act, 1978. The Interest Act provides as under:

> "3. *Power of court to allow interest.*—(1) In any proceedings for the recovery of any debt or damages or in any proceedings in which a claim for interest

1. (2006) 11 SCC 181: (2006) 2 (Supp) SCR 409: JT 2006 (11) 376: (2006) 6 SCALE 220: 2006 AIR SCW 3276.

in respect of any debt or damages already paid is made, the court may, if it thinks fit, allow interest to the person entitled to the debt or damages or to the person making such claim, as the case may be, at a rate not exceeding the current rate of interest, for the whole or part of the following period, that is to say,—

(a) If the proceedings relate to a debt payable by virtue of written instrument at a certain time, then, from the date when the debt is payable to the date of institution of the proceedings;

(b) If the proceedings do not relate to any such debt, then, from the date mentioned in this regard in a written notice given by the person entitled or the person making the claim to the person liable that interest will be claimed, to the date of institution of the proceedings:

Provided that where the amount of the debt or damages has bean repaid before the institution of the proceedings, interest shall not be allowed under this section for the period after such repayment.

(2) Where, in any such proceedings as are mentioned in sub-section (1),—

(a) Judgment, order or award is given for a sum which, apart from interest on damages, exceeds four thousand rupees, and

(b) The sum represents or includes damages in respect of personal injuries to the plaintiff or any other person, or in respect of a person's death,

then, the power conferred by that sub-section shall be exercised so as to include all that sum interest on those damages or on such part of them as the court considers appropriate for the whole or part of the period from the date mentioned in the notice to the date of institution of the proceedings, unless the court is satisfied that there are special reasons why no interest should be given in respect of those damages.

(3) Nothing in this section,—

(a) Shall apply in relation to—

(i) Any debt or damages upon which interest is payable as of right by virtue of any agreement; or

(ii) Any debt or damages upon which payment of interest is barred, by virtue of all express agreement;

(b) Shall affect—

(i) The compensation recoverable for the dishonour of a bill of exchange, promissory note or cheque, as defined in the Negotiable Instruments Act, 1881 (26 of 1881); or

(ii) The provisions of rule 2 of Order 11 of the First Schedule to the Code of Civil Procedure, 1908 (5 of 1908);

(c) Shall empower the court to award interest upon interest."

If there is express provision in the contract against payment of interest, the arbitrator cannot award interest. In *M.B. Patel & Co.* v. *ONGC*[1], the Hon'ble

1. (2008) 8 SCC 251: (2008) 8 SCR 35: (2008) 8 SCALE 598.

Supreme Court struck down the interest *pendente lite* awarded by the arbitrator against the provisions of the contract.

The claimant can claim interest in case a where the contract is silent as regards payment of interest. In *Secretary, Irrigation Deptt., Govt. of Orissa* v. *G.C. Roy*[1], the Hon'ble Supreme Court held that:

> "Where the agreement between the parties does not prohibit grant of interest and where a party claims interest and that dispute (along with the claim for principal amount or independently) is referred to the arbitrator, he shall have the power to award interest *pendente lite*. This is for the reason that in such a case it must be presumed that interest was an implied term of the agreement between the parties and, therefore, when the parties refer all their disputes—or refer the dispute as to interest as such—to the arbitrator, he shall have the power to award interest."[2]

The Interest Act, however, requires a written notice to be given. If the claimant does not demand interest in terms of the Act, then interest cannot be given for a period prior to commencement of arbitration. If, the claimant claims interest only in the Statement of Claim, he may be granted interest *pendente lite*. Again, in these cases, it is the author's view that in terms of section 31(3) of the Arbitration and Conciliation Act, 1996, the arbitrator has to give reasons for the award of interest, including the rate of interest.

The rate of interest awarded cannot be *de hors* the provisions of the contract or the Interest Act. It has been noted by the Hon'ble Supreme Court in *Uttar Pradesh Coop. Federation Ltd.* v. *Three Circles*[3] that—

> "... However, as this power emanates from section 3 of the Interest Act, 1978, the High Court noted that the rate of interest cannot be more than "the current rate of interest" as stipulated by the said section...."

The rate of interest therefore should not exceed the 'current rate of interest'. It may be noted that under the Interest Act, 'current rate of interest' has been defined in section 2(b) of the Act as under:

> "2. (b) 'Current rate of interest' means the highest of the maximum rates at which interest may be paid on different classes of deposits (other than those maintained by charitable or religious institutions) by different classes of scheduled banks in accordance with the directions given or issued to banking companies generally by the Reserve Bank of India under the Banking Regulation Act, 1949 (10 of 1949)."

---

1. (1992) 1 SCC 508: AIR 1992 SC 732: (1992) 1 Arb LR 145: JT 1991 (6) SC 349: 1992 AIR SCW 389: 1992 (1) SCJ 434.
2. This overruled an earlier decision in *Executive Engineer (Irrigation)* v. *Abhaduta Jena*, (1988) 1 SCC 418: (1988) 1 SCR 253: AIR 1988 SC 1520: JT 1987 (5) SC 8: 1988 Bank J 102.
3. (2009) 10 SCC 374; *Pure Helium India Pvt. Ltd.* v. *Oil and Natural Gas Commission*, AIR 2003 SC 4519: (2003) 3 Arb LR 409: (2004) 13 AIC 421: (2003) 8 Supreme 264: 2003 AIR SCW 5274: (2003) 8 SCC 593: (2003) 8 SCALE 553.

The rate of interest awarded by the courts have been varied:

(i) In *Pure Helium India (P) Ltd.* v. *ONGC*[1], the Hon'ble Supreme Court had awarded interest at the rate of 6 per cent;

(ii) In *Mukand Ltd.* v. *Hindustan Petroleum Corpn. Ltd.*[2], the Hon'ble Supreme Court awarded interest at the rate of 7½ per cent;

(iii) In *McDermott International Inc.* v. *Burn Standard Co. Ltd.*[3], the Hon'ble Supreme Court awarded interest at the rate of 7½ per cent.

However, where no interest has been claimed, the arbitrator cannot award interest. He cannot also award interest in excess of the claim. It has been held by the Hon'ble Supreme Court in *J.C. Budhraja* v. *Chairman, Orissa Mining Corpn. Ltd.*[4], that 'making an award in excess of the claim itself ... is a clear act of exceeding the jurisdiction and amounts to a legal misconduct ....'

As regards interest on awarded amount, the upper limit imposed by the Arbitration and Conciliation Act, 1996 is eighteen per cent. However, here too the arbitrator should give his reasons for the rate of interest awarded.

---

1. (2003) 8 SCC 593: AIR 2003 SC 4519: (2003) 3 Arb LR 409: (2004) 13 AIC 421: (2003) 8 Supreme 264.
2. (2006) 9 SCC 383: (2006) 4 SCALE 453.
3. (2006) 11 SCC 181: (2006) 2 (Supp) SCR 409: JT 2006 (11) 376: (2006) 6 SCALE 220: 2006 AIR SCW 3276.
4. (2008) 2 SCC 444: AIR 2008 SC 1363: (2008) 1 Arb LR 238: JT 2008 (1) SC 514: (2008) 8 MLJ 179: (2008) 1 SCR 821: 2008 AIR SCW 800: (2008) 1 SCALE 597.

CHALLENGE TO AWARD

SYNOPSIS

1. **Grounds for Challenge of Award**
2. **Appealable Orders**
3. **Public Policy of India**

1. Grounds for Challenge of Award

The grounds for setting aside the award are specific. They are given in section 34 of the 1996 Act. The petitioner who files an application has to plead the facts necessary to make out the ingredients of any of the grounds mentioned in sub-section (2) and prove the same. Therefore, the only question that arises in an application under section 34 of the Act is whether the award requires to be set aside on any of the specified grounds in sub-section (2) thereof. Sub-section (2) also clearly places the burden of proof on the person who makes the application.

The courts do not interfere with the conclusion of the arbitrator even with regard to construction of a contract, if it is a possible view of the matter. The words "no award shall be set aside" in section 30 mandate the courts not to set aside the award on the ground other than those specified in section 30.

It has been held by the Hon'ble Supreme Court in *SAIL* v. *Gupta Brother Steel Tubes Ltd.*,[1] that—

> "The legal position is no more *res integra* that the arbitrator having been made the final arbiter of resolution of disputes between the parties, the award is not open to challenge on the ground that arbitrator has reached at a wrong conclusion."

An award is open to interference by the court[2] under section 34(2) of the Act if it is:

(i) contrary to substantive provisions of law; or
(ii) the provisions of the Arbitration and Conciliation Act, 1996; or
(iii) against the terms of the respective contract; or
(iv) patently illegal[3]; or
(v) prejudicial to the rights of the parties.

In addition to the above five grounds, following the *Renusagar* case, it was held by the Apex Court in *Oil & Natural Gas Corpn. Ltd.* v. *SAW Pipes Ltd.*[4] that an arbitral award could be set aside if it is contrary to:

---

1. (2009) 10 SCC 63.
2. *DDA* v. *R.S. Sharma and Co.*, (2008) 13 SCC 80.
3. The illegality must go to the root of the matter. But if the illegality is of trivial nature it cannot be held that award is against the public policy.
4. AIR 2003 SC 2629: (2003) 2 Arb LR 5: JT 2003 (4) SC 171: (2003) 3 Supreme 449: (2003) 5 SCC 705: 2003 AIR SCW 3041: (2003) 4 SCALE 92..

(vi) fundamental policy of Indian law; or

(vii) the interest of India; or

(viii) justice or morality[1].

The jurisdiction or the power of the arbitral tribunal is prescribed under the Act and if the award is *de hors* the said provisions, it would be, on the face of it, illegal. The decision of the tribunal must be within the bounds of its jurisdiction conferred under the Act or the contract. It is open to the court to consider whether the award is against the specific terms of contract[2] and if so, interfere with it on the ground that it is patently illegal and opposed to the public policy of India.

In exercising jurisdiction, the arbitral tribunal cannot act in breach of some provision of substantive law or the provisions of the Act[3]. It was, therefore, decided that if the award is contrary to the substantive provisions of law or the provisions of the Act or against the terms of the contract, it would be patently illegal, which could be interfered under section 34.

In the recent case of *Fiza Developers & Inter-Trade P. Ltd.* v. *AMCI(I) Pvt. Ltd.*[4], the Hon'ble Supreme Court dealt with the question of 'framing of issues' in a proceeding under section 34 of the Arbitration and Conciliation Act, 1996. It observed as follows:

> "Framing of issues is necessary only where different types of material propositions of fact or law are affirmed by one party and are denied by the other and it is therefore necessary for the court to identify the issues and specify the party on whom the burden to prove the same lies. When this exercise has already been done by the statute, there is no need for framing the issues. In other words, an application under section 34 of the Act is a single issue proceeding, where the very fact that the application has been instituted under that particular provision declares the issue involved. Any further exercise to frame issues will only delay the proceedings. It is thus clear that issues need not be framed in applications under section 34 of the Act."

An important shortcoming in the procedure for challenge of an award becomes very much apparent from a bare reading of the Arbitration and Conciliation Act, 1996. There is no provision made for expediting proceedings in the courts, when applications are filed for setting aside awards. The aggrieved party has to start the process of challenging the award from the District Court onwards.[5]

---

1. It could also be set aside if it is so unfair and unreasonable that it shocks the conscience of the court.
2. Excess of jurisdiction.
3. *Oil & Natural Gas Corpn. Ltd.* v. *SAW Pipes Ltd.*, (2003) 5 SCC 705: AIR 2003 SC 2629: (2003) 2 Arb LR 5: JT 2003 (4) SC 171: (2003) 3 Supreme 449: 2003 AIR SCW 3041: (2003) 4 SCALE 92.
4. (2009) INSC 1285 Civil Appeal No. 5139 of 2009, decided on July 27, 2009 [Arising out of SLP(C) No. 16281 of 2009].
5. *Centrotrade Minerals & Metals Inc.* v. *Hindustan Copper Ltd.*, (2006) 11 SCC 245: JT 2006 (5) SC 507: (2006) 2 (Supp) SCR 146: (2006) 5 SCALE 535.

2. Appealable Orders

Section 37 of the Arbitration and Conciliation Act, 1996 lists the types of orders against which appeals can be preferred before a court of competent jurisdiction:

(a) granting or refusing to grant any interim measure[1];

(b) setting aside or refusing to set aside an arbitral award[2];

(c) accepting the plea that the arbitrator does not have jurisdiction, or that he is exceeding his authority[3]; or

(d) granting or refusing to grant an interim measure[4].

There can be no second appeal against such order, but that does not affect or take away any right to appeal to the Supreme Court.

3. Public Policy of India

As stated earlier, in the *Oil & Natural Gas Corpn.* v. *SAW Pipes* case, 'public policy' has been defined to be:

(a) fundamental policy of Indian law; or

(b) the interest of India; or

(c) justice or morality; or

(d) statutory provisions.

The award would therefore be considered to be against 'statutory provisions' if it can be proved that it suffered from any of the following defects:

(i) It is patently against the statutory provisions of substantive law which is in force in India, or

(ii) It has been passed without giving an opportunity of hearing to the parties as provided under section 24, or

(iii) The award does not state any reason, in a case where parties have not agreed that no reasons are to be recorded.

Such an award, which is against statutory provisions, is liable to be set aside on the ground of 'patent illegality'. In all such cases, the award is required to be set aside on the ground of 'patent illegality'.

In *Venture Global Engg.* v. *Satyam Computer Services Ltd.*[5], the Apex Court has observed that—

> "In any event, to apply section 34 to foreign international awards would not be inconsistent with section 48 of the Act, or any other provision of Part II as a situation may arise, where, even in respect of properties situate in India and where an award would be invalid if opposed to the public policy of India, merely because the judgment-debtor resides abroad, the award can be enforced against properties in India through personal compliance of the

---

1. Section 9.
2. Section 34.
3. Section 16, sub-sections (2) and (3).
4. Section 17.
5. (2008) 4 SCC 190: (2008) 1 Arb LR 137: (2008) 3 MPLJ 329: AIR 2008 SC 1061: 2008 AIR SCW 667: (2008) 1 SCALE 214.

> judgment-debtor and by holding out the threat of contempt as is being sought to be done in the present case. In such an event, the judgment-debtor cannot be deprived of his right under section 34 to invoke the public policy of India, to set aside the award. As observed earlier, the public policy of India includes—(a) the fundamental policy of India; or (b) the interests of India; or (c) justice or morality; or (d) in addition, if it is patently illegal. This extended definition of public policy can be bypassed by taking the award to a foreign country for enforcement."

To avert such a palpably untenable situation, the Apex Court decided that '*the provisions of Part I of the Act would apply to all arbitrations including international commercial arbitrations and to all proceedings relating thereto. We further hold that where such arbitration is held in India, the provisions of Part I would compulsorily apply and parties are free to deviate to the extent permitted by the provisions of Part I. It is also clear that even in the case of international commercial arbitrations held out of India provisions of Part I would apply unless the parties by agreement, express or implied, exclude all or any of its provisions.*'

ENFORCEMENT OF AWARD

SYNOPSIS

1. Finality of 'Domestic Award'

The ultimate objective of the arbitral process is to secure an award, and thereafter, if required, have it enforced.

Section 2(2) read with section 2(7) makes it clear that Part I applies to an arbitration which is held in India, and the award of the arbitrator in such a case is regarded as 'domestic award'. Again, an award made in an international commercial arbitration held in a non-convention country is also considered to be a "domestic award"[1].

As regards 'finality' of award, section 35 of the Act provides as follows:

> "35. *Finality of arbitral awards.*—Subject to this Part an arbitral award shall be final and binding on the parties and persons claiming under them respectively."

The award is thus 'final and binding'. It does not need any further *imprimatur* or endorsement by a court of law, *i.e.*, it does not need to be made a rule or decree of court.

But as has been seen in an earlier chapter, an arbitration award may be challenged. The limitation for filing an application for setting aside an award runs out three months after receiving the award. Thereafter, the award becomes enforceable. Under the 1996 Act, the award does not have to be made a decree of the court; it has the same force as a decree of the court. By a fiction of law, the award thus becomes an executable decree after the time has expired for filing appeal against the award under section 34 of the Act.

A domestic award is subject to the supervision of a court of law in India. It has been noted by the Apex Court in *Centrotrade Minerals & Metals Inc.* v. *Hindustan Copper Ltd.*[2] that:

> "An award can be set aside only if the court comes to the conclusion that one or the other grounds contained in section 34 of the Act exist. A

1. *Bhatia International* v. *Bulk Trading S.A.,* (2002) 4 SCC 105: AIR 2002 SC 1432: JT 2002 (3) SC 150: (2002) 1 Arb LR 675: (2003) 1 Jab LJ 264: (2002) 2 SCALE 612: (2002) 2 Supreme 395.
2. (2006) 11 SCC 245: 2006 AIR SCW 3172: JT 2006 (5) SC 507: (2006) 3 Arb LR 201.

challenge to the domestic award can, thus, be made only before a national court designated by the Act itself and on the grounds specified in section 34 of the Act. A *fortiori*, the validity of a domestic award cannot be questioned before any other forum including the forum chosen by the parties, if any."

The aspect of challenge to the award has been dealt with separately in this book.

2. Enforcement of 'Domestic' Arbitral Award

A 'domestic' arbitration award in a commercial arbitration normally consists of an award of damages to the injured party. The injured party would be compensated by receiving the awarded amount or assets from the party in breach. It would be an ideal situation if the amount is paid voluntarily by the other party; but it is often not the case. The manner of 'enforcement' of the award has therefore been given in section 36 of the Act:

> "36. *Enforcement*.—Where the time for making an application to set aside the arbitral award under section 34 has expired, or such application having been made, it has been refused, the award shall be enforced under the Code of Civil Procedure, 1908 in the same manner as if it were a decree of the court."

The above provision of the Arbitration and Conciliation Act, 1996 is consistent with the legal fiction created by the Act that the award of the arbitral tribunal has the same status as a decree of the competent court after expiry of the period of limitation for filing appeal against the award.

3. Jurisdiction of Court for Execution of Arbitral Award

The concerned party may approach the court having territorial and fiscal jurisdiction with respect to the arbitral proceedings for attachment of immovable property.

> "54. *Attachment of immovable property*.—(1) Where the property is immovable, the attachment shall be made by an order prohibiting the judgment-debtor from transferring or charging the property in any way, and all persons from taking any benefit from such transfer or charge."

It has been stated by the Hon'ble Supreme Court[1] that:

> "Section 136[2] of the Code provides for an order of attachment in respect of a property outside the jurisdiction of the court and sending the order of

1. *Mohit Bhargava* v. *Bharat Bhushan Bhargava*, (2007) 4 SCC 795: AIR 2007 SC 1717: (2007) 55 AIC 89: (2007) 2 Jab LJ 383: (2007) 3 MPLJ 419: (2007) 4 MLJ 508: 2007 AIR SCW 2707: (2007) 6 SCALE 38: 2007 (3) Supreme 828.
2. *Procedure where person to be arrested or property to be attached is outside district*.—(1) Where an application is made that any person shall be arrested or that any property shall be attached under any provision of this Code not relating to the execution of decrees, and such person resides or such property is situate outside the local limits of the jurisdiction of the Court to which the application is made, the Court may, in its discretion, issue a warrant of arrest or make an order of attachment, and send to the District Court within the local limits of whose jurisdiction such person or property reside or is situate a copy of the warrant or order, together with the probable amount of the costs of the arrest or attachment.

attachment to the District Court within whose local limits the property sought to be attached is situate, as provided for therein."

In the case of attachment of immovable property situated outside the territorial jurisdiction of the executing court, the court will proceed in accordance with section 46 of the Civil Procedure Code, 1908 ('CPC' for short), and issue a 'precept' to the court within whose territorial jurisdiction the property is situate:

> "46. *Precepts.*—(1) Upon the application of the decree-holder the Court which passed the decree may, whenever it thinks fit, issue a precept to any other Court which would be competent to execute such decree to attach any property belonging to the judgment-debtor and specified in the precept."

Thereupon, such *transferee* court would proceed with 'attachment' of the property.

If execution proceedings are to be drawn up, these too would be initiated in the court having jurisdiction with regard to the arbitral proceedings. But, if the immovable property concerned is outside the territorial jurisdiction of the executing court, the proceedings would have to be transferred by that court to the court having territorial jurisdiction.

In the above *Bhargava* case[1], the Hon'ble Supreme Court has ruled that:

> "Section 136 clearly excludes execution of decrees from within its purview. An execution against immovable property lying outside the jurisdiction of the executing court is possible in terms of Order 21, rule 3 of the Code which governs a case where the particular item of immovable property, forms one estate or tenure situate within the local limits of jurisdiction of two or more courts, and one of those courts is approached for execution of the decree against that property".

The Hon'ble Supreme Court further clarified that—

> "A decree could be executed by the court which passed the decree so long as it is confined to the assets within its own jurisdiction or as authorised by Order 21, rule 3 or Order 21, rule 48 of the Code or the judgment-debtor is within its jurisdiction, if it is a decree for personal obedience by the judgment-debtor.'[1]

Section 39(4) of CPC makes this position amply clear:

> "39. Transfer of decree.
>
> ... ...
>
> (4) Nothing in this section shall be deemed to authorise the Court which passed a decree to execute such decree against any person or property outside the local limits of its jurisdiction."

However, after transfer of the proceedings, the execution proceedings will continue before the court having territorial jurisdiction with respect to the property in question.

---

1. *Mohit Bhargava* v. *Bharat Bhushan Bhargava,* (2007) 4 SCC 795: AIR 2007 SC 1717: (2007) 55 AIC 89: (2007) 2 Jab LJ 383: (2007) 3 MPLJ 419: (2007) 4 MLJ 508: 2007 AIR SCW 2707: (2007) 6 SCALE 38: 2007 (3) Supreme 828.

4. Enforcement of 'Foreign Award'

In *Fuerst Day Lawson Ltd.* v. *Jindal Exports Ltd.*[1], it has been held by the Hon'ble Supreme Court that:

> "... in our view, a party holding a foreign award can apply for enforcement of it but the court before taking further effective steps for the execution of the award has to proceed in accordance with sections 47 to 49."

It was held that in one proceeding there could be different stages:

- In the first stage the court may have to decide about the enforceability of the award having regard to the requirement of the said provisions.
- Once the court decides that the foreign award is enforceable, it can proceed to take further effective steps for execution of the same. There arises no question of making foreign award a rule of court/decree again.

It was felt that if the object and purpose could be served in the same proceedings, there was no need to take two separate proceedings resulting in multiplicity of litigation. Every final arbitral award is to be enforced as if it were a decree of the court. It was therefore held that:

> "In our opinion, for enforcement of a foreign award there is no need to take separate proceedings, one for deciding the enforceability of the award to make it a rule of the court or decree and the other to take up execution thereafter. In one proceeding, as already stated above, the court enforcing a foreign award can deal with the entire matter...."

In *Venture Global*[2], the Hon'ble Supreme Court has held that Part I of the Arbitration and Conciliation Act, 1996 would apply even to a 'foreign award'. Such an award can challenged under section 34, and also enforced through a court of competent jurisdiction.

---

1. (2001) 6 SCC 356: AIR 2001 SC 2293: JT 2001 (1) (Supp) SC 263: (2001) 91 DLT 373: (2001) 4 Supreme 141: 2001 AIR SCW 2087: 2001 (4) SCJ 206: (2001) 3 SCALE 708.
2. (2008) 4 SCC 190: AIR 2008 SC 1061: (2008) 1 Arb LR 137: (2008) 2 MLJ 289: (2008) 1 SCALE 214: 2008 AIR SCW 667.

ANNEXURE A

ICA: ARBITRATION RULES

The Indian Council of Arbitration recommends to all parties desirous of making reference to arbitration by the Indian Council of Arbitration, the use of the following arbitration clause in writing in their contracts:

"Any dispute or difference whatsoever arising between the parties out of or relating to the construction, meaning, scope, operation or effect of this contract or the validity or the breach thereof shall be settled by arbitration in accordance with the Rules of Arbitration of the Indian Council of Arbitration and the award made in pursuance thereof shall be binding on the parties."

DEFINITIONS

Rule 1

(i) These rules may be called the "Rules of Arbitration of the Indian Council of Arbitration."

(ii) These rules shall apply where parties have agreed in writing that (a) a dispute has arisen, or (b) a dispute which may arise between them in respect of defined legal relationship whether contractual or not, shall be settled under the Rules of Arbitration.

Rule 2

In these rules, the following words have the following meanings:

(i) "Arbitral Tribunal" means an arbitrator or arbitrators appointed for determining a particular dispute or difference.

(ii) "Arbitral Award" includes an interim award.

(iii) "Committee" means the Arbitration Committee of the Council as provided for hereinafter.

(iv) "Council" means the Indian Council of Arbitration.

(v) "Governing Body" means the Governing Body of the Council.

(vi) "Guidelines" means the guidelines for arbitrators and the parties to arbitration for expeditious conduct of the arbitration proceedings, given in the Annexure to these Rules.

(vii) "International Commercial Arbitration" means an arbitration relating to disputes arising out of legal relationships, whether contractual or not, considered as commercial under the law in force in India and where at least one of the parties is (a) an individual who is a national of, or habitually resident in, any country other than India; or (b) a body corporate which is incorporated in any country other than India; or (c) a company or an association or a body of individuals whose central management and control is exercised in any country other than India; or (d) the Government of a foreign country.

(viii) "Party" means a party to an arbitration agreement. It shall include any individual, firm, company, Government, Government organisation or Government Undertaking.

(ix) "Panel" means the Panel of Arbitrators maintained by the Council.

(x) "Registrar" means the Registrar for the time being appointed by the Committee and includes such other persons as the Committee may nominate for carrying out the duties of the Registrar under these rules.

(xi) "Rules" means the Rules of Arbitration of the Council.

(xii) "Rules of Conciliation" means the Rules of Conciliation of the Council.

(xiii) "Fast Track Arbitration" means arbitration in accordance with rule 44.

(xiv) Words importing the singular number include, where the context admits or requires, the plural number and *vice versa*.

ARBITRATION COMMITTEE

Rule 3

(a) The Governing Body of the Council shall constitute an Arbitration Committee for performing the functions prescribed under these Rules. The Committee shall consist of the President of the Council, who shall be the *ex-officio* Chairman of the Committee and three members of the Governing Body of the Council elected by the Governing Body from amongst themselves. The Committee shall hold office for a year.

(b) The Committee may co-opt not more than two persons to be additional members of the Committee during its terms of office. Persons who are not members of the Governing Body may also be co-opted to be members of the Committee.

(c) The Committee or the Chairman of the Committee may delegate to the Registrar the power to take certain decisions, provided that any such decision shall be reported to the Chairman or the Committee, as the case may be.

RULES APPLICABLE

Rule 4

(a) Any dispute relating to any commercial matter including shipping, sale, purchase, banking, insurance, building construction, engineering, technical assistance, know-how, patents, trade marks, management consultancy, commercial agency, or labour, arising between two or more parties in India or a party or parties in India and a party or parties in a foreign country or between foreign parties who agree or have agreed for arbitration by the Council, or under the Rules of Arbitration of the Council, shall be determined and settled in accordance with these Rules.

(b) The Council shall also be competent to administer the conduct of arbitration in any dispute or difference relating to a commercial transaction between parties as mentioned in sub-clause (a) where they have agreed to have their dispute arbitrated under any other Rules of Arbitration and have agreed to have such arbitration administered by the Council, wholly or in respect of some matters arising out of such arbitration.

(c) In case the parties have provided different procedure for appointment of arbitrator or schedule of cost including the arbitrator's fee, the Council shall not be bound to process the case unless both the parties agree to follow the entire procedure of arbitration under Rules of Arbitration of the Council.

(d) The Council shall be competent to function as Appointing Authority as contemplated under the Arbitration Rules of the United Nations Commission on International Trade Law (UNCITRAL).

Rule 5

Wherever the Parties have provided or agreed for arbitration by the Indian Council of Arbitration or for arbitration under the Rules of Arbitration of the Council, these rules or any amendment thereof, in the form obtaining at the time the dispute is referred to arbitration of the Council, shall apply.

Rule 6

If one or both of the parties to a dispute which is referred to arbitration by the Council belong to a country or countries other than India, in the absence of an agreement by the Parties on the substantive law to be applied, it will be determined by the arbitral tribunal. The procedural law shall be the laws of India and parties shall be deemed to have submitted to the jurisdiction of the Courts in India.

Rule 7

Any chamber of commerce, trade association or any arbitral or other organisation may adopt these Rules by making them generally available to its members or by applying them to any dispute in which any of its members may be parties or by normally conducting its arbitration under these Rules.

INTERPRETATION OF THE RULES

Rule 8

The decision of the Committee on any question relating to interpretation of these rules or any procedural matter thereunder shall be final and binding on the parties.

PANEL OF ARBITRATORS

Rule 9

A Panel of Arbitrators shall be appointed by the Committee from amongst persons who are qualified and possesses knowledge and experience in their respective field of profession and arbitration law and procedure and are willing to serve as arbitrators generally or in specific fields and who are from time-to-time recommended by the members of the Council or any other person or organisation.

All the members of the Panel will carry equal status and parties will not have any right to challenge the appointment of the arbitrator on the ground that its nominee arbitrator has higher status than the Presiding Arbitrator.

Rule 10

The Registrar shall prepare and maintain an up-to-date Panel of arbitrators together with adequate information as to their qualifications and experience. Separate lists may be kept and maintained of arbitrators included in the Panel for disputes in general and for each of the fields of international trade and/or business transactions in which the Governing Body decides that the Council will offer arbitration facilities under the Rules.

The parties to a dispute or the Registrar where he appoints the arbitrator may choose any person from the panel with reference to any dispute. If any party appoints a foreigner/person residing abroad, as arbitrator from the panel, that party will have to meet the travel and stay expenses of the person appointed as arbitrator at the venue of arbitration. The arbitral tribunal may, however, make any order in regard thereto in the award. The panel of arbitrators shall be open to inspection by all persons with the permission of the Registrar.

Rule 11

The Committee may at any time add the name of any person to the list of arbitrators included in the Panel or delete the name of any person from the panel.

Rule 12

The Chairman of the Committee may include the name of any person in the panel, in case it is required in any particular case. His continuance in the Panel will be decided by the Committee.

Rule 13

The persons who have attained the age of more than 80 years will automatically cease to be member of the Panel of Arbitrators. In the case of a person, who has been appointed as arbitrator before attainment of the age of 80 years, his panel membership will continue till the pronouncement of the Award in pending arbitration matters referred to him.

DUTIES OF THE REGISTRAR

Rule 14

(a) The Registrar shall receive applications for arbitration by the Council, receive payment of fees and deposits, appoint, in consultation with the Chairman of the Committee, and in his absence in consultation with the member of the Governing Body designated by him, an arbitrator or arbitrators as hereinafter provided. The Registrar shall also receive all communications made to the arbitral tribunal by the parties and communicate to them the orders and directions of the arbitral tribunal, keep a register of applications to the Council and of awards made by the arbitral tribunal, keep such other books or memoranda and make such other records or returns as the Committee shall from time-to-time require and generally carry out the directions of an arbitral tribunal so constituted under these rules and take such other steps as may be necessary to assist such arbitral tribunal in the carrying out of its functions.

(b) The Registrar may delegate to any officer of the Council, Chambers of Commerce or Trade Association at the premises of which the arbitration proceedings are taking place, to discharge such of the functions and administrative duties of the Registrar as are deemed proper and necessary from time-to-time, with reference to a particular case or cases.

INITIATION OF ARBITRATION

Rule 15

(i) Any Party wishing to commence arbitration proceedings under these rules (Claimant) shall give a notice of request for arbitration to the Registrar of ICA and to the Respondent.

(ii) The notice of request (application) for arbitration to the Registrar shall be accompanied by:—

(a) the names and full addresses of the parties to the dispute.

(b) statement of the claim and facts supporting the claim, points at issue and relief or remedies sought with other details of the claimant's case.

(c) original or duly certified copies of the arbitration agreement, any contract or agreement out of or in connection with which the dispute has arisen and such other documents and information relevant or relied upon.

(d) Registration fee of Rs. 2,500 for claim upto Rs. One Crore and Rs. 5,000 for claim more than Rs. One Crore.

(e) The arbitration shall be deemed to have commenced on the day the application for arbitration, registration fee and statement of claim are received in the office of the Council.

Rule 16

If any Court makes an order directing that an arbitration be held under these rules, in addition to the documents listed in rule 15, the order of that Court or a copy thereof shall accompany the application for arbitration.

Rule 17

(a) On receipt of an application for arbitration, the Registrar shall have absolute discretion to accept or reject the said application. The Registrar is not bound to give reasons for the exercise of his discretion. Before deciding on the acceptability of an application for arbitration, the Registrar may ask the parties for further information and particulars of their claims.

(b) Similarly, if any information or particulars regarding the arbitration agreement furnished by claimant with the application for arbitration are found to be incorrect or false, at any time subsequently, the Registrar shall have a like power to reject the application for arbitration.

(c) Any Party aggrieved by the decision of the Registrar, in accepting or rejecting an application for arbitration as above, may apply to the Court for suitable directions.

DEFENCE STATEMENT

Rule 18

(a) On receipt of the application together with the claim statement, the Registrar shall send to the other Party (Respondent) a copy of the claim statement and attached documents and ask such other party to furnish within thirty days or within any extended date, a defence statement setting out his case accompanied by all documents and information in support of or bearing on the matter.

(b) Any communication sent by the Registrar under Registered Post to the respondent on the address appearing in the Arbitration Agreement/the contract between the parties, as per the information supplied to the Council, will be deemed to be duly served on the Respondent, if it is delivered to the addressee personally or at his place of business, habitual residence or mailing address last known, even if the respondent refuses to accept the said communication or if it is returned to the Council by the postal authorities as unclaimed by the said party. The Registrar may proceed further with the arbitration proceedings as per the rules as if such communication had been duly served on the concerned party. The Registrar may in such cases make an additional communication to the Parties by Registered Letter or by other means which may provide a record of attempts to deliver it.

(c) A copy of the defence statement and all appended documents, if any, shall be sent to the claimant for information.

(d) The communication is deemed to have been received on the day it is so delivered.

COUNTER-CLAIM AND REPLY TO COUNTER-CLAIM

Rule 19

(a) The respondent may make a counter-claim against the claimant provided the counter-claim arises under the same transaction as the original claim. He must submit the counter-claim with full details supported by all documents and information as in the case of the claim under rule 15 within the period laid down for the defence statement to the claim and the claimant may within twenty-one days of the notification of the counter-claim or within such extended time submit a statement in reply to the counter-claim. The arbitral tribunal appointed to adjudicate upon the original claim shall also adjudicate upon the counter-claim and there will be no change in the number of members of arbitral tribunal already constituted on the basis of original claim.

(b) Copy of the reply of the claimant to the counter-claim and all appended documents, if any, shall be sent to the respondent for information.

COPIES OF STATEMENTS, ETC.

Rule 20

All statements, replies and other documents and papers submitted by the parties and all appended documents must be supplied in triplicate. Where there is more than one arbitrator or more than one opposing party, the parties shall within the time specified to furnish the Registrar such number of further copies as may be required by the Registrar.

CONSTITUTION OF THE ARBITRAL TRIBUNAL

Rule 21

On receipt of the application for arbitration, the Registrar shall take necessary steps to have the arbitral tribunal constituted for the adjudication of the dispute or difference as provided hereunder.

Rule 22

The number of arbitrators to hear a dispute shall be determined as under:

(a) Where the claim including determination of interest, if any, being claimed upto the date of commencement of arbitration in terms of rule 15, does not exceed Rs. One crore and where the arbitration agreement does not specify three arbitrators, the reference shall be deemed to be to a sole arbitrator, unless the parties to the dispute agree to refer the dispute to three arbitrators within thirty days from the date of notification of request for arbitration.

(b) Where the claim including determination of interest, if any, being claimed upto the date of commencement of arbitration in terms of rule 15 exceeds Rs. One crore, the dispute will be heard and determined by three arbitrators, unless the parties to the dispute agree to refer the dispute to a sole arbitrator within thirty days from the date of the notification of the request for arbitration.

(c) Where three arbitrators have to be appointed as per the above sub-rule and any of the parties to the dispute fails to make the necessary deposit towards the cost and expenses of arbitration, instead of three arbitrators, the Registrar may appoint a sole arbitrator, where the claim is upto Rs. One crore. Where the claim is for more than Rs. One crore, the Registrar may appoint arbitrator/s on behalf of the respondent as well the as presiding arbitrator.

Rule 23

The appointment of sole arbitrator or three arbitrators shall be made in the following manner:

(a) In case a sole arbitrator has to be appointed, the Registrar shall, by a notice in writing, call upon the parties to the dispute to forward the name of an agreed arbitrator from among the panel of arbitrators. The said notice shall specify the period within which the nomination shall be made which shall not be more than thirty days from the date of the said notice to the respective parties. If the parties fail to agree on the person to be appointed as Sole Arbitrator within the time granted by the Registrar, the Registrar in consultation with the Chairman of the Committee and in his absence in consultation with the member of the Governing Body designated by the Chairman, shall appoint the sole arbitrator from among the Panel of Arbitrators. If one of the parties is a national or resident of a country other than India, the sole arbitrator shall, as far as possible, be chosen or appointed by the Registrar from among the nationals of a country other than that of either of the parties. The sole arbitrator so nominated shall constitute the arbitral tribunal to hear the dispute and shall be appointed as such in writing by the Registrar. The Registrar shall give notice to the Parties of the constitution of the arbitral tribunal.

(b) Where the reference is to three arbitrators, the Registrar shall in the first instance call upon the parties to nominate one arbitrator each from among the Panel of Arbitrators by a notice in writing, sent to them. The said notice shall specify the period within which the nomination shall be made which shall not be more than thirty days from the date of the said notice to the respective Parties. If a Party to the dispute refuses or neglects to appoint an arbitrator on his behalf within the period specified or if he requests the Registrar to nominate an arbitrator on behalf of that party, the Registrar in consultation with the Chairman of the Arbitration Committee and in his absence in consultation with the members of the Governing Body designated by the Chairman shall appoint the arbitrator from the Panel of Arbitrators on behalf of that party. On receipt of the nominations from the respective parties or on the appointment as aforesaid by the Registrar, the Registrar shall appoint another person as the Presiding Arbitrator of the arbitral tribunal in consultation with Chairman of the Committee and in his absence in consultation with members of the Governing Body designated by the Chairman, from among the panel of arbitrators to be additional arbitrator to act as Presiding Arbitrator of the arbitral tribunal.

(c) If one of the parties is a national or resident of a country other than India, the additional arbitrator shall, as far as possible, be chosen or appointed from among the nationals of a country other than that of either of the parties. The arbitrators so nominated or appointed shall constitute the arbitral tribunal and shall be appointed as such in writing by the Registrar. The additional arbitrator appointed by the Registrar shall act as Presiding Arbitrator of the arbitral tribunal. The Registrar shall give notice to the parties of the constitution of the arbitral tribunal.

Rule 24

The parties will obtain the consent from the persons nominated by them as arbitrator and intimate the Council accordingly. The Registrar will obtain the consent from person(s) nominated by him. After a person gives his consent for appointment as arbitrator, he will be duly intimated about his appointment to decide the dispute, by a Memo in writing under the hand of the Registrar about the constitution of the arbitral tribunal. The appointment of the arbitrator will take effect from the date of such intimation about the constitution of the arbitral tribunal.

Rule 25

Before accepting his nomination the prospective arbitrator shall disclose any circumstances such as financial or personal interest in the outcome of the award, likely to disqualify him as an impartial arbitrator. Upon receipt of such information, the Registrar shall disclose it to the parties, who if willing to proceed under the circumstances disclosed, shall advise the Registrar accordingly. If either party declines to waive the presumptive disqualification, the prospective arbitrator shall be disqualified from acting as arbitrator and the vacancy so created shall be filled, in accordance with the applicable provision of these rules.

Rule 26

Any Party shall have the right to challenge the appointment of an arbitrator on receipt of the notice of his appointment for reasons which disqualify the arbitrator. The challenge of an arbitrator shall be made within 30 days after his appointment has been communicated to the challenging party or within 30 days of his becoming aware of the reasons for which the challenge is made. Copies of the communication of challenge shall be sent to the other Parties and the arbitrators. The Committee shall be the sole judge of the grounds of challenge and its decision shall be final and binding on the Parties.

Rule 27

(a) If any appointed arbitrator resigns or dies or becomes incapable of acting or neglects or fails to act expeditiously, prior to or during the arbitration hearings, or if he fails to make the award within the prescribed time and the Parties do not agree to extend the time for making the award, the Registrar in consultation with the Arbitration Committee may terminate the authority of such an appointed arbitrator and inform him accordingly.

(b) In case of the resignation or death or termination of authority of an appointed arbitrator under sub-rule (a) above, a new arbitrator will be appointed in his place by the Registrar in case he had appointed the original arbitrator. Where the appointment was made by the Parties, the Registrar shall call upon the Party who had appointed the arbitrator to nominate another arbitrator in his place. If any Party refuses or neglects to nominate an arbitrator within 15 days of the date of notice requiring him to nominate the arbitrator or within such extended time, the Registrar shall nominate the arbitrator on behalf of that Party from among the Panel of Arbitrators.

(c) The arbitrator(s) appointed as above will be informed about the reconstitution of the arbitral tribunal and the reconstituted arbitral tribunal shall make the award expeditiously within the time prescribed under rule 63 from the date when the reconstituted arbitral tribunal enters on the reference. The reconstituted arbitral tribunal shall proceed with the arbitration with the liberty to act on the record of evidence and proceedings as then existing or to commence the proceedings *de novo*.

DEPOSITS

Rule 28

The Registrar may require the Parties before passing the case on to the arbitrators under rule 38, to deposit in advance in one or more instalments such sums of money as he deems necessary to defray expenses of the arbitration including the administrative charges and arbitrator's fee. As a general rule, the deposits shall be called for in equal shares from the Claimant(s) and the Respondent(s). The arbitral tribunal may, during the course of the arbitration proceedings or in the arbitration award, require further sums to be deposited by the Parties or any one of them to meet the expenses of the arbitration. When one of the Parties neglects or refuses to make the deposit, the Registrar or the arbitral tribunal, as the case may be, may require such deposit whether in relation to a claim or a counter-claim, to be made by the other Party to the dispute (Claimant or respondent, as the case may be). Should the whole or part of the deposit be not made by the Parties or any one of them, the Registrar shall inform the Parties or the Party concerned that the claim or counter-claim, as the case may be, will not be the subject-matter of the reference. The arbitral tribunal shall proceed only in respect of those claims or counter-claims for which the deposits has been duly paid to the Council and otherwise may order the suspension or termination of the arbitral proceedings.

All deposits towards costs and expenses shall be made with the Council and no payment shall be released to the arbitrators directly by the parties. The deposit made shall be taken into account by the arbitral tribunal in apportioning the cost while making the award. Any deposit made in excess shall be refunded to such of parties as the arbitral tribunal may direct. The Council shall have a lien for the arbitral award on any unpaid cost of the arbitration.

FEES AND EXPENSES

Rule 29

The arbitral tribunal shall be entitled to allow fees and expenses of witnesses, expenses connected with the selection and carriage of sample and examination of goods, Licensed Measures Department charges, conveyance, hire, cost of legal or technical advice or proceedings in respect of any matter arising out of the arbitration incurred by the arbitral tribunal, and any other incidental expenses and charges in connection with or arising out of the reference or award as the arbitral tribunal shall, in its absolute discretion, think fit.

Rule 30

The costs of the reference and the award including charges, fees and other expenses shall be in the discretion of the arbitral tribunal, which may direct to and by whom, and in what proportion, such charges, fees and other expenses and any part thereof shall be borne and paid, and may tax and settle the amount of costs to be so paid or any part thereof and may award costs to be paid as between solicitor and client. In the event, any administrative fees and expenses are due to the Council, the arbitral tribunal may award them in favour of the Council.

Rule 31

The fees, costs and expenses incidental to the reference and the award shall include the following:

(1) Registration Fee

The Registration fee shall be payable with regard to the amount in dispute in each case as hereunder. The registration fee will not be refunded and becomes the property of the Council:

Rs. 2,500 upto Rs. One Crore claim

Rs. 5,000 more than Rs. One Crore claim

(2) Administrative Fee and Arbitrator's Fee

The Administrative fee (of ICA) and Arbitrator's fee (for each arbitrator) will be fixed separately with regard to the amount in dispute including determined interest in each case, as under:

Amount in Dispute	Arbitrator's Fee	Administrative Fee
Upto ₹ 5 lakh (₹ 5,00,000)	₹ 30,000	₹ 15,000
From ₹ 5 lakh one to ₹ 25 lakh (₹ 5,00,001 to 25,00,000)	₹ 30,000 plus ₹ 15,000 per lakh or part thereof subject to a ceiling of ₹ 60,000	₹ 15,000 plus ₹ 750 per lakh or part thereof subject to a ceiling of ₹ 30,000
From ₹ 25 lakh one to ₹ 1 crore (₹ 2,500,001 to ₹ 10,000,000)	₹ 60,000 plus ₹ 1,200 per lakh or part thereof subject to a ceiling of ₹ 1,50,000	₹ 30,000 plus ₹ 600 per lakh or part thereof subject to a ceiling of ₹ 75,000

Amount in Dispute	Arbitrator's Fee	Administrative Fee
From ₹ 1 crore one to ₹ 5 crore (₹ 1,00,00,001 to ₹ 5,00,00,000)	₹ 1,50,000 plus ₹ 22,500 per crore or part thereof subject to a ceiling of ₹ 2,40,000	₹ 75,000 plus ₹ 11,250 per crore or part thereof subject to a ceiling or ₹ 1,20,000
From ₹ 5 crore one to ₹ 10 crore (₹ 5,00,00,001 to ₹ 10,00,00,000)	₹ 2,40,000 plus ₹ 15,000 per crore or part thereof subject to a ceiling of ₹ 3,15,000	₹ 1,20,000 plus ₹ 8,000 per crore or part thereof subject to a ceiling of ₹ 1,60,000
Over ₹ 10 crore (₹ 1,00,000,000)	₹ 3,15,000 plus ₹ 12,000 per crore or part thereof	₹ 1,60,000 plus ₹ 6,000 per crore or part thereof.

(3) In addition to the above the ICA will be entitled to receive a Special Fee of Rs. 2,500 per hearing for providing facilities of hearing rooms, for arbitration hearings and secretarial assistance etc., at the arbitration hearing.

(4) Notwithstanding the provisions in sub-rule (2) of this rule, the Committee/ Chairman of the Committee may prescribe the Arbitrator's Fees and the Administrative Fees of the Council at a figure higher than those prescribed in the said sub-rules, if in the exceptional circumstances of the case this appears to be necessary.

(5) Notwithstanding the provision in sub-rule (2) hereinabove, in arbitration cases to which rule 39 applies, the Arbitrator's fee and the Administrative fee of the ICA will be fixed by computing the fee applicable to larger claim in addition to 60 per cent. of the applicable fees of all claims being tried jointly. Provided that the Committee will have the power to prescribe the arbitrator's fee and administrative fee under this sub-rule in any other manner, having regard to the nature and facts of the matters under reference.

Rule 32

Other expenses: The arbitrator may be paid an amount of Rs. 750 towards local conveyance for attending each arbitration hearing in the city of his residence. In respect of joint trial, the hearing will be treated as one irrespective of the number of cases. Any travelling and other expenses incurred by the arbitrator or the Registrar for attending the arbitration hearings in a city other than the place of residence, shall also be reimbursed to him as provided hereinafter. All the above expenses shall form part of the arbitration costs.

Rule 33

(1) An arbitrator who has to travel shall be paid travelling expenses by air or rail (air-conditioned wherever available) or car (when neither air nor rail transport is available) at actuals. In addition, he may be paid out-of-pocket expenses at actuals for boarding, lodging and local transport subject to maximum of Rs. 6,000 per day in metropolitan towns, Rs. 3,000 in class A cities and Rs. 2,000 in other cities. An arbitrator who makes his own arrangements for boarding, lodging, local transport etc., may be paid out-of-pocket expenses at the rate of Rs. 1,000 per day, without production of vouchers. The limits for stay of the Registry officials will be of those applicable to arbitrators.

(2) The cost to be incurred on payment of expenses referred to in sub-rule (1) to an arbitrator nominated by a party will be borne and paid by the party nominating the arbitrator. However, if an appointed arbitrator changes his residence after his nomination

by a party, he will not be entitled to reimbursement of any enhanced expenses for attending the arbitration hearing, unless the party nominating him agrees to reimburse the same to him. The expenses payable to the third arbitrator or sole arbitrator appointed by the Council under rules 23(a) and (b) will be borne and paid by both the parties in equal proportion or in such other manner as may be determined by the arbitral tribunal.

Rule 34

Where the arbitration proceedings under an *ad hoc* arbitration or under the rules of arbitration of any other arbitral organisation or otherwise are administered by the Council wholly or in respect of some matters arising out of such arbitration, the Council may charge an appropriate fee for such administration and other services.

Rule 35

The amount of the claim shall be stated in the application by the party applying for arbitration. If the amount is stated in a currency other than the rupee, it shall be converted into rupees, at the current official rate of exchange.

Rule 36

Where the sum under dispute is not stated or in arbitration proceedings where the relief claimed is other than a money claim, *viz.*, a declaratory claim, the Registrar and the arbitral tribunal under rule 28, may require such deposits as may be deemed necessary to be paid by such of the parties as may be required subject to later adjustment.

Rule 37

The amount of interest, wherever specified, will be included in the claim amount for the purpose of calculation of administrative fee. Further, claims and counter-claims referred for arbitration shall be taken into consideration separately for the purpose of calculation of arbitrator as well as administrative fees under sub-rule 31(2).

SUBMISSION OF THE CASE TO THE ARBITRAL TRIBUNAL

Rule 38

The Registrar shall send copies of all papers relating to arbitration such as claim statement, defence statement, counter-claims, reply, statements, or other documents received from the parties to the dispute to the arbitrator/arbitrators constituting the arbitral tribunal under rule 22 with a request to proceed with the arbitration and the arbitral tribunal shall be deemed to have entered on the reference on the day on which applications, defence statement, counter-claims, replies, documents, etc., have been despatched to the arbitrator/arbitrators. Intimation shall be given to the Parties of the day on which the arbitral tribunal is deemed to have entered on the reference.

If the claimant does not file all the requisite documents, papers, etc., or does not deposit the appropriate fees as per the rules after having been given due opportunity for the purpose by the Registrar or the arbitral tribunal, the Registrar or the arbitral tribunal may dismiss/close the case on file for lack of pursual by the claimant. Similarly, if the respondent fails to produce any requisite documents, papers including the statement of defence or information or fails to deposit administrative fees, or arbitrators fees, etc., after having been given due opportunity for the purpose by the Registrar or the arbitral tribunal, the Registrar or the arbitral tribunal may proceed further with the arbitration proceedings as per the rules, notwithstanding such failure or refusal by the Respondent.

Rule 39

Where there are two or more applications for arbitration by the Council and the issue involved in the dispute arises out of same transactions, the Registrar may, if he thinks proper to do so and with the consent of the Parties, fix the hearings of the disputes to be heard jointly or refer the applications to the same Tribunal. The awards, however, shall be given separately in each case.

NOTIFICATIONS AND/OR COMMUNICATIONS FROM THE REGISTRAR

Rule 40

All applications which the parties desire to make to the arbitral tribunal and all notices to be given to the Parties before or during the course of arbitration or otherwise in relation thereto shall be made through and sent by the Registrar who shall communicate the orders and directions of the arbitral tribunal thereon to the Parties.

AMENDMENT OF CLAIMS, ETC.

Rule 41

Amendment of the claim, defence statement, counter-claim or reply submitted to the arbitral tribunal must be formulated in writing by the Party so desiring. The arbitral tribunal will decide whether such amendments should be allowed or not. The Administrative Fee and Arbitrator's Fee (for each Arbitrator) shall get revised to the extent of increase for such additional claims/counter-claims. The Party making such additional claim/counter-claim shall deposit the entire fees payable in respect of such increase of additional claim as set out in the schedule of fees in rule 31(2).

PLACE OF ARBITRATION

Rule 42

The place or venue of arbitration shall be India. The arbitration proceedings shall be held at such place or places in India as the arbitral tribunal may determine having regard to the convenience of the arbitrators and the Parties. In a case in which one or both the Parties are from overseas, the arbitration proceedings may also be held at any place outside India at the discretion of the arbitral tribunal.

PROCEEDINGS BEFORE THE ARBITRAL TRIBUNAL CONCILIATION

Rule 43

Optional Conciliation: The parties may opt for conciliation and request the arbitral tribunal before the commencement of the arbitration proceedings unless they have already agreed otherwise, to settle their dispute through conciliation as per rules of Conciliation of the Council.

FAST TRACK ARBITRATION

Rule 44

Fast Track Arbitration: The Parties may opt for Fast Track Arbitration and request the arbitral tribunal, before the commencement of the arbitration proceedings, to decide the reference in a fixed time-frame of 3 to 6 months or any other time agreed between the Parties, according to the Fast Track Arbitration procedure, as under:

(1) The arbitral tribunal will be authorised to decide the dispute on the written pleadings, documents and written submissions filed by the Parties without any oral hearings.

(2) The arbitral tribunal shall have power to call for any further information/ clarification from the Parties in addition to the pleading and documents filed by them.

(3) An oral hearing may be held if both the Parties make a joint request or if the arbitration tribunal considers an oral hearing necessary in any particular case.

(4) If an oral hearing is held, the arbitral tribunal may dispense with any technical formalities and adopt such procedure as it deems appropriate and necessary for economic and expeditious disposal of the case.

Rule 45

At a hearing, a party shall be entitled to appear by counsel, attorney, advocate or a duly authorised adviser or representative or personally. However, where the dispute is purely of a commercial nature, the parties shall have no right to be represented by lawyers except where, having regard to the nature or complexity of the dispute, the arbitral tribunal considers it necessary in the interest of justice that the parties should be allowed to be represented by counsel, attorney or advocate.

Rule 46

The arbitral tribunal may proceed with the reference notwithstanding any failure by a party to comply with any of the directions of the arbitral tribunal and may also proceed with the arbitral proceedings in the absence of any or both the Parties who fail or neglect to attend at the time and place appointed by the arbitral tribunal, in spite of due notice.

Rule 47

The parties shall do all acts necessary to enable the arbitral tribunal to make an award expeditiously and shall not do or cause or allow to be done, any act which will delay the proceedings or prevent arbitral tribunal from making an award expeditiously, and if any party does cause or allow to be done any such act, that party shall pay such costs as the arbitral tribunal deems reasonable.

Rule 48

The arbitration session will go on as far as possible on a day-to-day basis from 10.30 a.m. to 4.30 p.m once the hearing begins after completion of all the formalities. The arbitral tribunal shall not ordinarily adjourn a hearing at the request of any Party, except where the circumstances are beyond the control of the Party and the Arbitral Tribunal is satisfied that reasons and circumstances for the adjournment are justified. While granting an adjournment, the arbitral tribunal may make such orders regarding payment of costs by one or both of the Parties, as it deems fit and reasonable.

Rule 49

If the Parties have agreed to submit their case to arbitration under these rules and any Party refuses or fails to take part in the arbitration proceedings, the arbitral tribunal may proceed with the arbitration notwithstanding such refusal or absence.

Rule 50

The arbitral tribunal may at its discretion at any time or times before making the final award and at the expense of the parties concerned, consult any person having special knowledge relating to the particular industry, commodity, produce or branch of trade concerned in the reference or any expert or qualified accountant and may also at the like expenses of the Parties, consult solicitors, counsel or advocates upon any technical question of law, evidence, practice or procedure arising in the course of the reference. If the parties agree, the arbitral tribunal may, at the expense of the Parties, appoint any expert, accountant, or lawyers to sit with as an assessor and take into account the advice of such assessor.

Rule 51

The Parties to the reference and any witness on their behalf shall, subject to the provisions of any law for the time being in force:

(a) submit to be examined by the arbitral tribunal on oath or affirmation in relation to the matters in dispute;

(b) produce before the arbitral tribunal all books, deeds, papers, accounts, writings and documents in their possession or power respectively which may be required or called for by the arbitral tribunal;

(c) comply with the requirements of the arbitral tribunal as to the production or selection of samples; and

(d) generally do all other things which, during the pendency of the reference, the arbitral tribunal may require.

Rule 52

The arbitral tribunal will consider, as far as possible, to receive the evidence of witnesses by affidavit: Provided that the witness whose affidavit is admitted in evidence is made available for cross-examination at the request of the opposite Party, the arbitral tribunal may:

(a) administer an oath or affirmation to the Parties or witnesses appearing and giving evidence;

(b) make any award conditional or in the alternative;

(c) correct in any award, any clerical mistake or error arising from, or incidental to, any slip or omission;

(d) administer to the Parties to the arbitration such interrogatories as it may consider necessary;

(e) decide all objections to its jurisdiction including any objection regarding the existence or validity of the arbitration clause or the arbitration agreement, without prejudice to the right of the parties to have the matter decided by the Court of Law;

(f) decide the law governing:

 (i) the contract or the matter in dispute,

 (ii) the arbitration agreement, and

 (iii) the arbitration procedure.

(g) award interest including *pendente lite* interest.

Rule 53

When substantially the same dispute or questions of law and facts are likely to arise in more than one contract or agreement (Chain Contracts), the arbitral tribunal may invite all parties involved to agree to submit to an award in one arbitration between such two or more of the parties as are named for the purpose.

Rule 54

(i) The arbitral tribunal may by the award dismiss the application or claim:

 (a) if the claimant does not prosecute the arbitration proceedings or file the papers within the time granted; or

 (b) neglects or refuses to pay the dues or deposits ordered to be paid by the arbitral tribunal or the Registrar.

(ii) The arbitral tribunal may make an *ex parte* award:

 (a) if the respondent neglects or refuses to appear or make his defence or fails to file the papers within the time granted; or

 (b) neglects or refuses to pay the dues or deposits ordered to be paid by the arbitral tribunal or the Registrar.

Rule 55

The Registrar shall make necessary arrangements for a stenographic record of evidence whenever such record is required by a Party. The cost of the stenographic record and all transcripts thereof, if any, shall form part of the costs of the reference.

Rule 56

The language of the arbitration proceedings shall be English unless otherwise agreed by the parties. If any documents filed by a Party are in a language other than English, the Party filing such documents shall simultaneously furnish an English translation of the documents. The Registrar may make arrangements for the service of an interpreter at the request of one or more of the parties and costs thereof shall form part of the costs of the reference.

Rule 57

The arbitral tribunal may issue such orders or directions as it may deem necessary for safeguarding, interim custody, preservation, protection, storage, sale or disposal of the whole or part of the subject-matter of the dispute or for its inspection or sampling without prejudice to the rights of the Parties or the final determination of the dispute.

WAIVER OF RULES

Rule 58

Any party who proceeds with the arbitration with the knowledge that any provision or requirement of these rules has not been complied with and who fails to state his objection thereto in writing, shall be deemed to have waived his right to object.

RETURN OF DOCUMENTS

Rule 59

Unless required to be filed in a Court of Law, the arbitral tribunal shall have full discretion to retain/to return all books, documents or papers produced before it and may direct at any time that the books, documents or papers produced before it or any of them may be returned to the parties producing them on such terms and conditions, as the arbitral tribunal may impose.

AWARD

Rule 60

No award shall be made by the arbitral tribunal unless the case of the party applying for arbitration has been brought to the notice of the other party and until after the lapse of such specified time within which he has been asked to submit his defence statement under rule 18.

Rule 61

Whenever there is more than one arbitrator, the award of the majority shall prevail and be taken as the decision of arbitral tribunal. Failing a majority, the Presiding Arbitrator of the arbitral tribunal alone shall make the award.

Rule 62

Should the Parties arrive at a settlement of the dispute by common agreement before the arbitral tribunal and the arbitral tribunal is satisfied that such agreement is genuine and not to defeat the purpose of any law, the arbitral tribunal shall render an award as per agreement of the Parties. Otherwise, the arbitral tribunal shall make the award on the basis of the documents, evidence, etc., filed before it by the Parties.

Rule 63

The arbitral tribunal shall make the award as expeditiously as possible, preferably within six months, according to the guidelines, from the date of the reference subject to a maximum limit of two years from the date of commencement of the arbitral proceedings. If necessary, the maximum limit of two years for making the award may be extended by agreement between the parties to the dispute or by the Committee.

Rule 64

The arbitral award shall state the reasons upon which it is based, unless:

(i) the parties have agreed that no reasons are to be given, or

(ii) the award is an arbitral award on agreed terms.

Rule 65

The arbitral award shall state its date and the place of arbitration and the award shall be deemed to have been made at that place.

Rule 66

The arbitral tribunal may make an interim award, and may, by an award, determine and order what shall be done by either or any of the Parties, respecting the matters referred.

Rule 67

The arbitrators constituting the arbitral tribunal or the Presiding Arbitrator where rule 61 is applicable, shall sign the award and the Registrar shall give notice in writing to the Parties of the making and signing thereof and of the amount of fees and charges payable in respect of the arbitration and the award. The arbitrators fee shall be payable by the Council on receipt of the award and requisite deposit made by the parties.

Rule 68

(a) When an award has been made, the Registrar shall furnish a true copy of the award to the parties by registered post provided the arbitration costs have been fully paid to the Council by the parties or by one of them.

(b) The Registrar may require either Party to notify him of the compliance with the award.

(c) The arbitral tribunal and the Registrar of the Council shall assist the parties in complying with any formalities that may be necessary for the enforcement of the award or for other purposes.

(d) The council may print, publish or otherwise circulate any award made under its rules or under its auspices, in any arbitration journal, magazine, report, etc., for the purpose of creating arbitration jurisprudence or precedents for the benefit and guidance of future arbitrations. No party to the arbitration shall have any objection to the publication of awards as above provided that the names and addresses of any Party to the dispute will be omitted from such publication and its identity duly concerned if so desired by such party.

Rule 69

Additional copies of the award certified true by the Registrar shall be made available to the parties but to no one else, at all times at request and on payment as fixed by the Registrar.

Rule 70

A party shall in all things abide by and obey the award which shall be binding on the Parties and their respective representatives, notwithstanding the death of any party before or after the making of the award and such death shall not operate as revocation of the submission or reference. To avoid delays and further litigation, the arbitrators/Registrar shall ask the Parties to agree that the award made by the arbitrator/s shall be final and binding on the Parties and neither Party shall be entitled to challenge it in the Court of Law.

FILING OF AWARD

Rule 71

The arbitral tribunal shall at the request of any of the Parties to the proceedings or of any person claiming under a Party or if so directed by the Court and upon payment of fees and charges due in respect of the arbitration and award and of the costs and charges of filing the award, cause the award or a signed copy thereof together with the deposition or documents which may have been taken and proved before it to be filed before the Court.

Rule 72

A fee of Rs. 1,000 plus incidental expenses at actuals in addition to the court-fees, on the scale for the time being in force is payable by the party requiring the award to be filed.

STAMP DUTIES

Rule 73

Stamp duties are to be paid by the parties in equal share in all cases in accordance with the scale of stamp duties for the time being imposed by law.

COPIES OF PROCEEDINGS

Rule 74

No party is entitled as of right to copies of proceedings before the arbitral tribunal. In case the Registrar is required to furnish copies of depositions and/or documents which have been taken or proved before the arbitrator, a charge as demanded by the Registrar shall be paid by the party requiring such copies.

Rule 75

The Registrar shall, upon the written request of a party, furnish to such party at his expense certified facsimile of any documents filed in the arbitration proceedings.

CASES WITHDRAWN

Rule 76

When the party instituting a case desires to withdraw it before an arbitral tribunal has been constituted, the Registrar shall return to him any deposits made by him, under rule 28, after deducting such charges as he might have incurred in connection with the cases. The registration fee, however, shall not be refundable.

Rule 77

If the arbitration is terminated by the act or default of any parties after constitution of the arbitral tribunal and before the award is made, any fees, charges and expenses incurred by the Council shall be paid by the parties in such proportion as per schedule of fees prescribed in the Rules of Arbitration of the Council.

INDEMNITY OF SECRETARIAT AND ARBITRATORS

Rule 78

The Council, the Arbitration Committee and officers of the Council shall not be liable for any act or omission in whatever capacity they may have acted in connection with or in relation to an arbitration under these rules. Parties are themselves required to contest the proceedings regarding the validity of the arbitration agreement before the court.

Rule 79

No party shall bring or prosecute any suit or proceedings whatsoever against the arbitral tribunal, or any member thereof, for or in respect of any matter or thing purporting to be done under these rules nor any suit or proceedings in respect thereof (save for enforcement of the award) against the other party.

AMENDMENT OF RULES

Rule 80

The Governing Body may revise, amend or alter these rules or the schedule of fees and other monies to be charged and paid as and when expedient and necessary.

Annexure I

ICA Guidelines for Arbitrators and Parties for Expeditious Conduct of Arbitration Proceedings

1. The arbitrators and the parties to arbitration are expected to follow these guidelines to ensure economic and expeditious disposal of arbitration cases.

For Arbitrators

2. The arbitrators must take up the arbitration expeditiously on receipt of the request from the Council and should also complete the same with reasonable despatch. Serious efforts should be made to settle arbitration cases expeditiously within a period of 6 months where the amount of claim exceeds 1 crore and within a period of 4 months where the amount of claim is less than Rs. 1 crore.

3. When accepting his mandate, the arbitrator shall be able to perform his task with the necessary competence according to his professional qualifications.

4. When giving notice of his acceptance, the arbitrator shall disclose in writing in the printed format as under:

- any relationship with the parties or their counsel which may affect his independence and impartiality;
- any personal or economic interest, either direct or indirect, in the subject matter of the dispute;
- any prejudice or reservation as to the subject-matter of the dispute which may affect his impartiality.

Where necessary due to supervening facts, this Statement shall be repeated in the course of the entire arbitral proceedings until the award is filed.

5. Where facts that should have been disclosed are subsequently discovered, the arbitrator may either withdraw or be challenged or the Indian Council of Arbitration may refuse to appoint him in other arbitral proceedings on this ground.

6. The arbitrator may at all stages suggest the possibility of a settlement to the parties but may not influence their decision by indicating that he has already reached a decision on the dispute.

7. In the course of the arbitral proceedings, the arbitrator shall refrain from all unilateral contact with the parties or their counsel which is not notified to the Indian Council of Arbitration so that the ICA can inform the other parties and arbitrators.

8. The arbitrator shall refrain from giving the parties, either directly or through their counsel, notice of decisions in the evidence taking place or on the merits; notice of these decisions may be given exclusively by the ICA.

9. The arbitrator shall neither request nor accept any direct arrangement on costs or fees with the party which has designated him. The arbitrator is entitled to reimbursement of expenses and a fee as exclusively determined by the ICA according to its schedule of fees, which is deemed to be approved by the arbitrator when accepting his mandate.

10. The arbitrator shall encourage a serene and positive development of the arbitral proceedings. In particular, he shall decide on the date and manner of the hearings in such a way as to allow both parties to fully participate therein, in compliance with the principle of equal treatment and adversarial proceedings.

11. The first hearing of the arbitral tribunal should be convened within 15 days of the receipt of the complete reply of the respondent when the arbitral tribunal may issue necessary directions. Admission and denial of the documents may be got done by the Registrar. Issues if any to be framed, may be done at the same or at the next hearing. The arbitrators should hold arbitration hearings continuously on day-to-day basis during office hours.

12. The parties should be asked to furnish a list of their witness, if any, in advance and they should be asked to file affidavits of witness on the date fixed for evidence preferably within a week of the settlement of issues, cross-examination of such of the deponent's witnesses whose presence is demanded by the opposite party should be completed at a hearing to be fixed within 15 days.

13. Arguments preferably should be heard within 15 days of the completion of evidence, to be followed by submission of written arguments, if any.

14. Adjournments of duly fixed hearing should not be granted except for unavoidable reasons which should be spelt out in the adjournment order.

15. The arbitrator should make the award expeditiously after the close of the hearings, preferably within 15 days.

16. The arbitrator who does not comply with the provisions of these guidelines may be replaced by the Committee. Where it is not appropriate to replace the arbitrator in order not to cause delay in the arbitral proceedings, the ICA may also take such action after the conclusion of the arbitral proceedings, by refusing to confirm him in subsequent arbitral proceedings.

For Parties

17. The claimant should file the applications or demand for arbitration to the Registrar of the Council with all the information and papers as per rules, full statement of claim and copies of documents relied upon, in 3 sets in case of a Sole Arbitrator and in 5 sets in case of three arbitrators.

18. The respondent should file his reply to the claim with complete information and documents relied upon, in 3 or 5 sets as above as early as possible, within, the prescribed time. Fresh documentation/claims should not be entertained at a later stage of the proceedings unless the arbitral tribunal is satisfied about the reasons for granting such permission.

19. If any party to arbitration, particularly in cases where any arbitrator, advocate or any of the parties has to come from outstation to participate in arbitration proceedings, desires to seek adjournment on any valid ground, it must submit a written request to the Registrar at least before 5 working days stating the grounds which compel it to request for postponement of the hearing so that the Council is in a position to take necessary steps to inform the Parties, Arbitrators and Advocates regarding postponement of the hearing. Parties seeking adjournment will have to pay cost as may be determined by the arbitral tribunal.

20. Parties should deposit arbitration and administrative fees with the Council (ICA) within the stipulated time, as per the rules and no extension should be sought in this behalf except for compelling reasons.

21. To avoid excessive costs in arbitration proceedings, the parties are advised to choose their arbitrators from the Panel, as far as possible from the place where the arbitration hearings have to be held. In case, a party still chooses an arbitrator from a place other than the place of hearing, the concerned party will bear the entire extra cost to be incurred on stay TA/DA etc., of the arbitrator nominated by it.

For Arbitration Committee

22. The Arbitration Committee of the Council may examine the arbitration case file, from time-to-time to evaluate the progress of the proceedings and to ascertain whether the arbitrators have granted adjournments only on reasonable grounds.

23. The Arbitration Committee shall be sole judge of the grounds of violation of the guidelines and its decision shall be final and binding on the arbitral tribunal as well as the parties.

ANNEXURE B

RULES OF ARBITRATION OF THE INTERNATIONAL CHAMBER OF COMMERCE

As in force from 1st January, 1998
Costs scales effective as of 1st July, 2003

INTRODUCTORY PROVISIONS

Article 1: International Court of Arbitration

1. The International Court of Arbitration (the "Court") of the International Chamber of Commerce (the "ICC") is the arbitration body attached to the ICC. The statutes of the Court are set forth in Appendix I. Members of the Court are appointed by the World Council of the ICC. The function of the Court is to provide for the settlement by arbitration of business disputes of an international character in accordance with the Rules of Arbitration of the International Chamber of Commerce (the "Rules"). If so empowered by an arbitration agreement, the Court shall also provide for the settlement by arbitration in accordance with these Rules of business disputes not of an international character.

2. The Court does not itself settle disputes. It has the function of ensuring the application of these Rules. It draws up its own Internal Rules (Appendix II).

3. The Chairman of the Court or, in the Chairman's absence or otherwise at his request, one of its Vice-Chairmen shall have the power to take urgent decisions on behalf of the Court, provided that any such decision is reported to the Court at its next session.

4. As provided for in its Internal Rules, the Court may delegate to one or more committees composed of its members the power to take certain decisions, provided that any such decision is reported to the Court at its next session.

5. The Secretariat of the Court (the "Secretariat") under the direction of its Secretary-General (the "Secretary-General") shall have its seat at the headquarters of the ICC.

Article 2: Definitions

In these Rules:

(i) "Arbitral Tribunal" includes one or more arbitrators.

(ii) "Claimant" includes one or more claimants and "Respondent" includes one or more respondents.

(iii) "Award" includes, *inter alia*, an interim, partial or final Award.

Article 3: Written Notifications or Communications; Time Limits

1. All pleadings and other written communications submitted by any party, as well as all documents annexed thereto, shall be supplied in a number of copies sufficient to provide one copy for each party, plus one for each arbitrator, and one for the Secretariat. A copy of any communication from the arbitral tribunal to the parties shall be sent to the Secretariat.

2. All notifications or communications from the Secretariat and the arbitral tribunal shall be made to the last address of the party or its representative for whom the same are intended, as notified either by the party in question or by the other party. Such notification or communication may be made by delivery against receipt, registered post, courier, facsimile transmission, telex, telegram or any other means of telecommunication that provides a record of the sending thereof.

3. A notification or communication shall be deemed to have been made on the day it was received by the party itself or by its representative, or would have been received if made in accordance with the preceding paragraph.

4. Periods of time specified in or fixed under the present Rules, shall start to run on the day following the date a notification or communication is deemed to have been made in accordance with the preceding paragraph. When the day next following such date is an official holiday, or a non-business day in the country where the notification or communication is deemed to have been made, the period of time shall commence on the first following business day. Official holidays and non-business days are included in the calculation of the period of time. If the last day of the relevant period of time granted is an official holiday or a non-business day in the country where the notification or communication is deemed to have been made, the period of time shall expire at the end of the first following business day.

COMMENCING THE ARBITRATION

Article 4: Request for Arbitration

1. A party wishing to have recourse to arbitration under these Rules shall submit its Request for Arbitration (the "Request") to the Secretariat, which shall notify the claimant and respondent of the receipt of the Request and the date of such receipt.

2. The date on which the Request is received by the Secretariat shall, for all purposes, be deemed to be the date of the commencement of the arbitral proceedings.

3. The Request shall, *inter alia,* contain the following information:

(a) the name in full, description and address of each of the parties;

(b) a description of the nature and circumstances of the dispute giving rise to the claim(s);

(c) a statement of the relief sought, including, to the extent possible, an indication of any amount(s) claimed;

(d) the relevant agreements and, in particular, the arbitration agreement;

(e) all relevant particulars concerning the number of arbitrators and their choice in accordance with the provisions of articles 8, 9 and 10, and any nomination of an arbitrator required thereby; and

(f) any comments as to the place of arbitration, the applicable rules of law and the language of the arbitration.

4. Together with the Request, the claimant shall submit the number of copies thereof required by article 3(1) and shall make the advance payment on administrative expenses required by Appendix III ("Arbitration Costs and Fees") in force on the date the Request is submitted. In the event that the claimant fails to comply with either of these requirements, the Secretariat may fix a time-limit within which the claimant must comply, failing which the file shall be closed without prejudice to the right of the claimant to submit the same claims at a later date in another Request.

5. The Secretariat shall send a copy of the Request and the documents annexed thereto to the respondent for its Answer to the Request once the Secretariat has sufficient copies of the Request and the required advance payment.

6. When a party submits a Request in connection with a legal relationship in respect of which arbitration proceedings between the same parties are already pending under these Rules, the Court may, at the request of a party, decide to include the claims contained in the Request in the pending proceedings provided that the Terms of Reference have not been signed or approved by the Court. Once the Terms of Reference have been signed or approved by the Court, claims may only be included in the pending proceedings subject to the provisions of article 19.

Article 5: Answer to the Request; Counter-claims

1. Within 30 days from the receipt of the Request from the Secretariat, the respondent shall file an Answer (the "Answer") which shall, *inter alia*, contain the following information:

(a) its name in full, description and address;

(b) its comments as to the nature and circumstances of the dispute giving rise to the claim(s);

(c) its response to the relief sought;

(d) any comments concerning the number of arbitrators and their choice in light of the claimant's proposals and in accordance with the provisions of articles 8, 9 and 10, and any nomination of an arbitrator required thereby; and

(e) any comments as to the place of arbitration, the applicable rules of law and the language of the arbitration.

2. The Secretariat may grant the respondent an extension of the time for filing the Answer, provided the application for such an extension contains the Respondent's comments concerning the number of arbitrators and their choice and, where required by articles 8, 9 and 10, the nomination of an arbitrator. If the respondent fails to do so, the Court shall proceed in accordance with these Rules.

3. The Answer shall be supplied to the Secretariat in the number of copies specified by article 3(1).

4. A copy of the Answer and the documents annexed thereto shall be communicated by the Secretariat to the claimant.

5. Any counter-claim(s) made by the respondent shall be filed with its Answer and shall provide:

(a) a description of the nature and circumstances of the dispute giving rise to the counter-claim(s); and

(b) a statement of the relief sought, including, to the extent possible, an indication of any amount(s) counter-claimed.

6. The claimant shall file a reply to any counter-claim within 30 days from the date of receipt of the counter-claim(s) communicated by the Secretariat. The Secretariat may grant the claimant an extension of time for filing the reply.

Article 6: Effect of the Arbitration Agreement

1. Where the parties have agreed to submit to arbitration under the Rules, they shall be deemed to have submitted *ipso facto* to the Rules in effect on the date of commencement of the arbitration proceedings, unless they have agreed to submit to the Rules in effect on the date of their arbitration agreement.

2. If the respondent does not file an Answer, as provided by article 5, or if any party raises one or more pleas concerning the existence, validity or scope of the arbitration agreement, the Court may decide, without prejudice to the admissibility or merits of the plea or pleas, that the arbitration shall proceed if it is *prima facie* satisfied that an arbitration

agreement under the rules may exist. In such a case, any decision as to the jurisdiction of the arbitral tribunal shall be taken by the arbitral tribunal itself. If the Court is not so satisfied, the parties shall be notified that the arbitration cannot proceed. In such a case, any party retains the right to ask any court having jurisdiction whether or not there is a binding arbitration agreement.

3. If any of the parties refuses or fails to take part in the arbitration or any stage thereof, the arbitration shall proceed notwithstanding such refusal or failure.

4. Unless otherwise agreed, the arbitral tribunal shall not cease to have jurisdiction by reason of any claim that the contract is *null* and *void* or allegation that it is non-existent, provided that the arbitral tribunal upholds the validity of the arbitration agreement. The arbitral tribunal shall continue to have jurisdiction to determine the respective rights of the parties and to adjudicate their claims and pleas even though the contract itself may be non-existent or *null* and *void*.

THE ARBITRAL TRIBUNAL

Article 7: General Provisions

1. Every arbitrator must be and remain independent of the parties involved in the arbitration.

2. Before appointment or confirmation, a prospective arbitrator shall sign a statement of independence and disclose in writing to the Secretariat any facts or circumstances which might be of such a nature as to call into question the arbitrator's independence in the eyes of the parties. The Secretariat shall provide such information to the parties in writing and fix a time-limit for any comments from them.

3. An arbitrator shall immediately disclose in writing to the Secretariat and to the parties any facts or circumstances of a similar nature which may arise during the arbitration.

4. The decisions of the Court as to the appointment, confirmation, challenge or replacement of an arbitrator shall be final and the reasons for such decisions shall not be communicated.

5. By accepting to serve, every arbitrator undertakes to carry out his responsibilities in accordance with these Rules.

6. Insofar as the parties have not provided otherwise, the arbitral tribunal shall be constituted in accordance with the provisions of articles 8, 9 and 10.

Article 8: Number of Arbitrators

1. The disputes shall be decided by a sole arbitrator or by three arbitrators.

2. Where the parties have not agreed upon the number of arbitrators, the Court shall appoint a sole arbitrator, save where it appears to the Court that the dispute is such as to warrant the appointment of three arbitrators. In such case, the claimant shall nominate an arbitrator within a period of 15 days from the receipt of the notification of the decision of the Court, and the respondent shall nominate an arbitrator within a period of 15 days from the receipt of the notification of the nomination made by the Claimant.

3. Where the parties have agreed that the dispute shall be settled by a sole arbitrator, they may, by agreement, nominate the sole arbitrator for confirmation. If the parties fail to nominate a sole arbitrator within 30 days from the date when the Claimant's Request for Arbitration has been received by the other party, or within such additional time as may be allowed by the Secretariat, the sole arbitrator shall be appointed by the Court.

4. Where the dispute is to be referred to three arbitrators, each party shall nominate in the Request and the Answer, respectively, one arbitrator for confirmation. If a party

fails to nominate an arbitrator, the appointment shall be made by the Court. The third arbitrator, who will act as chairman of the arbitral tribunal, shall be appointed by the Court, unless the parties have agreed upon another procedure for such appointment, in which case the nomination will be subject to confirmation pursuant to article 9. Should such procedure not result in a nomination within the time-limit fixed by the parties or the Court, the third arbitrator shall be appointed by the Court.

Article 9: Appointment and Confirmation of the Arbitrators

1. In confirming or appointing arbitrators, the Court shall consider the prospective arbitrator's nationality, residence and other relationships with the countries of which the parties or the other arbitrators are nationals and the prospective arbitrator's availability and ability to conduct the arbitration in accordance with these rules. The same shall apply where the Secretary-General confirms arbitrators pursuant to article 9(2).

2. The Secretary-General may confirm as co-arbitrators, sole arbitrators and chairmen of arbitral tribunals persons nominated by the parties or pursuant to their particular agreements, provided they have filed a statement of independence without qualification or a qualified statement of independence has not given rise to objections. Such confirmation shall be reported to the Court at its next session. If the Secretary-General considers that a co-arbitrator, sole arbitrator or chairman of an arbitral tribunal should not be confirmed, the matter shall be submitted to the Court.

3. Where the Court is to appoint a sole arbitrator or the chairman of an arbitral tribunal, it shall make the appointment upon a proposal of a National Committee of the ICC that it considers to be appropriate. If the Court does not accept the proposal made, or if the National Committee fails to make the proposal requested within the time-limit fixed by the Court, the Court may repeat its request or may request a proposal from another National Committee that it considers to be appropriate.

4. Where the Court considers that the circumstances so demand, it may choose the sole arbitrator or the chairman of the arbitral tribunal from a country where there is no National Committee, provided that neither of the parties objects within the time-limit fixed by the Court.

5. The sole arbitrator or the chairman of the arbitral tribunal shall be of a nationality other than those of the parties. However, in suitable circumstances and provided that neither of the parties objects within the time-limit fixed by the Court, the sole arbitrator or the chairman of the arbitral tribunal may be chosen from a country of which any of the parties is a national.

6. Where the Court is to appoint an arbitrator on behalf of a party which has failed to nominate one, it shall make the appointment upon a proposal of the National Committee of the country of which that party is a national. If the Court does not accept the proposal made, or if the National Committee fails to make the proposal requested within the time-limit fixed by the Court, or if the country of which the said party is a national has no National Committee, the Court shall be at liberty to choose any person whom it regards as suitable. The Secretariat shall inform the National Committee, if one exists, of the country of which such person is a national.

Article 10: Multiple Parties

1. Where there are multiple parties, whether as claimant or as Respondent, and where the dispute is to be referred to three arbitrators, the multiple Claimants, jointly, and the multiple Respondents, jointly, shall nominate an arbitrator for confirmation pursuant to article 9.

2. In the absence of such a joint nomination and where all parties are unable to agree to a method for the constitution of the arbitral tribunal, the Court may appoint each

member of the arbitral tribunal and shall designate one of them to act as chairman. In such case, the Court shall be at liberty to choose any person it regards as suitable to act as arbitrator, applying article 9 when it considers this appropriate.

Article 11: Challenge of Arbitrators

1. A challenge of an arbitrator, whether for an alleged lack of independence or otherwise, shall be made by the submission to the Secretariat of a written statement specifying the facts and circumstances on which the challenge is based.

2. For a challenge to be admissible, it must be sent by a party either within 30 days from receipt by that party of the notification of the appointment or confirmation of the arbitrator, or within 30 days from the date when the party making the challenge was informed of the facts and circumstances on which the challenge is based if such date is subsequent to the receipt of such notification.

3. The Court shall decide on the admissibility and, at the same time, if necessary, on the merits of a challenge after the Secretariat has afforded an opportunity for the arbitrator concerned, the other party or parties and any other members of the arbitral tribunal to comment in writing within a suitable period of time. Such comments shall be communicated to the parties and to the arbitrators.

Article 12: Replacement of Arbitrators

1. An arbitrator shall be replaced upon his death, upon the acceptance by the Court of the arbitrator's resignation, upon acceptance by the Court of a challenge or, upon the request of all the parties.

2. An arbitrator shall also be replaced on the Court's own initiative when it decides that he is prevented *de jure* or *de facto* from fulfilling his functions, or that he is not fulfilling his functions in accordance with the Rules or within the prescribed time-limits.

3. When, on the basis of information that has come to its attention, the Court considers applying article 12(2), it shall decide on the matter after the arbitrator concerned, the parties and any other members of the arbitral tribunal have had an opportunity to comment in writing within a suitable period of time. Such comments shall be communicated to the parties and to the arbitrators.

4. When an arbitrator is to be replaced, the Court has discretion to decide whether or not to follow the original nominating process. Once reconstituted, and after having invited the parties to comment, the arbitral tribunal shall determine if and to what extent prior proceedings shall be repeated before the reconstituted arbitral tribunal.

5. Subsequent to the closing of the proceedings, instead of replacing an arbitrator who has died or been removed by the Court pursuant to articles 12(1) and 12(2), the Court may decide, when it considers it appropriate, that the remaining arbitrators shall continue the arbitration. In making such determination, the Court shall take into account the views of the remaining arbitrators and of the parties and such other matters that it considers appropriate in the circumstances.

THE ARBITRAL PROCEEDINGS

Article 13: Transmission of the File to the arbitral tribunal

The Secretariat shall transmit the file to the arbitral tribunal as soon as it has been constituted, provided the advance on costs requested by the Secretariat at this stage has been paid.

Article 14: Place of the Arbitration

1. The place of the arbitration shall be fixed by the Court unless agreed upon by the parties.

2. The arbitral tribunal may, after consultation with the parties, conduct hearings and meetings at any location it considers appropriate unless otherwise agreed by the parties.

3. The arbitral tribunal may deliberate at any location it considers appropriate.

Article 15: Rules Governing the Proceedings

1. The proceedings before the arbitral tribunal shall be governed by these Rules, and, where these Rules are silent by any rules which the parties or, failing them, the arbitral tribunal may settle on, whether or not reference is thereby made to the rules of procedure of a national law to be applied to the arbitration.

2. In all cases, the arbitral tribunal shall act fairly and impartially and ensure that each party has a reasonable opportunity to present its case.

Article 16: Language of the Arbitration

In the absence of an agreement by the parties, the arbitral tribunal shall determine the language or languages of the arbitration, due regard being given to all relevant circumstances, including the language of the contract.

Article 17: Applicable Rules of Law

1. The parties shall be free to agree upon the rules of law to be applied by the arbitral tribunal to the merits of the dispute. In the absence of any such agreement, the arbitral tribunal shall apply the rules of law which it determines to be appropriate.

2. In all cases the arbitral tribunal shall take account of the provisions of the contract and the relevant trade usages.

3. The arbitral tribunal shall assume the powers of an *amiable compositeur* or decide *ex æquo et bono* only if the parties have agreed to give it such powers.

Article 18: Terms of Reference; Procedural Time-table

1. As soon as it has received the file from the Secretariat, the arbitral tribunal shall draw up, on the basis of documents or in the presence of the parties and in the light of their most recent submissions, a document defining its Terms of Reference. This document shall include the following particulars:

(a) the full names and descriptions of the parties;

(b) the addresses of the Parties to which notifications and communications arising in the course of the arbitration may be made;

(c) a summary of the Parties' respective claims and of the relief sought by each party, with an indication to the extent possible of the amounts claimed or counter-claimed;

(d) unless the arbitral tribunal considers it inappropriate, a list of issues to be determined;

(e) the full names, descriptions and addresses of the arbitrators;

(f) the place of the arbitration; and

(g) particulars of the applicable procedural rules and, if such is the case, reference to the power conferred upon the arbitral tribunal to act as *amiable compositeur* or to decide *ex æquo et bono*.

2. The Terms of Reference shall be signed by the parties and the arbitral tribunal. Within two months of the date on which the file has been transmitted to it, the arbitral tribunal shall transmit to the Court the Terms of Reference signed by it and by the parties. The Court may extend this time-limit pursuant to a reasoned request from the arbitral tribunal or on its own initiative if it decides it is necessary to do so.

3. If any of the parties refuses to take part in the drawing up of the Terms of Reference or to sign the same, they shall be submitted to the Court for approval. When the Terms of Reference have been signed in accordance with article 18(2) or approved by the Court, the arbitration shall proceed.

4. When drawing up the Terms of Reference, or as soon as possible thereafter, the arbitral tribunal, after having consulted the parties, shall establish in a separate document a provisional timetable that it intends to follow for the conduct of the arbitration and shall communicate it to the Court and the parties. Any subsequent modifications of the provisional time-table shall be communicated to the Court and the parties.

Article 19: New Claims

After the Terms of Reference have been signed or approved by the Court, no party shall make new claims or counter-claims which fall outside the limits of the Terms of Reference unless it has been authorised to do so by the arbitral tribunal, which shall consider the nature of such new claims or counter-claims, the stage of the arbitration and other relevant circumstances.

Article 20: Establishing the Facts of the Case

1. The arbitral tribunal shall proceed within as short a time as possible to establish the facts of the case by all appropriate means.

2. After studying the written submissions of the parties and all documents relied upon, the arbitral tribunal shall hear the parties together in person if any of them so requests or, failing such a request, it may of its own motion decide to hear them.

3. The arbitral tribunal may decide to hear witnesses, experts appointed by the parties or any other person, in the presence of the parties, or in their absence provided they have been duly summoned.

4. The arbitral tribunal, after having consulted the parties, may appoint one or more experts, define their terms of reference and receive their reports. At the request of a party, the parties shall be given the opportunity to question at a hearing any such expert appointed by the Tribunal.

5. At any time during the proceedings, the arbitral tribunal may summon any party to provide additional evidence.

6. The arbitral tribunal may decide the case solely on the documents submitted by the parties unless any of the parties requests a hearing.

7. The arbitral tribunal may take measures for protecting trade secrets and confidential information.

Article 21: Hearings

1. When a hearing is to be held, the arbitral tribunal, giving reasonable notice, shall summon the parties to appear before it on the day and at the place fixed by it.

2. If any of the parties, although duly summoned, fails to appear without valid excuse, the arbitral tribunal shall have the power to proceed with the hearing.

3. The arbitral tribunal shall be in full charge of the hearings, at which all the parties shall be entitled to be present. Save with the approval of the arbitral tribunal and the parties, persons not involved in the proceedings shall not be admitted.

4. The parties may appear in person or through duly authorised representatives. In addition, they may be assisted by advisers.

Article 22: Closing of the Proceedings

1. When it is satisfied that the parties have had a reasonable opportunity to present their cases, the arbitral tribunal shall declare the proceedings closed. Thereafter, no further

submission or argument may be made, or evidence produced, unless requested or authorised by the arbitral tribunal.

2. When the arbitral tribunal has declared the proceedings closed, it shall indicate to the Secretariat an approximate date by which the draft Award will be submitted to the Court for approval pursuant to article 27. Any postponement of that date shall be communicated to the Secretariat by the arbitral tribunal.

Article 23: Conservatory and Interim Measures

1. Unless the parties have otherwise agreed, as soon as the file has been transmitted to it, the arbitral tribunal may, at the request of a party, order any interim or conservatory measure it deems appropriate. The arbitral tribunal may make the granting of any such measure subject to appropriate security being furnished by the requesting party. Any such measure shall take the form of an order, giving reasons, or of an Award, as the arbitral tribunal considers appropriate.

2. Before the file is transmitted to the arbitral tribunal, and in appropriate circumstances even thereafter, the parties may apply to any competent judicial authority for interim or conservatory measures. The application of a party to a judicial authority for such measures or for the implementation of any such measures ordered by an arbitral tribunal shall not be deemed to be an infringement or a waiver of the arbitration agreement and shall not affect the relevant powers reserved to the arbitral tribunal. Any such application and any measures taken by the judicial authority must be notified without delay to the Secretariat. The Secretariat shall inform the arbitral tribunal thereof.

AWARDS

Article 24: Time Limit for the Award

1. The time-limit within which the arbitral tribunal must render its final Award is six months. Such time-limit shall start to run from the date of the last signature by the arbitral tribunal or by the parties of the Terms of Reference or, in the case of application of article 18(3), the date of the notification to the arbitral tribunal by the Secretariat of the approval of the Terms of Reference by the Court.

2. The Court may extend this time-limit pursuant to a reasoned request from the arbitral tribunal or on its own initiative if it decides it is necessary to do so.

Article 25: Making of the Award

1. When the arbitral tribunal is composed of more than one arbitrator, an Award is given by a majority decision. If there be no majority, the Award shall be made by the chairman of the arbitral tribunal alone.

2. The Award shall state the reasons upon which it is based.

3. The Award shall be deemed to be made at the place of the arbitration and on the date stated therein.

Article 26: Award by Consent

If the parties reach a settlement after the file has been transmitted to the arbitral tribunal in accordance with article 13, the settlement shall be recorded in the form of an Award made by consent of the parties if so requested by the parties and if the arbitral tribunal agrees to do so.

Article 27: Scrutiny of the Award by the Court

Before signing any Award, the arbitral tribunal shall submit it in draft form to the Court. The Court may lay down modifications as to the form of the Award and, without affecting the arbitral tribunal's liberty of decision, may also draw its attention to points of substance. No Award shall be rendered by the arbitral tribunal until it has been approved by the Court as to its form.

Article 28: Notification, Deposit and Enforceability of the Award

1. Once an Award has been made, the Secretariat shall notify to the parties the text signed by the arbitral tribunal, provided always that the costs of the arbitration have been fully paid to the ICC by the parties or by one of them.

2. Additional copies certified true by the Secretary-General shall be made available on request and at any time to the parties, but to no one else.

3. By virtue of the notification made in accordance with Paragraph 1 of this Article, the parties waive any other form of notification or deposit on the part of the arbitral tribunal.

4. An original of each Award made in accordance with the present Rules shall be deposited with the Secretariat.

5. The arbitral tribunal and the Secretariat shall assist the parties in complying with whatever further formalities may be necessary.

6. Every Award shall be binding on the parties. By submitting the dispute to arbitration under these Rules, the parties undertake to carry out any Award without delay and shall be deemed to have waived their right to any form of recourse insofar as such waiver can validly be made.

Article 29: Correction and Interpretation of the Award

1. On its own initiative, the arbitral tribunal may correct a clerical, computational or typographical error, or any errors of similar nature contained in an Award, provided such correction is submitted for approval to the Court within 30 days of the date of such Award.

2. Any application of a party for the correction of an error of the kind referred to in article 29(1), or for the interpretation of an Award, must be made to the Secretariat within 30 days of the receipt of the Award by such party, in a number of copies as stated in article 3(1). After transmittal of the application to the arbitral tribunal, the latter shall grant the other party a short-time-limit, normally not exceeding 30 days, from the receipt of the application by that party to submit any comments thereon. If the arbitral tribunal decides to correct, or interpret the Award, it shall submit its decision in draft form to the Court not later than 30 days following the expiration of the time-limit for the receipt of any comments from the other party or within such other period as the Court may decide.

3. The decision to correct or to interpret the Award shall take the form of an addendum and shall constitute part of the Award. The provisions of articles 25, 27 and 28 shall apply *mutatis mutandis.*

COSTS

Article 30: Advance to Cover the Costs of the Arbitration

1. After receipt of the Request, the Secretary-General may request the claimant to pay a provisional advance in an amount intended to cover the costs of arbitration until the Terms of Reference have been drawn up.

2. As soon as practicable, the Court shall fix the advance on costs in an amount likely to cover the fees and expenses of the arbitrators and the ICC administrative costs for the claims and counter-claims which have been referred to it by the parties. This amount may be subject to re-adjustment at any time during the arbitration. Where, apart from the claims, counter-claims are submitted, the Court may fix separate advances on costs for the claims and the counter-claims.

3. The advance on costs fixed by the Court shall be payable in equal shares by the claimant and the Respondent. Any provisional advance paid on the basis of article 30(1) will be considered as a partial payment thereof. However, any party shall be free to pay the whole of the advance on costs in respect of the principal claim or the counter-claim should the other party fail to pay its share. When the Court has set separate advances on costs in accordance with article 30(2), each of the parties shall pay the advance on costs corresponding to its claims.

4. When a request for an advance on costs has not been complied with, and after consultation with the arbitral tribunal, the Secretary-General may direct the arbitral tribunal to suspend its work and set a time-limit, which must be not less than 15 days, on the expiry of which the relevant claims, or counter-claims, shall be considered as withdrawn. Should the party in question wish to object to this measure, it must make a request within the aforementioned period for the matter to be decided by the Court. Such party shall not be prevented, on the ground of such withdrawal, from reintroducing the same claims or counter-claims at a later date in another proceeding.

5. If one of the parties claims a right to a set-off with regard to either claims or counter-claims, such set-off shall be taken into account in determining the advance to cover the costs of arbitration in the same way as a separate claim insofar as it may require the arbitral tribunal to consider additional matters.

Article 31: Decision as to the Costs of the Arbitration

1. The costs of the arbitration shall include the fees and expenses of the arbitrators and the ICC administrative expenses fixed by the Court, in accordance with the scale in force at the time of the commencement of the arbitral proceedings, as well as the fees and expenses of any experts appointed by the arbitral tribunal and the reasonable legal and other costs incurred by the parties for the arbitration.

2. The Court may fix the fees of the arbitrators at a figure higher or lower than that which would result from the application of the relevant scale should this be deemed necessary due to the exceptional circumstances of the case. Decisions on costs other than those fixed by the Court may be taken by the arbitral tribunal at any time during the proceedings.

3. The final Award shall fix the costs of the arbitration and decide which of the parties shall bear them or in what proportion they shall be borne by the parties.

MISCELLANEOUS

Article 32: Modified Time Limits

1. The parties may agree to shorten the various time-limits set out in these rules. Any such agreement entered into subsequent to the constitution of an arbitral tribunal shall become effective only upon the approval of the arbitral tribunal.

2. The Court, on its own initiative, may extend any time-limit which has been modified pursuant to article 32(1) if it decides that it is necessary to do so in order that the arbitral tribunal or the Court may fulfil their responsibilities in accordance with these Rules.

Article 33: Waiver

A party which proceeds with the arbitration without raising its objection to a failure to comply with any provision of these rules, or of any other rules applicable to the proceedings, any direction given by the arbitral tribunal, or any requirement under the arbitration agreement relating to the constitution of the arbitral tribunal, or to the conduct of the proceedings, shall be deemed to have waived its right to object.

Article 34: Exclusion of Liability

Neither the arbitrators, nor the Court and its members, nor the ICC and its employees, nor the ICC National Committees shall be liable to any person for any act or omission in connection with the arbitration.

Article 35: General Rule

In all matters not expressly provided for in these Rules, the Court and the arbitral tribunal shall act in the spirit of these Rules and shall make every effort to make sure that the Award is enforceable at law.

APPENDIX I

STATUTES OF THE INTERNATIONAL COURT OF ARBITRATION

Article 1: Function

1. The function of the International Court of Arbitration of the International Chamber of Commerce (the "Court") is to ensure the application of the Rules of Arbitration of the International Chamber of Commerce, and it has all the necessary powers for that purpose.

2. As an autonomous body, it carries out these functions in complete independence from the ICC and its organs.

3. Its members are independent from the ICC National Committees.

Article 2: Composition of the Court

The Court shall consist of a Chairman, Vice-Chairmen, and members and alternate members (collectively designated as members). In its work it is assisted by its Secretariat (Secretariat of the Court).

Article 3: Appointment

1. The Chairman is elected by the ICC World Council upon the recommendation of the Executive Board of the ICC.

2. The ICC World Council appoints the Vice-Chairmen of the Court from among the members of the Court or otherwise.

3. Its members are appointed by the ICC World Council on the proposal of National Committees, one member for each Committee.

4. On the proposal of the Chairman of the Court, the World Council may appoint alternate members.

5. The term of office of all members is three years. If a member is no longer in a position to exercise his functions, his successor is appointed by the World Council for the remainder of the term.

Article 4: Plenary Session of the Court

The Plenary Sessions of the Court are presided over by the Chairman or, in his absence, by one of the Vice-Chairmen designated by him. The deliberations shall be valid when at least six members are present. Decisions are taken by a majority vote, the Chairman having a casting vote in the event of a tie.

Article 5: Committees

The Court may set-up one or more Committees and establish the functions and organisation of such Committees.

Article 6: Confidentiality

The work of the Court is of a confidential nature which must be respected by everyone who participates in that work in whatever capacity. The Court lays down the rules regarding the persons who can attend the meetings of the Court and its Committees and who are entitled to have access to the materials submitted to the Court and its Secretariat.

Article 7: Modification of the Rules of Arbitration

Any proposal of the Court for a modification of the Rules is laid before the Commission on Arbitration before submission to the Executive Board and the World Council of the ICC for approval.

APPENDIX II

INTERNAL RULES OF THE INTERNATIONAL COURT OF ARBITRATION

Article 1: Confidential Character of the Work of the International Court of Arbitration

1. The sessions of the Court, whether plenary or those of a Committee of the Court, are open only to its members and to the Secretariat.

2. However, in exceptional circumstances, the Chairman of the Court may invite other persons to attend. Such persons must respect the confidential nature of the work of the Court.

3. The documents submitted to the Court, or drawn up by it in the course of its proceedings, are communicated only to the members of the Court and to the Secretariat and to persons authorised by the Chairman to attend Court sessions.

4. The Chairman or the Secretary-General of the Court may authorise researchers undertaking work of a scientific nature on international trade law to acquaint themselves with awards and other documents of general interest, with the exception of memoranda, notes, statements and documents remitted by the parties within the framework of arbitration proceedings.

5. Such authorisation shall not be given unless the beneficiary has undertaken to respect the confidential character of the documents made available and to refrain from any publication in their respect without having previously submitted the text for approval to the Secretary-General of the Court.

6. The Secretariat will in each case submitted to arbitration under the Rules retain in the archives of the Court all Awards, Terms of Reference, and decisions of the Court, as well as copies of the pertinent correspondence of the Secretariat.

7. Any documents, communications or correspondence submitted by the parties or the arbitrators may be destroyed unless a party or an arbitrator requests in writing within a period fixed by the Secretariat the return of such documents. All related costs and expenses for the return of those documents shall be paid by such party or arbitrator.

Article 2: Participation of Members of the International Court of Arbitration in ICC Arbitration

1. The Chairman and the members of the Secretariat of the Court may not act as arbitrators or as counsel in cases submitted to ICC arbitration.

2. The Court shall not appoint Vice-Chairmen or members of the Court as arbitrators. They may, however, be proposed for such duties by one or more of the parties, or pursuant to any other procedure agreed upon by the parties, subject to confirmation.

3. When the Chairman, a Vice-Chairman or a member of the Court or of the Secretariat is involved in any capacity whatsoever in proceedings pending before the Court, such person must inform the Secretary-General of the Court upon becoming aware of such involvement.

4. Such person must refrain from participating in the discussions or in the decisions of the Court concerning the proceedings and must be absent from the courtroom whenever the matter is considered.

5. Such person will not receive any material documentation or information pertaining to such proceedings.

Article 3: Relations between the Members of the Court and the ICC National Committees

1. By virtue of their capacity, the members of the Court are independent of the ICC National Committees which proposed them for appointment by the ICC World Council.

2. Furthermore, they must regard as confidential, *vis-à-vis* the said National Committees, any information concerning individual cases with which they have become acquainted in their capacity as members of the Court, except when they have been requested by the Chairman of the Court or by its Secretary-General to communicate specific information to their respective National Committee.

Article 4: Committee of the Court

1. In accordance with the provisions of article 1(4) of the Rules and article 5 of its Statutes (Appendix I), the Court hereby establishes a Committee of the Court.

2. The members of the Committee consist of a Chairman and at least two other members. The Chairman of the Court acts as the Chairman of the Committee. If absent, the Chairman may designate a Vice-Chairman of the Court or, in exceptional circumstances, another member of the Court as Chairman of the Committee.

3. The other two members of the Committee are appointed by the Court from among the Vice-Chairmen or the other members of the Court. At each Plenary Session the Court appoints the members who are to attend the meetings of the Committee to be held before the next Plenary Session.

4. The Committee meets when convened by its Chairman. Two members constitute a quorum.

5. (a) The Court shall determine the decisions that may be taken by the Committee.
   (b) The decisions of the Committee are taken unanimously.
   (c) When the Committee cannot reach a decision or deems it preferable to abstain, it transfers the case to the next Plenary Session, making any suggestions it deems appropriate.
   (d) The Committee's decisions are brought to the notice of the Court at its next Plenary Session.

Article 5: Court Secretariat

1. In case of absence, the Secretary-General may delegate to the General Counsel and Deputy Secretary-General the authority to confirm arbitrators, to certify true copies of Awards and to request the payment of a provisional advance, respectively provided for in articles 9(2), 28(2) and 30(1) of the Rules.

2. The Secretariat may, with the approval of the Court, issue notes and other documents for the information of the parties and the arbitrators, or as necessary for the proper conduct of the arbitral proceedings.

3. Branches of the Secretariat may be established outside the headquarters of the ICC. The Secretariat shall keep a list of offices designated as branches by the Secretary-General. Requests for Arbitration may be submitted to the Secretariat at its seat or at any of its branches, and the Secretariat's functions under the Rules may be carried out from its seat or any of its branches, as instructed by the Secretary-General, Deputy-Secretary-General or General Counsel.

Article 6: Scrutiny of Arbitral Awards

When the Court scrutinizes draft Awards in accordance with article 27 of the Rules, it considers, to the extent practicable, the requirements of mandatory law at the place of arbitration.

APPENDIX III

ARBITRATION COSTS AND FEES

Article 1: Advance on Costs

1. Each request to commence an arbitration pursuant to the rules must be accompanied by an advance payment of US$ 2,500 on the administrative expenses. Such payment is non-refundable, and shall be credited to the Claimant's portion of the advance on costs.

2. The provisional advance fixed by the Secretary-General according to article 30(1) of the rules shall normally not exceed the amount obtained by adding together the administrative expenses, the minimum of the fees (as set out in the scale hereinafter) based upon the amount of the claim and the expected reimbursable expenses of the arbitral tribunal incurred with respect to the drafting of the Terms of Reference. If such amount is not quantified, the provisional advance shall be fixed at the discretion of the Secretary-General. Payment by the claimant shall be credited to its share of the advance on costs fixed by the Court.

3. In general, after the Terms of Reference have been signed or approved by the Court and the provisional time-table has been established, the arbitral tribunal shall, in accordance with article 30(4) of the Rules, proceed only with respect to those claims or counterclaims in regard to which the whole of the advance on costs has been paid.

4. The advance on costs fixed by the Court according to article 30(2) of the Rules comprises the fees of the arbitrator or arbitrators (hereinafter referred to as "arbitrator"), any arbitration-related expenses of the arbitrator and the administrative expenses.

5. Each party shall pay in cash its share of the total advance on costs. However, if its share exceeds an amount fixed from time-to-time by the Court, a party may post a bank guarantee for this additional amount.

6. A party that has already paid in full its share of the advance on costs fixed by the Court may, in accordance with article 30(3) of the Rules, pay the unpaid portion of the advance owed by the defaulting party by posting a bank guarantee.

7. When the Court has fixed separate advances on costs pursuant to article 30(2) of the Rules, the Secretariat shall invite each party to pay the amount of the advance corresponding to its respective claim(s).

8. When, as a result of the fixing of separate advances on costs, the separate advance fixed for the claim of either party exceeds one half of such global advance as was previously fixed (in respect of the same claims and counter-claims that are the subject of separate advances), a bank guarantee may be posted to cover any such excess amount. In the event that the amount of the separate advance is subsequently increased, at least one half of the increase shall be paid in cash.

9. The Secretariat shall establish the terms governing all bank guarantees which the parties may post pursuant to the above provisions.

10. As provided in article 30(2) of the Rules, the advance on costs may be subject to readjustment at any time during the arbitration, in particular to take into account fluctuations in the amount in dispute, changes in the amount of the estimated expenses of the arbitrator, or the evolving difficulty or complexity of arbitration proceedings.

11. Before any expertise ordered by the arbitral tribunal can be commenced, the parties, or one of them, shall pay an advance on costs fixed by the arbitral tribunal

sufficient to cover the expected fees and expenses of the expert as determined by the arbitral tribunal. The arbitral tribunal shall be responsible for ensuring the payment by the parties of such fees and expenses.

Article 2: Costs and Fees

1. Subject to article 31(2) of the Rules, the Court shall fix the fees of the arbitrator in accordance with the scale hereinafter set out or, where the sum in dispute is not stated, at its discretion.

2. In setting the arbitrator's fees, the Court shall take into consideration the diligence of the arbitrator, the time spent, the rapidity of the proceedings, and the complexity of the dispute so as to arrive at a figure within the limits specified or, in exceptional circumstances [Article 31(2) of the Rules], at a figure higher or lower than those limits.

3. When a case is submitted to more than one arbitrator, the Court, at its discretion, shall have the right to increase the total fees up to a maximum which shall normally not exceed three times the fees of one arbitrator.

4. The arbitrator's fees and expenses shall be fixed exclusively by the Court as required by the Rules. Separate fee arrangements between the parties and the arbitrator are contrary to the Rules.

5. The Court shall fix the administrative expenses of each arbitration in accordance with the scale hereinafter set out or, where the sum in dispute is not stated, at its discretion. In exceptional circumstances, the Court may fix the administrative expenses at a lower or higher figure than that which would result from the application of such scale, provided that such expenses shall normally not exceed the maximum amount of the scale. Further, the Court may require the payment of administrative expenses in addition to those provided in the scale of administrative expenses as a condition to holding an arbitration in abeyance at the request of the parties or of one of them with the acquiescence of the other.

6. If an arbitration terminates before the rendering of a final Award, the Court shall fix the costs of the arbitration at its discretion, taking into account the stage attained by the arbitral proceedings and any other relevant circumstances.

7. In the case of an application under article 29(2) of the Rules, the Court may fix an advance to cover additional fees and expenses of the arbitral tribunal and may make the transmission of such application to the arbitral tribunal subject to the prior cash payment in full to the ICC of such advance. The Court shall fix at its discretion any possible fees of the arbitrator when approving the decision of the arbitral tribunal.

8. When an arbitration is preceded by an attempt at amicable resolution pursuant to the ICC ADR Rules, one half of the administrative expenses paid for such ADR proceedings shall be credited to the administrative expenses of the arbitration.

9. Amounts paid to the arbitrator do not include any possible value added taxes (VAT) or other taxes or charges and imposts applicable to the arbitrator's fees. Parties have a duty to pay any such taxes or charges; however, the recovery of any such charges or taxes is a matter solely between the arbitrator and the parties.

Article 3: ICC as Appointing Authority

Any request received for an authority of the ICC to act as appointing authority will be treated in accordance with the Rules of ICC as Appointing Authority in UNCITRAL or other *Ad Hoc* Arbitration Proceedings and shall be accompanied by a non-refundable sum of US$ 2,500. No request shall be processed unless accompanied by the said sum. For additional services, ICC may at its discretion fix administrative expenses, which shall be commensurate with the services provided and shall not exceed the maximum sum of US$ 10,000.

Article 4: Scales of Administrative Expenses and Arbitrator's Fees

1. The Scales of Administrative Expenses and Arbitrator's Fees set forth below shall be effective as of 1st May, 2010 in respect of all arbitrations commenced on or after such date, irrespective of the version of the Rules applying to such arbitrations.

2. To calculate the administrative expenses and the arbitrator's fees, the amounts calculated for each successive slice of the sum in dispute must be added together, except that where the sum in dispute is over US$ 80 million, a flat amount of US$ 88,800 shall constitute the entirety of the administrative expenses.

A. ADMINISTRATIVE EXPENSES

Sum in dispute (in US Dollars)				Administrative expenses(*)
up to			50,000	$3,000
from	50,001	to	100,000	4.73%
from	100,001	to	200,000	2.53%
from	200,001	to	500,000	2.09%
from	500,001	to	1,000,000	1.51%
from	1,000,001	to	2,000,000	0.95%
from	2,000,001	to	5,000,000	0.46%
from	5,000,001	to	10,000,000	0.25%
from	10,000,001	to	30,000,000	0.10%
from	30,000,001	to	50,000,000	0.09%
from	50,000,001	to	80,000,000	0.01%
from	80,000,001	to	500,000,000	0.0035%
over	500,000,000			$113,215

(*) For illustrative purposes only, the table on the following page indicates the resulting administrative expenses in US$ when the proper calculations have been made.

B. ARBITRATOR'S FEES

Sum in dispute (in US Dollars)				Fees (**) minimum	maximum
up to			50,000	$53,000	18.0200%
from	50,001	to	100,000	2.6500%	13.5680%
from	100,001	to	200,000	1.4310%	7.6850%
from	200,001	to	500,000	1.3670%	6.8370%
from	500,001	to	1,000,000	0.9540%	4.0280%
from	1,000,001	to	2,000,000	0.6890%	3.6040%
from	2,000,001	to	5,000,000	0.3750%	1.3910%
from	5,000,001	to	10,000,000	0.1280%	0.9100%
from	10,000,001	to	30,000,000	0.0640%	0.2410%
from	30,000,001	to	50,000,000	0.0590%	0.2280%
from	50,000,001	to	80,000,000	0.0330%	0.1570%
from	80,000,001	to	100,000,000	0.0210%	0.1150%
from	100,000,001	to	500,000,000	0.0110%	0.0580%
over	500,000,000			0.0100%	0.0400%

(**) For illustrative purposes only, the table on the following page indicates the resulting range of fees in US$ when the proper calculations have been made.

Sun Dispute (in US Dollars)			A. Administrative Expenses (*) (in US Dollars)			B. Arbitrator's Fees(*) (in US Dollars)			
						Minimum		Maximum	
Upto		50,000	3,000			3,000		18.200% of amount in dispute	
from	50,001 to	10,000	3,000 +	4.73% of amt. over	50,000	3,000 + 2.6500% of amt. over	50,000	9,010 + 13.5680% of amt. over	50,000
from	100,001 to	200,000	5,365 +	2.53% of amt. over	100,000	4,325 + 1.4310% of amt. over	100,000	15,794 + 7.6850% of amt. over	100,000
from	200,001 to	500,000	7,895 +	2.09% of amt. over	200,000	5,756 + 1.3670% of amt. over	200,000	23,479 + 6.8370% of amt. over	200,000
from	500,001 to	1,000,000	14,165 +	1.51% of amt. over	500,000	9,857 + 0.9540% of amt. over	500,000	43,990 + 4.0280% of amt. over	500,000
from	1,000,001 to	2,000,000	21,715 +	0.95% of amt. over	1,000,000	14,627 + 0.6890% of amt. over	1,000,000	64,130 + 3.6040% of amt. over	1,000,000
from	2,000,001 to	5,000,000	31,215 +	0.46% of amt. over	2,000,000	21,517 + 03750% of amt. over	2,000,000	100,170 + 1.3910% of amt. over	2,000,000
from	5,000,001 to	10,000,000	45,015 +	0.25% of amt. over	5,000,000	32,767 + 0.1280% of amt. over	5,000,000	141,900 + 0.9100% of amt. over	5,000,000
from	10,000,001 to	30,000,000	57,515 +	0.10% of amt. over	10,000,000	39,167 + 0.0640% of amt. over	10,000,000	187,400 + 0.2410% of amt. over	10,000,000
from	30,000,001 to	50,000,000	77,515 +	0.09% of amt. over	30,000,000	51,967 + 0.0590% of amt. over	30,000,000	235,600 + 0.2280% of amt. over	30,000,000
from	50,000,001 to	80,000,000	95,515 +	0.01% of amt. over	50,000,000	63,767 + 0.0330% of amt. over	50,000,000	281,200 + 0.1570% of amt. over	50,000,000
from	80,000,001 to	100,000,000	98,515 +	0.0035% of amt. over	80,000,000	73,667 + 0.0210% of amt. over	80,000,000	328,300 + 0.1150% of amt. over	80,000,000
from	100,000,001 to	500,000,000	99,215 +	0.0035% of amt. over	100,000,000	77,867 + 0.0110% of amt. over	100,000,000	351,300 + 0.0580% of amt. over	100,000,000
from	500,000,000		113,215			121,867 + 0.0100% of amt. over	500,000,000	583,300 + 0.0400% of amt. over	500,000,000

ANNEXURE C

LCIA ARBITRATION RULES

(adopted to take effect for arbitrations
commencing on or after 1st January, 1998)

Where any agreement, submission or reference provides in writing and in whatsoever manner for arbitration under the rules of the LCIA or by the Court of the LCIA ("the LCIA Court"), the parties shall be taken to have agreed in writing that the arbitration shall be conducted in accordance with the following rules ("the rules") or such amended rules as the LCIA may have adopted hereafter to take effect before the commencement of the arbitration. The rules include the Schedule of Costs in effect at the commencement of the arbitration, as separately amended from time-to-time by the LCIA Court.

Article 1: The Request for Arbitration

1.1 Any party wishing to commence an arbitration under these Rules ("the Claimant") shall send to the Registrar of the LCIA Court ("the Registrar") a written request for arbitration ("the Request"), containing or accompanied by:

(a) the names, addresses, telephone, facsimile, telex and e-mail numbers (if known) of the parties to the arbitration and of their legal representatives;

(b) a copy of the written arbitration clause or separate written arbitration agreement invoked by the claimant ("the Arbitration Agreement"), together with a copy of the contractual documentation in which the arbitration clause is contained or in respect of which the arbitration arises;

(c) a brief statement describing the nature and circumstances of the dispute, and specifying the claims advanced by the claimant against another party to the arbitration ("the Respondent");

(d) a statement of any matters [such as the seat or language(s) of the arbitration, or the number of arbitrators, or their qualifications or identities] on which the parties have already agreed in writing for the arbitration or in respect of which the claimant wishes to make a proposal;

(e) if the Arbitration Agreement calls for party nomination of arbitrators, the name, address, telephone, facsimile, telex and e-mail numbers (if known) of the Claimant's nominee;

(f) the fee prescribed in the Schedule of Costs (without which the Request shall be treated as not having been received by the Registrar and the arbitration as not having been commenced);

(g) confirmation to the Registrar that copies of the Request (including all accompanying documents) have been or are being served simultaneously on all other parties to the arbitration by one or more means of service to be identified in such confirmation.

1.2 The date of receipt by the Registrar of the Request shall be treated as the date on which the arbitration has commenced for all purposes. The Request (including all accompanying documents) should be submitted to the Registrar in two copies where a sole arbitrator should be appointed, or, if the parties have agreed or the claimant considers that three arbitrators should be appointed, in four copies.

Article 2: The Response

2.1 Within 30 days of service of the Request on the Respondent, (or such lesser period fixed by the LCIA Court), the respondent shall send to the Registrar a written response to the Request ("the Response"), containing or accompanied by:

(a) confirmation or denial of all or part of the claims advanced by the claimant in the Request;

(b) a brief statement describing the nature and circumstances of any counter-claims advanced by the respondent against the Claimant;

(c) comment in response to any statements contained in the Request, as called for under article 1.1(d), on matters relating to the conduct of the arbitration;

(d) if the Arbitration Agreement calls for party nomination of arbitrators, the name, address, telephone, facsimile, telex and e-mail numbers (if known) of the Respondent's nominee; and

(e) confirmation to the Registrar that copies of the Response (including all accompanying documents) have been or are being served simultaneously on all other parties to the arbitration by one or more means of service to be identified in such confirmation.

2.2 The Response (including all accompanying documents) should be submitted to the Registrar in two copies, or if the parties have agreed or the respondent considers that three arbitrators should be appointed, in four copies.

2.3 Failure to send a Response shall not preclude the respondent from denying any claim or from advancing a counter-claim in the arbitration. However, if the Arbitration Agreement calls for party nomination of arbitrators, failure to send a Response or to nominate an arbitrator within time or at all shall constitute an irrevocable waiver of that party's opportunity to nominate an arbitrator.

Article 3: The LCIA Court and Registrar

3.1 The functions of the LCIA Court under these Rules shall be performed in its name by the President or a Vice-President of the LCIA Court or by a division of three or five members of the LCIA Court appointed by the President or a Vice-President of the LCIA Court, as determined by the President.

3.2 The functions of the Registrar under these Rules shall be performed by the Registrar or any deputy Registrar of the LCIA Court under the supervision of the LCIA Court.

3.3 All communications from any party or arbitrator to the LCIA Court shall be addressed to the Registrar.

Article 4: Notices and Periods of Time

4.1 Any notice or other communication that may be or is required to be given by a party under these Rules shall be in writing and shall be delivered by registered postal or courier service or transmitted by facsimile, telex, e-mail or any other means of telecommunication that provide a record of its transmission.

4.2 A party's last-known residence or place of business during the arbitration shall be a valid address for the purpose of any notice or other communication in the absence of any notification of a change to such address by that party to the other parties, the arbitral tribunal and the Registrar.

4.3 For the purpose of determining the date of commencement of a time-limit, a notice or other communication shall be treated as having been received on the day it is delivered or, in the case of telecommunications, transmitted in accordance with articles 4.1 and 4.2.

4.4 For the purpose of determining compliance with a time-limit, a notice or other communication shall be treated as having been sent, made or transmitted if it is despatched in accordance with articles 4.1 and 4.2 prior to or on the date of the expiration of the time-limit.

4.5 Notwithstanding the above, any notice or communication by one party may be addressed to another party in the manner agreed in writing between them or, failing such agreement, according to the practice followed in the course of their previous dealings or in whatever manner ordered by the arbitral tribunal.

4.6 For the purpose of calculating a period of time under these Rules, such period shall begin to run on the day following the day when a notice or other communication is received. If the last day of such period is an official holiday or a non-business day at the residence or place of business of the addressee, the period is extended until the first business day which follows. Official holidays or non-business days occurring during the running of the period of time are included in calculating that period.

4.7 The arbitral tribunal may at any time extend (even where the period of time has expired) or abridge any period of time prescribed under these Rules or under the Arbitration Agreement for the conduct of the arbitration, including any notice or communication to be served by one party on any other party.

Article 5: Formation of the arbitral tribunal

5.1 The expression "the arbitral tribunal" in these Rules includes a sole arbitrator or all the arbitrators where more than one. All references to an arbitrator shall include the masculine and feminine. (References to the President, Vice-President and members of the LCIA Court, the Registrar or Deputy-Registrar, expert, witness, party and legal representative shall be similarly understood).

5.2 All arbitrators conducting an arbitration under these Rules shall be and remain at all times impartial and independent of the parties; and none shall act in the arbitration as advocates for any party. No arbitrator, whether before or after appointment, shall advise any party on the merits or outcome of the dispute.

5.3 Before appointment by the LCIA Court, each arbitrator shall furnish to the Registrar a written résumé of his past and present professional positions; he shall agree in writing upon fee rates conforming to the Schedule of Costs; and he shall sign a declaration to the effect that there are no circumstances known to him likely to give rise to any justified doubts as to his impartiality or independence, other than any circumstances disclosed by him in the declaration. Each arbitrator shall thereby also assume a continuing duty forthwith to disclose any such circumstances to the LCIA Court, to any other members of the arbitral tribunal and to all the parties if such circumstances should arise after the date of such declaration and before the arbitration is concluded.

5.4 The LCIA Court shall appoint the arbitral tribunal as soon as practicable after receipt by the Registrar of the Response or after the expiry of 30 days following service of the Request upon the respondent if no Response is received by the Registrar (or such lesser period fixed by the LCIA Court). The LCIA Court may proceed with the formation of the arbitral tribunal notwithstanding that the Request is incomplete or the Response is missing, late or incomplete. A sole arbitrator shall be appointed unless the parties have agreed in writing otherwise, or unless the LCIA Court determines that in view of all the circumstances of the case a three-member tribunal is appropriate.

5.5 The LCIA Court alone is empowered to appoint arbitrators. The LCIA Court will appoint arbitrators with due regard for any particular method or criteria of selection agreed in writing by the parties. In selecting arbitrators consideration will be given to the nature of the transaction, the nature and circumstances of the dispute, the nationality, location and languages of the parties and (if more than two) the number of parties.

5.6 In the case of a three-member arbitral tribunal, the chairman (who will not be a party-nominated arbitrator) shall be appointed by the LCIA Court.

Article 6: Nationality of Arbitrators

6.1 Where the parties are of different nationalities, a sole arbitrator or chairman of the arbitral tribunal shall not have the same nationality as any party unless the parties who are not of the same nationality as the proposed appointee all agree in writing otherwise.

6.2 The nationality of parties shall be understood to include that of controlling shareholders or interests.

6.3 For the purpose of this Article, a person who is a citizen of two or more states shall be treated as a national of each State; and citizens of the European Union shall be treated as nationals of its different Member States and shall not be treated as having the same nationality.

Article 7: Party and Other Nominations

7.1 If the parties have agreed that any arbitrator is to be appointed by one or more of them or by any third person, that agreement shall be treated as an agreement to nominate an arbitrator for all purposes. Such nominee may only be appointed by the LCIA Court as arbitrator subject to his prior compliance with article 5.3. The LCIA Court may refuse to appoint any such nominee if it determines that he is not suitable or independent or impartial.

7.2 Where the parties have howsoever agreed that the respondent or any third person is to nominate an arbitrator and such nomination is not made within time or at all, the LCIA Court may appoint an arbitrator notwithstanding the absence of the nomination and without regard to any late nomination. Likewise, if the Request for Arbitration does not contain a nomination by the claimant where the parties have howsoever agreed that the claimant or a third person is to nominate an arbitrator, the LCIA Court may appoint an arbitrator notwithstanding the absence of the nomination and without regard to any late nomination.

Article 8: Three or More Parties

8.1 Where the Arbitration Agreement entitles each party howsoever to nominate an arbitrator, the parties to the dispute number more than two and such parties have not all agreed in writing that the disputant parties represent two separate sides for the formation of the arbitral tribunal as claimant and respondent respectively, the LCIA Court shall appoint the arbitral tribunal without regard to any party's nomination.

8.2 In such circumstances, the Arbitration Agreement shall be treated for all purposes as a written agreement by the parties for the appointment of the arbitral tribunal by the LCIA Court.

Article 9: Expedited Formation

9.1 In exceptional urgency, on or after the commencement of the arbitration, any party may apply to the LCIA Court for the expedited formation of the arbitral tribunal, including the appointment of any replacement arbitrator under articles 10 and 11 of these rules.

9.2 Such an application shall be made in writing to the LCIA Court, copied to all other parties to the arbitration; and it shall set out the specific grounds for exceptional urgency in the formation of the arbitral tribunal.

9.3 The LCIA Court may, in its complete discretion, abridge or curtail any time-limit under these Rules for the formation of the arbitral tribunal, including service of the Response and of any matters or documents adjudged to be missing from the Request. The LCIA Court shall not be entitled to abridge or curtail any other time-limit.

Article 10: Revocation of Arbitrator's Appointment

10.1 If either (a) any arbitrator gives written notice of his desire to resign as arbitrator to the LCIA Court, to be copied to the parties and the other arbitrators (if any) or (b) any arbitrator dies, falls seriously ill, refuses, or becomes unable or unfit to act, either upon challenge by a party or at the request of the remaining arbitrators, the LCIA Court may revoke that arbitrator's appointment and appoint another arbitrator. The LCIA Court shall decide upon the amount of fees and expenses to be paid for the former arbitrator's services (if any) as it may consider appropriate in all the circumstances.

10.2 If any arbitrator acts in deliberate violation of the Arbitration Agreement (including these Rules) or does not act fairly and impartially as between the parties or does not conduct or participate in the arbitration proceedings with reasonable diligence, avoiding unnecessary delay or expense, that arbitrator may be considered unfit in the opinion of the LCIA Court.

10.3 An arbitrator may also be challenged by any party if circumstances exist that give rise to justifiable doubts as to his impartiality or independence. A party may challenge an arbitrator it has nominated, or in whose appointment it has participated, only for reasons of which it becomes aware after the appointment has been made.

10.4 A party who intends to challenge an arbitrator shall, within 15 days of the formation of the arbitral tribunal or (if later) after becoming aware of any circumstances referred to in article 10.1, 10.2 or 10.3, send a written statement of the reasons for its challenge to the LCIA Court, the arbitral tribunal and all other parties. Unless the challenged arbitrator withdraws or all other parties agree to the challenge within 15 days of receipt of the written statement, the LCIA Court shall decide on the challenge.

Article 11: Nomination and Replacement of Arbitrators

11.1 In the event that the LCIA Court determines that any nominee is not suitable or independent or impartial or if an appointed arbitrator is to be replaced for any reason, the LCIA Court shall have a complete discretion to decide whether or not to follow the original nominating process.

11.2 If the LCIA Court should so decide, any opportunity given to a party to make a re-nomination shall be waived if not exercised within 15 days (or such lesser time as the LCIA Court may fix), after which the LCIA Court shall appoint the replacement arbitrator.

Article 12: Majority Power to Continue Proceedings

12.1 If any arbitrator on a three-member arbitral tribunal refuses or persistently fails to participate in its deliberations, the two other arbitrators shall have the power, upon their written notice of such refusal or failure to the LCIA Court, the parties and the third arbitrator, to continue the arbitration (including the making of any decision, ruling or award), notwithstanding the absence of the third arbitrator.

12.2 In determining whether to continue the arbitration, the two other arbitrators shall take into account the stage of the arbitration, any explanation made by the third arbitrator for his non-participation and such other matters as they consider appropriate in the circumstances of the case. The reasons for such determination shall be stated in any award, order or other decision made by the two arbitrators without the participation of the third arbitrator.

12.3 In the event that the two other arbitrators determine at any time not to continue the arbitration without the participation of the third arbitrator missing from their deliberations, the two arbitrators shall notify in writing the parties and the LCIA Court of such determination; and in that event, the two arbitrators or any party may refer the matter to the LCIA Court for the revocation of that third arbitrator's appointment and his replacement under article 10.

Article 13: Communications between Parties and the arbitral tribunal

13.1 Until the arbitral tribunal is formed, all communications between parties and arbitrators shall be made through the Registrar.

13.2 Thereafter, unless and until the arbitral tribunal directs that communications shall take place directly between the arbitral tribunal and the parties (with simultaneous copies to the Registrar), all written communications between the parties and the arbitral tribunal shall continue to be made through the Registrar.

13.3 Where the Registrar sends any written communication to one party on behalf of the arbitral tribunal, he shall send a copy to each of the other parties. Where any party sends to the Registrar any communication (including Written Statements and Documents under article 15), it shall include a copy for each arbitrator; and it shall also send copies direct to all other parties and confirm to the Registrar in writing that it has done or is doing so.

Article 14: Conduct of the Proceedings

14.1 The parties may agree on the conduct of their arbitral proceedings and they are encouraged to do so, consistent with the arbitral tribunal's general duties at all times:

(i) to act fairly and impartially as between all parties, giving each a reasonable opportunity of putting its case and dealing with that of its opponent; and

(ii) to adopt procedures suitable to the circumstances of the arbitration, avoiding unnecessary delay or expense, so as to provide a fair and efficient means for the final resolution of the parties' dispute.

Such agreements shall be made by the parties in writing or recorded in writing by the arbitral tribunal at the request of and with the authority of the parties.

14.2 Unless otherwise agreed by the parties under article 14.1, the arbitral tribunal shall have the widest discretion to discharge its duties allowed under such law(s) or rules of law as the arbitral tribunal may determine to be applicable; and at all times the parties shall do everything necessary for the fair, efficient and expeditious conduct of the arbitration.

14.3 In the case of a three-member arbitral tribunal the chairman may, with the prior consent of the other two arbitrators, make procedural rulings alone.

Article 15: Submission of Written Statements and Documents

15.1 Unless the parties have agreed otherwise under article 14.1 or the arbitral tribunal should determine differently, the written stage of the proceedings shall be as set out below.

15.2 Within 30 days of receipt of written notification from the Registrar of the formation of the arbitral tribunal, the claimant shall send to the Registrar a Statement of Case setting out in sufficient detail the facts and any contentions of law on which it relies, together with the relief claimed against all other parties, save and insofar as such matters have not been set out in its Request.

15.3 Within 30 days of receipt of the Statement of Case or written notice from the claimant that it elects to treat the Request as its Statement of Case, the respondent shall send to the Registrar a Statement of Defence setting out in sufficient detail which of the facts and contentions of law in the Statement of Case or Request (as the case may be) it admits or denies, on what grounds and on what other facts and contentions of law it relies. Any counter-claims shall be submitted with the Statement of Defence in the same manner as claims are to be set out in the Statement of Case.

15.4 Within 30 days of receipt of the Statement of Defence, the claimant shall send to the Registrar a Statement of Reply which, where there are any counter-claims, shall include a Defence to Counter-claim in the same manner as a defence is to be set out in the Statement of Defence.

15.5 If the Statement of Reply contains a Defence to Counter-claim, within 30 days of its receipt the respondent shall send to the Registrar a Statement of Reply to Counter-claim.

15.6 All Statements referred to in this article shall be accompanied by copies (or, if they are especially voluminous, lists) of all essential documents on which the party concerned relies and which have not previously been submitted by any party, and (where appropriate) by any relevant samples and exhibits.

15.7 As soon as practicable following receipt of the Statements specified in this Article, the arbitral tribunal shall proceed in such manner as has been agreed in writing by the parties or pursuant to its authority under these Rules.

15.8 If the respondent fails to submit a Statement of Defence or the claimant a Statement of Defence to Counter-claim, or if at any point any party fails to avail itself of the opportunity to present its case in the manner determined by articles 15.2 to 15.6 or directed by the arbitral tribunal, the arbitral tribunal may nevertheless proceed with the arbitration and make an award.

Article 16: Seat of Arbitration and Place of Hearings

16.1 The parties may agree in writing the seat (or legal place) of their arbitration. Failing such a choice, the seat of arbitration shall be London, unless and until the LCIA Court determines in view of all the circumstances, and after having given the parties an opportunity to make written comment, that another seat is more appropriate.

16.2 The arbitral tribunal may hold hearings, meetings and deliberations at any convenient geographical place in its discretion; and if elsewhere than the seat of the arbitration, the arbitration shall be treated as an arbitration conducted at the seat of the arbitration and any award as an award made at the seat of the arbitration for all purposes.

16.3 The law applicable to the arbitration (if any) shall be the arbitration law of the seat of arbitration, unless and to the extent that the parties have expressly agreed in writing on the application of another arbitration law and such agreement is not prohibited by the law of the arbitral seat.

Article 17: Language of Arbitration

17.1 The initial language of the arbitration shall be the language of the Arbitration Agreement, unless the parties have agreed in writing otherwise and providing always that a non-participating or defaulting party shall have no cause for complaint if communications to and from the Registrar and the arbitration proceedings are conducted in English.

17.2 In the event that the Arbitration Agreement is written in more than one language, the LCIA Court may, unless the Arbitration Agreement provides that the arbitration proceedings shall be conducted in more than one language, decide which of those languages shall be the initial language of the arbitration.

17.3 Upon the formation of the arbitral tribunal and unless the parties have agreed upon the language or languages of the arbitration, the Arbitration Tribunal shall decide upon the language(s) of the arbitration, after giving the parties an opportunity to make written comment and taking into account the initial language of the arbitration and any other matter it may consider appropriate in all the circumstances of the case.

17.4 If any document is expressed in a language other than the language(s) of the arbitration and no translation of such document is submitted by the party relying upon the document, the arbitral tribunal or (if the arbitral tribunal has not been formed) the LCIA Court may order that party to submit a translation in a form to be determined by the arbitral tribunal or the LCIA Court, as the case may be.

Article 18: Party Representation

18.1 Any party may be represented by legal practitioners or any other representatives.

18.2 At any time the arbitral tribunal may require from any party proof of authority granted to its representative(s) in such form as the arbitral tribunal may determine.

Article 19: Hearings

19.1 Any party which expresses a desire to that effect has the right to be heard orally before the arbitral tribunal on the merits of the dispute, unless the parties have agreed in writing on documents.—only arbitration.

19.2 The arbitral tribunal shall fix the date, time and physical place of any meetings and hearings in the arbitration, and shall give the parties reasonable notice thereof.

19.3 The arbitral tribunal may in advance of any hearing submit to the parties a list of questions which it wishes them to answer with special attention.

19.4 All meetings and hearings shall be in private unless the parties agree otherwise in writing or the arbitral tribunal directs otherwise.

19.5 The arbitral tribunal shall have the fullest authority to establish time-limits for meetings and hearings, or for any parts thereof.

Article 20: Witnesses

20.1 Before any hearing, the arbitral tribunal may require any party to give notice of the identity of each witness that party wishes to call (including rebuttal witnesses), as well as the subject-matter of that witness's testimony, its content and its relevance to the issues in the arbitration.

20.2 The arbitral tribunal may also determine the time, manner and form in which such materials should be exchanged between the parties and presented to the arbitral tribunal; and it has a discretion to allow, refuse, or limit the appearance of witnesses (whether witness of fact or expert witness).

20.3 Subject to any order otherwise by the arbitral tribunal, the testimony of a witness may be presented by a party in written form, either as a signed statement or as a sworn affidavit.

20.4 Subject to articles 14.1 and 14.2, any party may request that a witness, on whose testimony another party seeks to rely, should attend for oral questioning at a hearing before the arbitral tribunal. If the arbitral tribunal orders that other party to produce the witness and the witness fails to attend the oral hearing without good cause, the arbitral tribunal may place such weight on the written testimony (or exclude the same altogether) as it considers appropriate in the circumstances of the case.

20.5 Any witness who gives oral evidence at a hearing before the arbitral tribunal may be questioned by each of the parties under the control of the arbitral tribunal. The arbitral tribunal may put questions at any stage of his evidence.

20.6 Subject to the mandatory provisions of any applicable law, it shall not be improper for any party or its legal representatives to interview any witness or potential witness for the purpose of presenting his testimony in written form or producing him as an oral witness.

20.7 Any individual intending to testify to the arbitral tribunal on any issue of fact or expertise shall be treated as a witness under these Rules notwithstanding that the individual is a party to the arbitration or was or is an officer, employee or shareholder of any party.

Article 21: Experts to the arbitral tribunal

21.1 Unless otherwise agreed by the parties in writing, the arbitral tribunal:

(a) may appoint one or more experts to report to the arbitral tribunal on specific issues, who shall be and remain impartial and independent of the parties throughout the arbitration proceedings; and

(b) may require a party to give any such expert any relevant information or to provide access to any relevant documents, goods, samples, property or site for inspection by the expert.

21.2 Unless otherwise agreed by the parties in writing, if a party so requests or if the arbitral tribunal considers it necessary, the expert shall, after delivery of his written or oral report to the arbitral tribunal and the parties, participate in one or more hearings at which the parties shall have the opportunity to question the expert on his report and to present expert witnesses in order to testify on the points at issue.

21.3 The fees and expenses of any expert appointed by the arbitral tribunal under this article shall be paid out of the deposits payable by the parties under article 24 and shall form part of the costs of the arbitration.

Article 22: Additional Powers of the arbitral tribunal

22.1 Unless the parties at any time agree otherwise in writing, the arbitral tribunal shall have the power, on the application of any party or of its own motion, but in either case only after giving the parties a reasonable opportunity to state their views:

(a) to allow any party, upon such terms (as to costs and otherwise) as it shall determine, to amend any claim, counter-claim, defence and reply;

(b) to extend or abbreviate any time-limit provided by the Arbitration Agreement or these rules for the conduct of the arbitration or by the arbitral tribunal's own orders;

(c) to conduct such enquiries as may appear to the arbitral tribunal to be necessary or expedient, including whether and to what extent the arbitral tribunal should itself take the initiative in identifying the issues and ascertaining the relevant facts and the law(s) or rules of law applicable to the arbitration, the merits of the parties' dispute and the Arbitration Agreement;

(d) to order any party to make any property, site or thing under its control and relating to the subject-matter of the arbitration available for inspection by the arbitral tribunal, any other party, its expert or any expert to the arbitral tribunal;

(e) to order any party to produce to the arbitral tribunal, and to the other parties for inspection, and to supply copies of, any documents or classes of documents in their possession, custody or power which the arbitral tribunal determines to be relevant;

(f) to decide whether or not to apply any strict rules of evidence (or any other rules) as to the admissibility, relevance or weight of any material tendered by a party on any matter of fact or expert opinion; and to determine the time, manner and form in which such material should be exchanged between the parties and presented to the arbitral tribunal;

(g) to order the correction of any contract between the parties or the Arbitration Agreement, but only to the extent required to rectify any mistake which the arbitral tribunal determines to be common to the parties and then only if and to the extent to which the law(s) or rules of law applicable to the contract or Arbitration Agreement permit such correction; and

(h) to allow, only upon the application of a party, one or more third persons to be joined in the arbitration as a party provided any such third person and the applicant party have consented thereto in writing, and thereafter to make a single final award, or separate awards, in respect of all parties so implicated in the arbitration.

22.2 By agreeing to arbitration under these Rules, the parties shall be treated as having agreed not to apply to any State court or other judicial authority for any order available from the arbitral tribunal under article 22.1, except with the agreement in writing of all parties.

22.3 The arbitral tribunal shall decide the parties' dispute in accordance with the law(s) or rules of law chosen by the parties as applicable to the merits of their dispute. If and to the extent that the arbitral tribunal determines that the parties have made no such choice, the arbitral tribunal shall apply the law(s) or rules of law which it considers appropriate.

22.4 The arbitral tribunal shall only apply to the merits of the dispute principles deriving from *"ex æquo et bono"*, *"amiable compositeur"* or "honourable engagement" where the parties have so agreed expressly in writing.

Article 23: Jurisdiction of the arbitral tribunal

23.1 The arbitral tribunal shall have the power to rule on its own jurisdiction, including any objection to the initial or continuing existence, validity or effectiveness of the Arbitration Agreement. For that purpose, an arbitration clause which forms or was intended to form part of another agreement shall be treated as an arbitration agreement independent of that other agreement. A decision by the arbitral tribunal that such other agreement is non-existent, invalid or ineffective shall not entail *ipso jure* the non-existence, invalidity or ineffectiveness of the arbitration clause.

23.2 A plea by a respondent that the arbitral tribunal does not have jurisdiction shall be treated as having been irrevocably waived unless it is raised not later than the Statement of Defence; and a like plea by a respondent to counter-claim shall be similarly treated unless it is raised no later than the Statement of Defence to counter-claim. A plea that the arbitral tribunal is exceeding the scope of its authority shall be raised promptly after the arbitral tribunal has indicated its intention to decide on the matter alleged by any party to be beyond the scope of its authority, failing which such plea shall also be treated as having been waived irrevocably. In any case, the arbitral tribunal may nevertheless admit an untimely plea if it considers the delay justified in the particular circumstances.

23.3 The arbitral tribunal may determine the plea to its jurisdiction or authority in an award as to jurisdiction or later in an award on the merits, as it considers appropriate in the circumstances.

23.4 By agreeing to arbitration under these Rules, the parties shall be treated as having agreed not to apply to any State court or other judicial authority for any relief regarding the arbitral tribunal's jurisdiction or authority, except with the agreement in writing of all parties to the arbitration or the prior authorisation of the arbitral tribunal or following the latter's award ruling on the objection to its jurisdiction or authority.

Article 24: Deposits

24.1 The LCIA Court may direct the parties, in such proportions as it thinks appropriate, to make one or several interim or final payments on account of the costs of the arbitration. Such deposits shall be made to and held by the LCIA and from time-to-time may be released by the LCIA Court to the arbitrator(s), any expert appointed by the arbitral tribunal and the LCIA itself as the arbitration progresses.

24.2 The arbitral tribunal shall not proceed with the arbitration without ascertaining at all times from the Registrar or any Deputy-Registrar that the LCIA is in requisite funds.

24.3 In the event that a party fails or refuses to provide any deposit as directed by the LCIA Court, the LCIA Court may direct the other party or parties to effect a substitute payment to allow the arbitration to proceed (subject to any award on costs). In such circumstances, the party paying the substitute payment shall be entitled to recover that amount as a debt immediately due from the defaulting party.

24.4 Failure by a claimant or counter-claiming party to provide promptly and in full the required deposit may be treated by the LCIA Court and the arbitral tribunal as a withdrawal of the claim or counter-claim respectively.

Article 25: Interim and Conservatory Measures

25.1 The arbitral tribunal shall have the power, unless otherwise agreed by the parties in writing, on the application of any party:

(a) to order any respondent party to a claim or counter-claim to provide security for all or part of the amount in dispute, by way of deposit or bank guarantee or in any other manner and upon such terms as the arbitral tribunal considers appropriate. Such terms may include the provision by the claiming or counter-claiming party of a cross-indemnity, itself secured in such manner as the arbitral tribunal considers appropriate, for any costs or losses incurred by such respondent in providing security. The amount of any costs and losses payable under such cross-indemnity may be determined by the arbitral tribunal in one or more awards;

(b) to order the preservation, storage, sale or other disposal of any property or thing under the control of any party and relating to the subject-matter of the arbitration; and

(c) to order on a provisional basis, subject to final determination in an award, any relief which the arbitral tribunal would have power to grant in an award, including a provisional order for the payment of money or the disposition of property as between any parties.

25.2 The arbitral tribunal shall have the power, upon the application of a party, to order any claiming or counter-claiming party to provide security for the legal or other costs of any other party by way of deposit or bank guarantee or in any other manner and upon such terms as the arbitral tribunal considers appropriate. Such terms may include the provision by that other party of a cross-indemnity, itself secured in such manner as the arbitral tribunal considers appropriate, for any costs and losses incurred by such claimant or counter-claimant in providing security. The amount of any costs and losses payable under such cross-indemnity may be determined by the arbitral tribunal in one or more awards. In the event that a claiming or counter-claiming party does not comply with any order to provide security, the arbitral tribunal may stay that party's claims or counter-claims or dismiss them in an award.

25.3 The power of the arbitral tribunal under article 25.1 shall not prejudice howsoever any party's right to apply to any State court or other judicial authority for interim or conservatory measures before the formation of the arbitral tribunal and, in exceptional cases, thereafter. Any application and any order for such measures after the formation of the arbitral tribunal shall be promptly communicated by the applicant to the arbitral tribunal and all other parties. However, by agreeing to arbitration under these Rules, the parties shall be taken to have agreed not to apply to any State court or other judicial authority for any order for security for its legal or other costs available from the arbitral tribunal under article 25.2.

Article 26: The Award

26.1 The arbitral tribunal shall make its award in writing and, unless all parties agree in writing otherwise, shall state the reasons upon which its award is based. The award shall also state the date when the award is made and the seat of the arbitration; and it shall be signed by the arbitral tribunal or those of its members assenting to it.

26.2 If any arbitrator fails to comply with the mandatory provisions of any applicable law relating to the making of the award, having been given a reasonable opportunity to do so, the remaining arbitrators may proceed in his absence and state in their award the circumstances of the other arbitrator's failure to participate in the making of the award.

26.3 Where there are three arbitrators and the arbitral tribunal fails to agree on any issue, the arbitrators shall decide that issue by a majority. Failing a majority decision on any issue, the chairman of the arbitral tribunal shall decide that issue.

26.4 If any arbitrator refuses or fails to sign the award, the signatures of the majority or (failing a majority) of the chairman shall be sufficient, provided that the reason for the omitted signature is stated in the award by the majority or chairman.

26.5 The sole arbitrator or chairman shall be responsible for delivering the award to the LCIA Court, which shall transmit certified copies to the parties provided that the costs of arbitration have been paid to the LCIA in accordance with article 28.

26.6 An award may be expressed in any currency. The arbitral tribunal may order that simple or compound interest shall be paid by any party on any sum awarded at such rates as the arbitral tribunal determines to be appropriate, without being bound by legal rates of interest imposed by any State court, in respect of any period which the arbitral tribunal determines to be appropriate ending not later than the date upon which the award is complied with.

26.7 The arbitral tribunal may make separate awards on different issues at different times. Such awards shall have the same status and effect as any other award made by the arbitral tribunal.

26.8 In the event of a settlement of the parties' dispute, the arbitral tribunal may render an award recording the settlement if the parties so request in writing (a "Consent Award"), provided always that such award contains an express statement that it is an award made by the parties' consent. A Consent Award need not contain reasons. If the parties do not require a consent award, then on written confirmation by the parties to the LCIA Court that a settlement has been reached, the arbitral tribunal shall be discharged and the arbitration proceedings concluded, subject to payment by the parties of any outstanding costs of the arbitration under article 28.

26.9 All awards shall be final and binding on the parties. By agreeing to arbitration under these Rules, the parties undertake to carry out any award immediately and without any delay (subject only to article 27); and the parties also waive irrevocably their right to any form of appeal, review or recourse to any State court or other judicial authority, insofar as such waiver may be validly made.

Article 27: Correction of Awards and Additional Awards

27.1 Within 30 days of receipt of any award, or such lesser period as may be agreed in writing by the parties, a party may by written notice to the Registrar (copied to all other parties) request the arbitral tribunal to correct in the award any errors in computation, clerical or typographical errors or any errors of a similar nature. If the arbitral tribunal considers the request to be justified, it shall make the corrections within 30 days of receipt of the request. Any correction shall take the form of separate memorandum dated and signed by the arbitral tribunal or (if three arbitrators) those of its members assenting to it; and such memorandum shall become part of the award for all purposes.

27.2 The arbitral tribunal may likewise correct any error of the nature described in article 27.1 on its own initiative within 30 days of the date of the award, to the same effect.

27.3 Within 30 days of receipt of the final award, a party may by written notice to the Registrar (copied to all other parties), request the arbitral tribunal to make an additional award as to claims or counter-claims presented in the arbitration but not determined in any award. If the arbitral tribunal considers the request to be justified, it shall make the additional award within 60 days of receipt of the request. The provisions of article 26 shall apply to any additional award.

Article 28: Arbitration and Legal Costs

28.1 The costs of the arbitration (other than the legal or other costs incurred by the parties themselves) shall be determined by the LCIA Court in accordance with the Schedule of Costs. The parties shall be jointly and severally liable to the arbitral tribunal and the LCIA for such arbitration costs.

28.2 The arbitral tribunal shall specify in the award the total amount of the costs of the arbitration as determined by the LCIA Court. Unless the parties agree otherwise in writing, the arbitral tribunal shall determine the proportions in which the parties shall bear all or part of such arbitration costs. If the arbitral tribunal has determined that all or any part of the arbitration costs shall be borne by a party other than a party which has already paid them to the LCIA, the latter party shall have the right to recover the appropriate amount from the former party.

28.3 The arbitral tribunal shall also have the power to order in its award that all or part of the legal or other costs incurred by a party be paid by another party, unless the parties agree otherwise in writing. The arbitral tribunal shall determine and fix the amount of each item comprising such costs on such reasonable basis as it thinks fit.

28.4 Unless the parties otherwise agree in writing, the arbitral tribunal shall make its orders on both arbitration and legal costs on the general principle that costs should reflect the parties' relative success and failure in the award or arbitration, except where it appears to the arbitral tribunal that in the particular circumstances this general approach is inappropriate. Any order for costs shall be made with reasons in the award containing such order.

28.5 If the arbitration is abandoned, suspended or concluded, by agreement or otherwise, before the final award is made, the parties shall remain jointly and severally liable to pay to the LCIA and the arbitral tribunal the costs of the arbitration as determined by the LCIA Court in accordance with the Schedule of Costs. In the event that such arbitration costs are less than the deposits made by the parties, there shall be a refund by the LCIA in such proportion as the parties may agree in writing, or failing such agreement, in the same proportions as the deposits were made by the parties to the LCIA.

Article 29: Decisions by the LCIA Court

29.1 The decisions of the LCIA Court with respect to all matters relating to the arbitration shall be conclusive and binding upon the parties and the arbitral tribunal. Such decisions are to be treated as administrative in nature and the LCIA Court shall not be required to give any reasons.

29.2 To the extent permitted by the law of the seat of the arbitration, the parties shall be taken to have waived any right of appeal or review in respect of any such decisions of the LCIA Court to any State court or other judicial authority. If such appeals or review remain possible due to mandatory provisions of any applicable law, the LCIA Court shall, subject to the provisions of that applicable law, decide whether the arbitral proceedings are to continue, notwithstanding an appeal or review.

Article 30: Confidentiality

30.1 Unless the parties expressly agree in writing to the contrary, the parties undertake as a general principle to keep confidential all awards in their arbitration, together with all materials in the proceedings created for the purpose of the arbitration and all other documents produced by another party in the proceedings not otherwise in the public domain—save and to the extent that disclosure may be required of a party by legal duty, to protect or pursue a legal right or to enforce or challenge an award in *bona fide* legal proceedings before a State court or other judicial authority.

30.2 The deliberations of the arbitral tribunal are likewise confidential to its members, save and to the extent that disclosure of an arbitrator's refusal to participate in the arbitration is required of the other members of the arbitral tribunal under articles 10, 12 and 26.

30.3 The LCIA Court does not publish any award or any part of an award without the prior written consent of all parties and the arbitral tribunal.

Article 31: Exclusion of Liability

31.1 None of the LCIA, the LCIA Court (including its President, Vice-Presidents and individual members), the Registrar, any Deputy-Registrar, any arbitrator and any expert to the arbitral tribunal shall be liable to any party howsoever for any act or omission in connection with any arbitration conducted by reference to these Rules, save where the act or omission is shown by that party to constitute conscious and deliberate wrongdoing committed by the body or person alleged to be liable to that party.

31.2 After the award has been made and the possibilities of correction and additional awards referred to in article 27 have lapsed or been exhausted, neither the LCIA, the LCIA Court (including its President, Vice-Presidents and individual members), the Registrar, any Deputy-Registrar, any arbitrator or expert to the arbitral tribunal shall be under any legal obligation to make any statement to any person about any matter concerning the arbitration, nor shall any party seek to make any of these persons a witness in any legal or other proceedings arising out of the arbitration.

Article 32: General Rules

32.1 A party who knows that any provision of the Arbitration Agreement (including these rules) has not been complied with and yet proceeds with the arbitration without promptly stating its objection to such non-compliance, shall be treated as having irrevocably waived its right to object.

32.2 In all matters not expressly provided for in these rules, the LCIA Court, the arbitral tribunal and the parties shall act in the spirit of these rules and shall make every reasonable effort to ensure that an award is legally enforceable.

RECOMMENDED ARBITRATION CLAUSES

Future disputes

For contracting parties who wish to have future disputes referred to arbitration under the LCIA Rules, the following clause is recommended. Words/spaces in square brackets should be deleted/completed as appropriate.

> "Any dispute arising out of or in connection with this contract, including any question regarding its existence, validity or termination, shall be referred to and finally resolved by arbitration under the LCIA Rules, which Rules are deemed to be incorporated by reference into this clause.
>
> The number of arbitrators shall be [one/three].
>
> The seat, or legal place, of arbitration shall be [City and/or Country].
>
> The language to be used in the arbitral proceedings shall be [ ].
>
> The governing law of the contract shall be the substantive law of [ ]."

Existing disputes

If a dispute has arisen, but there is no agreement between the parties to arbitrate, or if the parties wish to vary a dispute resolution clause to provide for LCIA arbitration, the following clause is recommended. Words/spaces in square brackets should be deleted/completed as appropriate.

> "A dispute having arisen between the parties concerning [ ], the parties hereby agree that the dispute shall be referred to and finally resolved by arbitration under the LCIA Rules.
>
> The number of arbitrators shall be [one/three].
>
> The seat, or legal place, of arbitration shall be [City and/or Country].
>
> The language to be used in the arbitral proceedings shall be [ ].
>
> The governing law of the contract [is/shall be] the substantive law of [ ]."

SCHEDULE OF ARBITRATION COSTS

(effective 1st January, 2010)

For all arbitrations in which the LCIA provides services, whether as administrator, or as appointing authority only, and whether under the LCIA Rules, UNCITRAL Rules or other, *ad hoc*, rules or procedures agreed by the parties to the arbitration.

1. Administrative charges under LCIA Rules, UNCITRAL Rules, or other, *ad hoc*, rules or procedures*

1. (a) Registration Fee (payable in advance with Request for Arbitration non-refundable). **£1,500**

1.(b) Time spent** by the Secretariat of the LCIA in the administration of the arbitration.***

Registrar/Deputy-Registrar/Counsel	**£200 per hour**
Other Secretariat personnel	**£100 per hour**

1.(c) Time spent by members of the LCIA Court in carrying out their functions in deciding any challenge brought under the applicable rules.***

at hourly rates advised by members of the LCIA Court

1.(d) A sum equivalent to 5 per cent of the fees of the Tribunal (excluding expenses) in respect of the LCIA's general overhead.***

1.(e) Expenses incurred by the Secretariat and by members of the LCIA Court, in connection with the arbitration (such as postage, telephone, facsimile, travel, etc.), and additional arbitration support services, whether provided by the Secretariat or the members of the LCIA Court from their own resources or otherwise.***

at applicable hourly rates or at cost

1.(f) The LCIA's fees and expenses will be invoiced in sterling, but may be paid in other convertible currencies, at rates prevailing at the time of payment, provided that any transfer and/or currency exchange charges shall be borne by the payer.

2. Request to act as Appointing Authority only*

2.(a) Appointment Fee (payable in advance with request – non-refundable). **£1,000**

2.(b) As for 1(b) and 1(e), above.

3. Request to act in deciding challenges to arbitrators in non-LCIA arbitrations*

3.(a) As for 2(a) and 2(b), above; plus

3.(b) Time spent by members of the LCIA Court in carrying out their functions in deciding the challenges.

at hourly rates advised by members of the LCIA Court

4. Fees and expenses of the Tribunal*

4. (a) The Tribunal's fees will be calculated by reference to work done by its members in connection with the arbitration and will be charged at rates appropriate to the particular circumstances of the case, including its complexity and the special qualifications of the arbitrators. The Tribunal shall agree in writing upon fee rates conforming to this Schedule of Arbitration Costs prior to its appointment by the LCIA Court. The rates will be advised by the Registrar to the parties at the time of the appointment of the Tribunal, but may be reviewed annually if the duration of the arbitration requires.

Fees shall be at hourly rates not exceeding £400.

However, in exceptional cases, the rate may be higher provided that, in such cases, (a) the fees of the Tribunal shall be fixed by the LCIA Court on the recommendation of the Registrar, following consultations with the arbitrator(s), and (b) the fees shall be agreed expressly by all parties.

4. (b) The Tribunal's fees may include a charge for time spent travelling.

4. (c) The Tribunal's fees may also include a charge for time reserved but not used as a result of late postponement or cancellation, provided that the basis for such charge shall be advised in writing to, and approved by, the LCIA Court.

4. (d) The Tribunal may also recover such expenses as are reasonably incurred in connection with the arbitration, and as are in a reasonable amount, provided that claims for expenses should be supported by invoices or receipts.

4. (e) The Tribunal's fees may be invoiced either in the currency of account between the Tribunal and the Parties, or in sterling. The Tribunal's expenses may be invoiced in the currency in which they were incurred, or in sterling.

4. (f) In the event of the revocation of the appointment of any arbitrator, pursuant to the provisions of article 10 of the LCIA Rules, the LCIA Court shall decide upon the amount of fees and expenses to be paid for the former arbitrator's services (if any) as it may consider appropriate in all the circumstances.

5. Deposits

5. (a) The LCIA Court may direct the parties, in such proportions as it thinks appropriate, to make one or several interim or final payments on account of the costs of the arbitration. The LCIA Court may limit such payments to a sum sufficient to cover fees, expenses and costs for the next stage of the arbitration.

5. (b) The Tribunal shall not proceed with the arbitration without ascertaining at all times from the Registrar or any Deputy-Registrar that the LCIA is in requisite funds.

5. (c) In the event that a party fails or refuses to provide any deposit as directed by the LCIA Court, the LCIA Court may direct the other party or parties to effect a substitute payment to allow the arbitration to proceed (subject to any award on costs). In such circumstances, the party paying the substitute payment shall be entitled to recover that amount as a debt immediately due from the defaulting party.

5. (d) Failure by a claimant or counter-claiming party to provide promptly and in full the required deposit may be treated by the LCIA Court and the arbitral tribunal as a withdrawal of the claim or counter-claim, respectively.

5. (e) Funds lodged by the parties on account of the fees and expenses of the Tribunal and of the LCIA are held on trust in client bank accounts which are controlled by reference to each individual case and are disbursed by the LCIA, in accordance with the LCIA Rules and with this Schedule of Arbitration Fees and Costs. In the event that funds lodged by the parties exceed the costs of the arbitration at the conclusion of the arbitration, surplus monies will be returned to the parties as the ultimate default beneficiaries under the trust.

6. Interest on deposits

Interest on sums deposited shall be credited to the account of each party depositing them, at the rate applicable to an amount equal to the amount so credited.

7. Interim payments

7. (a) When interim payments are required to cover the LCIA's administrative costs, or the fees or expenses of members of the LCIA Court, or the Tribunal's fees or expenses, including the fees or expenses of any expert appointed by the Tribunal, such payments may be made out of deposits held, upon the approval of the LCIA Court.

7. (b) The LCIA may, in any event, submit interim invoices in respect of all current arbitrations, in March, June, September and December of each year, for payment direct by the parties or from funds held on deposit.

8. Registrar's authority

8. (a) For the purposes of sections 5(a) and 5(c) above, and of articles 24.1 and 24.3 of the LCIA Rules, the Registrar has the authority of the LCIA Court to make the directions referred to, under the supervision of the Court.

8. (b) For the purposes of section 7(a) above, and of article 24.1 of the LCIA Rules, the Registrar has the authority of the LCIA Court to approve the payments referred to.

8. (c) Any request by an arbitrator for payment on account of his fees shall be supported by a fee note, which shall include, or be accompanied by, details of the time spent at the rates that have been advised to the parties by the LCIA.

8. (d) Any dispute regarding administration costs or the fees and expenses of the Tribunal shall be determined by the LCIA Court.

9. Arbitration costs

9. (a) The parties shall be jointly and severally liable to the arbitral tribunal and the LCIA for the arbitration costs (other than the legal or other costs incurred by the parties themselves).

9. (b) The Tribunal's Award(s) shall be transmitted to the parties by the LCIA Court provided that the costs of the arbitration have been paid in accordance with article 28 of the LCIA Rules.

---

* Charges may be subject to Value Added Tax at the prevailing rate.

** Minimum unit of time in all cases: 15 minutes.

*** Items 1(b), 1(c), 1(d) and 1(e) above, are payable on interim invoice; with the award, or as directed by the LCIA Court under article 24.1 of the Rules.

ANNEXURE D

ARBITRATION RULES OF THE SINGAPORE INTERNATIONAL ARBITRATION CENTRE

SIAC Rules 3rd Edn., 1st July, 2007

1. Scope of Application and Interpretation

1.1 Where parties have agreed to refer their disputes to the SIAC for arbitration, the parties shall be deemed to have agreed that the arbitration shall be conducted and administered in accordance with these Rules. If any of these Rules is in conflict with a mandatory provision of the applicable law of the arbitration from which the parties cannot derogate, that provision shall prevail.

1.2 These Rules shall come into force on 1st July, 2010 and unless the parties have agreed otherwise, shall apply to any arbitration which is commenced on or after that date.

1.3 In these Rules—

"Award" means any decision of the Tribunal on the substance of the dispute and includes a partial or final award or an award by an Emergency Arbitrator pursuant to Schedule 1;

"Board" means the Board of Directors of the Centre;

"Centre" means the Singapore International Arbitration Centre, a company incorporated under the Companies Act of the Republic of Singapore as a company limited by guarantee;

"Chairman" means the Chairman of the Centre and includes the Deputy Chairman and the Chief Executive Officer;

"Committee of the Board" means a committee consisting of not less than two Board members appointed by the Chairman (which may include the Chairman);

"Registrar" means the Registrar of the Centre and includes any Deputy Registrar;

"Tribunal" includes a sole arbitrator or all the arbitrators where more than one is appointed;

Any pronoun shall be understood to be gender-neutral; and

Any singular noun shall be understood to refer to the plural in the appropriate circumstances.

2. Notice, Calculation of Periods of Time

2.1 For the purposes of these Rules, any notice, communication or proposal, shall be in writing. Any such written communication may be delivered or sent by registered postal or courier service or transmitted by any form of electronic communication (including electronic mail and facsimile) or delivered by any other means that provides an independent record of its delivery. It is deemed to have been received if it is delivered (i) to the addressee personally, (ii) to his habitual residence, place of business or designated address, (iii) to any address agreed by the parties, (iv) according to the practice of the parties in prior dealings, or (v) if none of these can be found after making reasonable inquiry, then at the addressee's last-known residence or place of business.

2.2 The notice, communication, or proposal is deemed to have been received on the day it is delivered.

2.3 For the purposes of calculating any period of time under these Rules, such period shall begin to run on the day following the day when a notice, communication or proposal is received. If the last day of such period is not a business day at the place of receipt pursuant to rule 2.1, the period is extended until the first business day which follows. Non-business days occurring during the running of the period of time are included in calculating the period.

2.4 The parties shall file with the Registrar a copy of any notice, communication or proposal concerning the arbitral proceedings.

3. Notice of Arbitration

3.1 A party wishing to commence an arbitration (the "Claimant") shall file with the Registrar a Notice of Arbitration which shall comprise:—

(a) a demand that the dispute be referred to arbitration;

(b) the names, addresses, telephone number(s), facsimile number(s) and electronic mail address(es), if known, of the parties to the arbitration and their representatives, if any;

(c) a reference to the arbitration clause or the separate arbitration agreement that is invoked and a copy of it;

(d) a reference to the contract out of or in relation to which the dispute arises and where possible, a copy of it;

(e) a brief statement describing the nature and circumstances of the dispute, specifying the relief claimed and, where possible, an initial quantification of the claim amount;

(f) a statement of any matters which the parties have previously agreed as to the conduct of the arbitration or with respect to which the Claimant wishes to make a proposal;

(g) a proposal for the number of arbitrator(s) if this is not specified in the arbitration agreement;

(h) unless the parties have agreed otherwise, the nomination of an arbitrator if the arbitration agreement provides for three arbitrators, or a proposal for a sole arbitrator if the arbitration agreement provides for a sole arbitrator;

(i) any comment as to the applicable rules of law;

(j) any comment as to the language of the arbitration; and

(k) payment of the requisite filing fee.

3.2 The Notice of Arbitration may also include the Statement of Claim referred to in rule 17.2.

3.3 The date of receipt of the complete Notice of Arbitration by the Registrar shall be deemed the date of commencement of the arbitration. For the avoidance of doubt, the Notice of Arbitration is deemed to be complete when all the requirements of rule 3.1 are fulfilled. The Centre shall notify the parties on the commencement of arbitration.

3.4 The Claimant shall at the same time send a copy of the Notice of Arbitration to the Respondent, and it shall notify the Registrar that it has done so, specifying the mode of service employed and the date of service.

4. Response to the Notice of Arbitration

4.1 The Respondent shall send to the Claimant a Response within 14 days of receipt of the Notice of Arbitration. The Response shall contain:

(a) a confirmation or denial of all or part of the claims;

(b) a brief statement describing the nature and circumstances of any counter-claim, specifying the relief claimed and, where possible, an initial quantification of the counterclaim amount;

(c) any comment in response to any statements contained in the Notice of Arbitration under rules 3.1(f), (g), (h), (i) and (j) or any comment with respect to the matters covered in such rules; and

(d) unless the parties have agreed otherwise, the nomination of an arbitrator if the arbitration agreement provides for three arbitrators or, if the arbitration agreement provides for a sole arbitrator, agreement with Claimant's proposal for a sole arbitrator or a counter-proposal.

4.2 The Response may also include the Statement of Defence and a Statement of Counter-claim, as referred to in rules 17.2 and 17.3.

4.3 The Respondent shall at the same time send a copy of the Response to the Registrar, together with the payment of the requisite filing fee for any counter-claim, and shall notify the Registrar of the mode of service of the Response employed and the date of service.

5. Expedited Procedure

5.1 Prior to the full constitution of the Tribunal, a party may apply to the Centre in writing for the arbitral proceedings to be conducted in accordance with the Expedited Procedure under this Rule where any of the following criteria is satisfied:

(a) the amount in dispute does not exceed the equivalent amount of S$5,000,000, representing the aggregate of the claim, counter-claim and any setoff defence;

(b) the parties so agree; or

(c) in cases of exceptional urgency.

5.2 When a party has applied to the Centre under rule 5.1, and when the Chairman determines, after considering the views of the parties, that the arbitral proceedings shall be conducted in accordance with the Expedited Procedure, the following procedure shall apply:

(a) The Registrar may shorten any time-limits under these Rules;

(b) The case shall be referred to a sole arbitrator, unless the Chairman determines otherwise;

(c) Unless the parties agree that the dispute shall be decided on the basis of documentary evidence only, the Tribunal shall hold a hearing for the examination of all witnesses and expert witnesses as well as for any argument;

(d) The award shall be made within six months from the date when the Tribunal is constituted unless, in exceptional circumstances, the Registrar extends the time; and

(e) The Tribunal shall state the reasons upon which the award is based in summary form, unless the parties have agreed that no reasons are to be given.

6. Number and Appointment of Arbitrators

6.1 A sole arbitrator shall be appointed unless the parties have agreed otherwise or unless it appears to the Registrar, giving due regard to any proposals by the parties, the complexity, the quantum involved or other relevant circumstances of the dispute, that the dispute warrants the appointment of three arbitrators.

6.2 If the parties have agreed that any arbitrator is to be appointed by one or more of the parties, or by any third person including the arbitrators already appointed, that agreement shall be treated as an agreement to nominate an arbitrator under these Rules.

6.3 In all cases, the arbitrators nominated by the parties, or by any third person including the arbitrators already appointed, shall be subject to appointment by the Chairman in his discretion.

6.4 The Chairman shall appoint an arbitrator as soon as practicable. Any decision by the Chairman to appoint an arbitrator under these Rules shall be final and not subject to appeal.

6.5 The Chairman is entitled in his discretion to appoint any nominee whose appointment has already been suggested or proposed by any party.

6.6 The terms of appointment of each arbitrator shall be fixed by the Registrar in accordance with these Rules and Practice Notes for the time being in force, or in accordance with the agreement of the parties.

7. Sole Arbitrator

7.1 If a sole arbitrator is to be appointed, either party may propose to the other the names of one or more persons, one of whom would serve as the sole arbitrator. Where the parties have reached an agreement on the nomination of a sole arbitrator, rule 6.3 shall apply.

7.2 If within 21 days after receipt by the Registrar of the Notice of Arbitration, the parties have not reached an agreement on the nomination of a sole arbitrator, or if at any time either party so requests, the Chairman shall make the appointment as soon as practicable.

8. Three Arbitrators

8.1 If three arbitrators are to be appointed, each party shall nominate one arbitrator.

8.2 If a party fails to make a nomination within 14 days after receipt of a party's nomination of an arbitrator, or in the manner otherwise agreed by the parties, the Chairman shall proceed to appoint the arbitrator on its behalf.

8.3 Unless the parties have agreed upon another procedure for appointing the third arbitrator, or if such agreed procedure does not result in a nomination within the time-limit fixed by the parties or by the Centre, the third arbitrator, who shall act as the presiding arbitrator, shall be appointed by the Chairman.

9. Multi-party Appointment of Arbitrator(s)

9.1 Where there are more than two parties in the arbitration, and three arbitrators are to be appointed, the Claimant shall jointly nominate one arbitrator and the Respondent shall jointly nominate one arbitrator. In the absence of both such joint nominations having been made within 28 days of the filing of the Notice of Arbitration or within the period agreed by the parties, the Chairman shall appoint all three arbitrators and shall designate one of them to act as the presiding arbitrator.

9.2 Where there are more than two parties in the arbitration, and one arbitrator is to be appointed, all parties are to agree on an arbitrator. In the absence of such a joint nomination having been made within 28 days of the filing of the Notice of Arbitration or within the period agreed by the parties, the Chairman shall appoint the arbitrator.

10. Qualifications of Arbitrators

10.1 Any arbitrator, whether or not nominated by the parties, conducting an arbitration under these Rules shall be and remain at all times independent and impartial, and shall not act as advocate for any party.

10.2 In making an appointment under these Rules, the Chairman shall have due regard to any qualifications required of the arbitrator by the agreement of the parties and to such considerations as are likely to secure the appointment of an independent and impartial arbitrator.

10.3 The Chairman shall also consider whether the arbitrator has sufficient availability to determine the case in a prompt and efficient manner appropriate to the nature of the arbitration.

10.4 An arbitrator shall disclose to the parties and to the Registrar any circumstance that may give rise to justifiable doubts as to his impartiality or independence as soon as reasonably practicable and in any event before appointment by the Chairman.

10.5 An arbitrator shall immediately disclose to the parties, to the other arbitrators and to the Registrar any circumstance of a similar nature that may arise during the arbitration.

10.6 If the parties have agreed on any qualifications required of an arbitrator, the arbitrator shall be deemed to meet such qualifications unless a party states that the arbitrator is not so qualified within 14 days after receipt by that party of the notification of the nomination of the arbitrator. In the event of such a challenge, the procedure for challenge and replacement of an arbitrator in rules 11 to 14 shall apply.

10.7 No party or anyone acting on its behalf shall have any *ex parte* communication relating to the case with any arbitrator or with any candidate for appointment as party-nominated arbitrator, except to advise the candidate of the general nature of the controversy and of the anticipated proceedings and to discuss the candidate's qualifications, availability or independence in relation to the parties, or to discuss the suitability of candidates for selection as a third arbitrator where the parties or party-designated arbitrators are to participate in that selection. No party or anyone acting on its behalf shall have any *ex parte* communication relating to the case with any candidate for presiding arbitrator.

11. Challenge of Arbitrators

11.1 Any arbitrator may be challenged if circumstances exist that give rise to justifiable doubts as to the arbitrator's impartiality or independence or if the arbitrator does not possess any requisite qualification on which the parties have agreed.

11.2 A party may challenge the arbitrator nominated by him only for reasons of which he becomes aware after the appointment has been made.

12. Notice of Challenge

12.1 A party who intends to challenge an arbitrator shall send a notice of challenge within 14 days after the receipt of the notice of appointment of the arbitrator who is being challenged or, except as provided in rule 10.6, within 14 days after the circumstances mentioned in rule 11.1 or 11.2 became known to that party.

12.2 The notice of challenge shall be filed with the Registrar and shall be sent simultaneously to the other party, the arbitrator who is being challenged and the other members of the Tribunal. The notice of challenge shall be in writing and shall state the reasons for the challenge. The Registrar may order a suspension of the arbitration until the challenge is resolved.

12.3 When an arbitrator is challenged by one party, the other party may agree to the challenge. The challenged arbitrator may also withdraw from his office. In neither case does this imply acceptance of the validity of the grounds for the challenge.

12.4 In instances referred to in rule 12.3, the procedure provided in rule 6 and rules 7, 8 or 9, as the case may be, shall be used for the appointment of the substitute arbitrator, even if during the process of appointing the challenged arbitrator, a party had failed to exercise his right to nominate. The time-limit provided in those Rules shall commence from the date of receipt of the agreement of the other party to the challenge or the challenged arbitrator's withdrawal.

13. Decision on Challenge

13.1 If, within 7 days of receipt of the notice of challenge, the other party does not agree to the challenge and the arbitrator who is being challenged does not withdraw voluntarily, a Committee of the Board shall decide on the challenge.

13.2 If the Committee of the Board sustains the challenge, a substitute arbitrator shall be appointed in accordance with the procedure provided in rule 6 and rules 7, 8 or 9, as the case may be, even if during the process of appointing the challenged arbitrator, a party had failed to exercise his right to nominate. The time-limit provided in those Rules shall commence from the date of the Registrar's notification to the parties of the decision by the Committee of the Board.

13.3 If the Committee of the Board denies the challenge, the arbitrator shall continue with the arbitration unless the Registrar ordered the suspension of the arbitration pursuant to rule 12.2. Pending the determination of the challenge by the Committee of the Board, the challenged arbitrator shall be entitled to proceed in the arbitration.

13.4 The Committee of the Board may fix the costs of the challenge and may direct by whom and how such costs should be borne.

13.5 The Committee of the Board's decision made under this Rule shall be final and not subject to appeal.

14. Replacement of an Arbitrator

14.1 In the event of the death or resignation of an arbitrator during the course of the arbitral proceedings, a substitute arbitrator shall be appointed in accordance with the procedure applicable to the nomination and appointment of the arbitrator being replaced.

14.2 In the event that an arbitrator refuses or fails to act or in the event of a *de jure* or *de facto* impossibility of him performing his functions or that he is not fulfilling his functions in accordance with the Rules or within prescribed time-limits, the procedure for challenge and replacement of an arbitrator provided in rules 11 to 13 and 14.1 shall apply.

14.3 After consulting with the parties, the Chairman may in his discretion remove an arbitrator who refuses or fails to act, or in the event of a *de jure* or *de facto* impossibility of him performing his functions, or if he is not fulfilling his functions in accordance with the Rules or within the prescribed time-limits.

15. Repetition of Hearings in the Event of Replacement of an Arbitrator

If under rules 12 to 14 the sole or presiding arbitrator is replaced, any hearings held previously shall be repeated unless otherwise agreed by the parties. If any other arbitrator is replaced, such prior hearings may be repeated at the discretion of the Tribunal after consulting with the parties. If the Tribunal has issued an interim or partial award, any hearings related solely to that award shall not be repeated, and the award shall remain in effect.

16. Conduct of the Proceedings

16.1 The Tribunal shall conduct the arbitration in such manner as it considers appropriate, after consulting with the parties, to ensure the fair, expeditious, economical and final determination of the dispute.

16.2 The Tribunal shall determine the relevance, materiality and admissibility of all evidence. Evidence need not be admissible in law.

16.3 As soon as practicable after the appointment of all arbitrators, the Tribunal shall conduct a preliminary meeting with the parties, in person or by any other means, to discuss the procedures that will be most appropriate and efficient for the case.

16.4 The Tribunal may in its discretion direct the order of proceedings, bifurcate proceedings, exclude cumulative or irrelevant testimony or other evidence and direct the parties to focus their presentations on issues the decision of which could dispose of all or part of the case.

16.5 A presiding arbitrator may make procedural rulings alone, subject to revision by the Tribunal.

16.6 All statements, documents or other information supplied to the Tribunal and the Registrar by one party shall simultaneously be communicated to the other party.

17. Submissions by the Parties

17.1 Unless the Tribunal determines otherwise, the submission of written statements shall proceed as set out in this Rule.

17.2 Unless already submitted pursuant to rule 3.2, the Claimant shall, within a period of time to be determined by the Tribunal, send to the Respondent and the Tribunal a Statement of Claim setting out in full detail

(a) a statement of facts supporting the claim;

(b) the legal grounds or arguments supporting the claim; and

(c) the relief claimed together with the amount of all quantifiable claims.

17.3 Unless already submitted pursuant to rule 4.2, the Respondent shall, within a period of time to be determined by the Tribunal, send to the Claimant a Statement of Defence setting out its full defence to the Statement of Claim, including without limitation, the facts and contentions of law on which it relies. The Statement of Defence shall also state any counter-claim, which shall comply with the requirements of rule 17.2.

17.4 If a counter-claim is made, the Claimant shall, within a period of time to be determined by the Tribunal, send to the Respondent a Statement of Defence to the Counter-claim stating in full detail which of the facts and contentions of law in the Statement of Counter-claim it admits or denies, on what grounds it denies the claims or contentions, and on what other facts and contentions of law it relies.

17.5 A party may amend its claim, counter-claim or other submissions unless the Tribunal considers it inappropriate to allow such amendment having regard to the delay in making it or prejudice to the other party or any other circumstances. However, a claim or counterclaim may not be amended in such a manner that the amended claim or counterclaim falls outside the scope of the arbitration agreement.

17.6 The Tribunal shall decide which further submissions shall be required from the parties or may be presented by them. The Tribunal shall fix the periods of time for communicating such submissions.

17.7 All submissions referred to in this Rule shall be accompanied by copies of all supporting documents which have not previously been submitted by any party.

17.8 If the Claimant fails within the time specified to submit its Statement of Claim, the Tribunal may issue an order for the termination of the arbitral proceedings or give such other directions as may be appropriate.

17.9 If the Respondent fails to submit a Statement of Defence, or if at any point any party fails to avail itself of the opportunity to present its case in the manner directed by the Tribunal, the Tribunal may proceed with the arbitration.

18. Seat of Arbitration

18.1 The parties may agree on the seat of arbitration. Failing such an agreement, the seat of arbitration shall be Singapore, unless the Tribunal determines, having regard to all the circumstances of the case, that another seat is more appropriate.

18.2 The Tribunal may hold hearings and meetings by any means it considers expedient or appropriate and at any location it considers convenient or appropriate.

19. Language of Arbitration

19.1 Unless the parties have agreed otherwise, the Tribunal shall determine the language to be used in the proceedings.

19.2 If a document is written in a language other than the language(s) of the arbitration, the Tribunal, or if the Tribunal has not been established, the Registrar, may order that party to submit a translation in a form to be determined by the Tribunal or the Registrar.

20. Party Representatives

Any party may be represented by legal practitioners or any other representatives, subject to such proof of authority as the Registrar or the Tribunal may require.

21. Hearings

21.1 Unless the parties have agreed on documents-only arbitration, the Tribunal shall, if either party so requests or the Tribunal so decides, hold a hearing for the presentation of evidence and/or for oral submissions on the merits of the dispute, including without limitation any issue as to jurisdiction.

21.2 The Tribunal shall fix the date, time and place of any meeting or hearing and shall give the parties reasonable notice.

21.3 If any party to the proceedings fails to appear at a hearing without showing sufficient cause for such failure, the Tribunal may proceed with the arbitration and may make the award based on the submissions and evidence before it.

21.4 Unless the parties agree otherwise, all meetings and hearings shall be in private, and any recordings, transcripts, or documents used shall remain confidential.

22. Witnesses

22.1 Before any hearing, the Tribunal may require any party to give notice of the identity of witnesses, including expert witnesses, whom it intends to produce, the subject-matter of their testimony and its relevance to the issues.

22.2 The Tribunal has discretion to allow, refuse or limit the appearance of witnesses.

22.3 Any witness who gives oral evidence may be questioned by each of the parties, their representatives and the Tribunal in such manner as the Tribunal shall determine.

22.4 The Tribunal may direct the testimony of witnesses to be presented in written form, either as signed statements or sworn affidavits or any other form of recording. Subject to rule 22.2, any party may request that such a witness should attend for oral examination. If the witness fails to attend, the Tribunal may place such weight on the written testimony as it thinks fit, disregard it or exclude it altogether.

22.5 Subject to the mandatory provisions of any applicable law, it shall be proper for any party or its representatives to interview any witness or potential witness prior to his appearance at any hearing.

23. Tribunal-Appointed Experts

23.1 Unless the parties have agreed otherwise, the Tribunal:

(a) may following consultation with the parties, appoint an expert to report on specific issues; and

(b) may require a party to give such expert any relevant information, or to produce or provide access to any relevant documents, goods or property for inspection.

23.2 Any expert so appointed shall submit a report in writing to the Tribunal. Upon receipt of such a written report, the Tribunal shall deliver a copy of the report to the parties and invite the parties to submit written comments on the report.

23.3 Unless the parties have agreed otherwise, if the Tribunal considers it necessary, any such expert shall, after delivery of his written report, participate in a hearing. At the hearing, the parties shall have the opportunity to question him.

24. Additional Powers of the Tribunal

In addition to the powers specified in these Rules and not in derogation of the mandatory rules of law applicable to the arbitration, the Tribunal shall have the power to:

(a) order the correction of any contract, but only to the extent required to rectify any mistake which it determines to have been made by all the parties to that contract. This is subject to the condition that the proper law of the contract allows rectification of such contract;

(b) upon the application of a party, allow one or more third parties to be joined in the arbitration, provided that such person is a party to the arbitration agreement, with the written consent of such third party, and thereafter make a single final award or separate awards in respect of all parties;

(c) except as provided in rules 28.2 and 29.4, extend or abbreviate any time-limits provided by these Rules or by its directions;

(d) conduct such enquiries as may appear to the Tribunal to be necessary or expedient;

(e) order the parties to make any property or item available, for inspection in the parties' presence, by the Tribunal or any expert;

(f) order the preservation, storage, sale or disposal of any property or item which is or forms part of the subject-matter of the dispute;

(g) order any party to produce to the Tribunal and to the other parties for inspection, and to supply copies of any document in their possession or control which the Tribunal considers relevant to the case and material to its outcome;

(h) issue an award for unpaid costs of arbitration;

(i) direct any party to give evidence by affidavit or in any other form;

(j) direct any party to ensure that any award which may be made in the arbitral proceedings is not rendered ineffectual by the dissipation of assets by a party;

(k) order any party to provide security for legal or other costs in any manner the Tribunal thinks fit;

(l) order any party to provide security for all or part of any amount in dispute in the arbitration;

(m) proceed with the arbitration notwithstanding the failure or refusal of any party to comply with these Rules, or with the Tribunal's orders or directions or any partial award or to attend any meeting or hearing, and to impose such sanctions as the Tribunal deems appropriate;

(n) determine the law applicable to the arbitral proceedings; and

(o) determine any claim of legal or other applicable privilege.

25. Jurisdiction of the Tribunal

25.1 If a party objects to the existence, validity or scope of the arbitration agreement or to the jurisdiction of the Centre over a claim or counter-claim or a claim relied on for the purpose of a set-off before the Tribunal is appointed, a Committee of the Board shall decide, without prejudice to the admissibility or merits of a claim or claims, if it is *prima facie* satisfied that an arbitration agreement under the Rules may exist. The arbitral proceedings shall be terminated if the Committee of the Board is not so satisfied.

25.2 The Tribunal shall have the power to rule on its own jurisdiction, including any objections with respect to the existence, termination or validity of the arbitration agreement. For that purpose, an arbitration agreement which forms part of a contract shall be treated as an agreement independent of the other terms of the contract. A decision by the Tribunal that the contract is null and void shall not entail *ipso jure* the invalidity of the arbitration agreement.

25.3 A plea that the Tribunal does not have jurisdiction shall be raised not later than in the Statement of Defence or in a Statement of Defence to a Counter-claim. A plea that the Tribunal is exceeding the scope of its jurisdiction shall be raised promptly after the Tribunal has indicated its intention to decide on the matter alleged to be beyond the scope of its jurisdiction. In either case the Tribunal may nevertheless admit a late plea under this Rule if it considers the delay justified. A party is not precluded from raising such a plea by the fact that he has nominated, or participated in the nomination of, an arbitrator.

25.4 The Tribunal may rule on a plea referred to in rule 25.3 either as a preliminary question or in an award on the merits.

25.5 A party may rely on a claim or defence for the purpose of a set-off to the extent permitted by the applicable law.

26. Interim and Emergency Relief

26.1 The Tribunal may, at the request of a party, issue an order or an award granting an injunction or any other interim relief it deems appropriate. The Tribunal may order the party requesting interim relief to provide appropriate security in connection with the relief sought.

26.2 A party in need of emergency interim relief prior to the Constitution of the Tribunal may apply for such relief pursuant to the procedures set forth in Schedule I.

26.3 A request for interim relief made by a party to a judicial authority prior to the Constitution of the Tribunal, or in exceptional circumstances thereafter, is not incompatible with these Rules.

27. Applicable law, *amiable compositeur*

27.1 The Tribunal shall apply the rules of law designated by the parties as applicable to the substance of the dispute. Failing such designation by the parties, the Tribunal shall apply the law which it determines to be appropriate.

27.2 The Tribunal shall decide as *amiable compositeur* or *ex æquo et bono* only if the parties have expressly authorised the Tribunal to do so.

27.3 In all cases, the Tribunal shall decide in accordance with the terms of the contract, if any, and shall take into account any usage of trade applicable to the transaction.

28. The Award

28.1 The Tribunal shall, after consulting with the parties, declare the proceedings closed if it is satisfied that the parties have no further relevant and material evidence to produce or submission to make. The Tribunal may, on its own motion or upon application of a party but before any award is made, reopen the proceedings.

28.2 Before issuing any award, the Tribunal shall submit it in draft form to the Registrar. Unless the Registrar extends time or the parties agree otherwise, the Tribunal shall submit the draft award to the Registrar within 45 days from the date on which the Tribunal declares the proceedings closed. The Registrar may, as soon as practicable, suggest modifications as to the form of the award and, without affecting the Tribunal's liberty of decision, may also draw its attention to points of substance. No award shall be issued by the Tribunal until it has been approved by the Registrar as to its form.

28.3 The Tribunal may make separate awards on different issues at different times.

28.4 If any arbitrator fails to co-operate in the making of the award, having been given a reasonable opportunity to do so, the remaining arbitrators shall proceed in his absence.

28.5 Where there is more than one arbitrator, the Tribunal shall decide by a majority. Failing a majority decision, the presiding arbitrator alone shall make the award for the Tribunal.

28.6 The award shall be delivered to the Registrar, who shall transmit certified copies to the parties upon the full settlement of the costs of arbitration.

28.7 The Tribunal may award simple or compound interest on any sum which is the subject of the arbitration at such rates as the parties may have agreed or, in the absence of such agreement, as the Tribunal determines to be appropriate, in respect of any period which the Tribunal determines to be appropriate ending not later than the date of the award.

28.8 In the event of a settlement, if any party so requests, the Tribunal may render a consent award recording the settlement. If the parties do not require a consent award, the parties shall confirm to the Registrar that a settlement has been reached. The Tribunal shall be discharged and the arbitration concluded upon payment of any outstanding costs of arbitration.

28.9 By agreeing to arbitration under these Rules, the parties undertake to carry out the award immediately and without delay (subject to rule 29), and they also irrevocably waive their rights to any form of appeal, review or recourse to any State court or other judicial authority, insofar as such waiver may be validly made. An award shall be final and binding on the parties from the date it is made.

29. Correction of Awards and Additional Awards

29.1 Within 30 days of receipt of the award, a party may, by written notice to the Registrar and to any other party, request the Tribunal to correct in the award any error in computation, any clerical or typographical error or any error of a similar nature. Any other party may comment on such request within 15 days of its receipt. If the Tribunal considers the request to be justified, it shall make the correction within 30 days of receipt of the request. Any correction, made in the original award or in a separate memorandum, shall constitute part of the award.

29.2 The Tribunal may correct any error of the type referred to in rule 29.1 on its own initiative within 30 days of the date of the award.

29.3 Within 30 days of receipt of the award, a party may, by written notice to the Registrar and to any other party, request the Tribunal to make an additional award as to claims presented in the arbitral proceedings but not dealt with in the award. Any other party may comment on such request within 15 days of its receipt. If the Tribunal considers the request to be justified, it shall make the additional award within 45 days of receipt of the request.

29.4 Within 30 days of the receipt of the award, a party may, by written notice to the Registrar and to any other party, request that the Tribunal give an interpretation of the award. Any other party may comment on such request within 15 days of its receipt. If the Tribunal considers the request to be justified, it shall give the interpretation in writing within 45 days after the receipt of the request. The interpretation shall form part of the award.

29.5 The Registrar may extend the time limits in this Rule.

29.6 The provisions of rule 28 shall apply in the same manner with the necessary or appropriate changes in relation to a correction of an award and to any additional award made.

30. Fees and Deposits

30.1 The Tribunal's fees and the Centre's fees shall be ascertained in accordance with the Schedule of Fees in force at the time of commencement of the arbitration. Alternative methods in determining the Tribunal's fees may be agreed by parties prior to the constitution of the Tribunal.

30.2 The Registrar shall fix the advances on costs of the arbitration. Unless the Registrar directs otherwise, 50 per cent of such advances shall be payable by the Claimant and the remaining 50 per cent of such advances shall be payable by the Respondent.

30.3 Where the amount of the claim or the counter-claim is not quantifiable at the time payment is due, a provisional estimate of the costs of the arbitration shall be made by the Registrar. Such estimate may be based on the nature of the controversy and the circumstances of the case. This may be adjusted in light of such information as may subsequently become available.

30.4 The Registrar may from time-to-time direct parties to make further advances towards costs of the arbitration incurred or to be incurred on behalf of or for the benefit of the parties.

30.5 If a party fails to make the advances or deposits directed, the Registrar may, after consultation with the Tribunal and the parties, direct the Tribunal to suspend the work and set a time-limit on the expiry of which the relevant claims or counter-claims shall be considered as withdrawn without prejudice to reintroducing the same claims or counterclaims in another proceeding.

30.6 Parties are jointly and severally liable for the costs of the arbitration. Any party is free to pay the whole of the advances or deposits on costs of the arbitration in respect of the claim or the counter-claim should the other party fail to pay its share. The Tribunal or the Registrar may suspend its work, in whole or in part, should the advances or deposits directed under this Rule remain either wholly or in part unpaid. On the application of a party, the Tribunal may issue an award for unpaid costs pursuant to rule 24(h).

30.7 If the arbitration is settled or disposed of without a hearing, the costs of arbitration shall be finally determined by the Registrar. The Registrar shall have regard to all the circumstances of the case, including the stage of proceedings at which the arbitration is settled or disposed of. In the event that the costs of arbitration determined are less than the deposits made, there shall be a refund in such proportions as the parties may agree, or failing an agreement, in the same proportions as the deposits were made.

30.8 All advances shall be made to and held by the Centre. Any interest which may accrue on such deposits shall be retained by the Centre.

31. Costs of Arbitration

31.1 The Tribunal shall specify in the award, the total amount of the costs of the arbitration. Unless the parties have agreed otherwise, the Tribunal shall determine in the award the apportionment of the costs of arbitration among the parties.

31.2 The term "costs of the arbitration" includes:

(a) the Tribunal's fees and expenses;

(b) the Centre's administrative fees and expenses; and

(c) the costs of expert advice and of other assistance required by the Tribunal.

32. Tribunal's Fees and Expenses

32.1 The fees of the Tribunal shall be fixed by the Registrar in accordance with the Schedule of Fees and the stage of the proceedings. In exceptional circumstances, the Registrar may allow an additional fee over that prescribed in the Schedule of Fees to be paid.

32.2 The Tribunal's reasonable out-of-pocket expenses necessarily incurred and other allowances shall be reimbursed in accordance with the Practice Notes for the time being in force.

33. Party's Legal and Other Costs

The Tribunal shall have the authority to order in its award that all or a part of the legal or other costs of a party (apart from the costs of the arbitration) be paid by another party.

34. Exclusion of Liability

34.1 The Centre including its directors, officers, employees or any arbitrator shall not be liable to any person for negligence, act or omission in connection with any arbitration governed by these Rules.

34.2 The Centre including its directors, officers, employees or any arbitrator shall not be under any obligation to make any statement in connection with any arbitration governed by these Rules. No party shall seek to make any director, officer, employee or arbitrator act as a witness in any legal proceedings in connection with any arbitration governed by these Rules.

35. Confidentiality

35.1 The parties and the Tribunal shall at all times treat all matters relating to the proceedings and the award as confidential.

35.2 A party or any arbitrator shall not, without the prior written consent of all the parties, disclose to third party any such matter except:

(a) for the purpose of making an application to any competent court of any State to enforce or challenge the award;

(b) pursuant to the order of or a *subpoena* issued by a court of competent jurisdiction;

(c) for the purpose of pursuing or enforcing a legal right or claim;

(d) in compliance with the provisions of the laws of any State which are binding on the party making the disclosure;

(e) in compliance with the request or requirement of any regulatory body or other authority; or

(f) pursuant to an order by the Tribunal on application by a party with proper notice to the other parties.

35.3 In this Rule, "matters relating to the proceedings" means the existence of the proceedings, and the pleadings, evidence and other materials in the arbitration proceedings and all other documents produced by another party in the proceedings or the award arising from the proceedings, but excludes any matter that is otherwise in the public domain.

35.4 The Tribunal has the power to take appropriate measures, including issuing an order or award for sanctions or costs, if a party breaches the provisions of this Rule.

36. General Provisions

36.1 A party who knows that any provision or requirement under these Rules has not been complied with and proceeds with the arbitration without promptly stating its objection shall be deemed to have waived its right to object.

36.2 In all matters not expressly provided for in these Rules, the Chairman, the Registrar and the Tribunal shall act in the spirit of these Rules and shall make every reasonable effort to ensure the fair, expeditious and economical conclusion of the arbitration and the enforceability of the award.

36.3 The Registrar may from time-to-time issue Practice Notes to supplement, regulate and implement these Rules for the purpose of facilitating the administration of arbitrations governed by these Rules.

SCHEDULE 1

Emergency Arbitrator

1. A party in need of emergency relief may, concurrent with or following the filing of a Notice of Arbitration but prior to the Constitution of the Tribunal, make an application for emergency interim relief. The party shall notify the Registrar and all other parties in writing of the nature of the relief sought and the reasons why such relief is required on an emergency basis. The application shall also set forth the reasons why the party is entitled to such relief. Such notice may be given by e-mail, facsimile transmission or other reliable means, but must include a statement certifying that all other parties have been notified or an explanation of the steps taken in good faith to notify other parties. The application shall also be accompanied by payment of any fees set by the Registrar for proceedings pursuant to this Schedule 1.

2. The Chairman shall, if he determines that the Centre should accept the application, seek to appoint an Emergency Arbitrator within one business day of receipt by the Registrar of such application and payment of any required fee.

3. Prior to accepting appointment, a prospective Emergency Arbitrator shall disclose to the Registrar any circumstance that may give rise to justifiable doubts as to his impartiality or independence. Any challenge to the appointment of the Emergency Arbitrator must be made within one business day of the communication by the Registrar to the parties of the appointment of the Emergency Arbitrator and the circumstances disclosed.

4. An Emergency Arbitrator may not act as an arbitrator in any future arbitration relating to the dispute, unless agreed by the parties.

5. The Emergency Arbitrator shall, as soon as possible but in any event within two business days of appointment, establish a schedule for consideration of the application for emergency relief. Such schedule shall provide a reasonable opportunity to all parties to be heard, but may provide for proceedings by telephone conference or on written submissions as alternatives to a formal hearing. The Emergency Arbitrator shall have the

powers vested in the Tribunal pursuant to these Rules, including the authority to rule on his own jurisdiction, and shall resolve any disputes over the applicability of this Schedule 1.

6. The Emergency Arbitrator shall have the power to order or award any interim relief that he deems necessary. The Emergency Arbitrator shall give reasons for his decision in writing. The Emergency Arbitrator may modify or vacate the interim award or order for good cause shown.

7. The Emergency Arbitrator shall have no further power to act after the Tribunal is constituted. The Tribunal may reconsider, modify or vacate the interim award or **22** SIAC Rules (4th Edn., 1 July, 2010)

order of emergency relief issued by the Emergency Arbitrator. The Tribunal is not bound by the reasons given by the Emergency Arbitrator. Any order or award issued by the Emergency Arbitrator shall, in any event, cease to be binding if the Tribunal is not constituted within 90 days of such order or award or when the Tribunal makes a final award or if the claim is withdrawn.

8. Any interim award or order of emergency relief may be conditioned on provision by the party seeking such relief of appropriate security.

9. An order or award pursuant to this Schedule 1 shall be binding on the parties when rendered. By agreeing to arbitration under these Rules, the parties undertake to comply with such an order or award without delay.

10. The costs associated with any application pursuant to this Schedule 1 shall initially be apportioned by the Emergency Arbitrator, subject to the power of the Tribunal to determine finally the apportionment of such costs.

11. These Rules shall apply as appropriate to any proceeding pursuant to this Schedule 1, taking into account the inherent urgency of such a proceeding. The Emergency Arbitrator may decide in what manner these Rules shall apply as appropriate, and his decision as to such matters is final and not subject to appeal. **23** SIAC Rules (4th Edn., 1 July, 2010).

SCHEDULE 2

SPECIAL PROVISIONS FOR SIAC DOMESTIC ARBITRATION RULES

Article 1—Repeal

The Domestic Arbitration Rules of the Singapore International Arbitration Centre, 2nd Edition, 1st September, 2002 (SIAC Domestic Arbitration Rules) shall cease to apply to arbitrations administered by the Centre.

Article 2—Transitional Provision

Where parties have by agreement expressly referred to arbitration under the SIAC Domestic Arbitration Rules, the agreement shall be deemed to be a reference to arbitration under these Rules and to this Schedule.

Article 3—Summary Award

1. Upon the expiry of the time-limit for the filing of Statement of Claim, Statement of Defence and Counterclaim under rule 17 of these Rules, but not later than 21 days after the expiry, if a party considers that there is no valid defence to its claim or any substantial part of its claim, it may file with the Tribunal and serve on the other party and the Registrar an application for a summary award on the claim or part of the claim. "Claim" in this Article includes a counter-claim.

2. The application shall be accompanied by an affidavit stating the full facts and detailed grounds in support of it.

3. Within 21 days after service of the application and affidavit, the other party must, if it wishes to contest the application, file and serve an affidavit in opposition. The applicant must file any reply affidavit within 14 days from receipt of the opposition. No further affidavit may be filed without leave of the Tribunal.

4. The Tribunal may on hearing the application:

(a) make an award summarily; or

(b) make an order dismissing the application; or

(c) make an order requiring security for the applicant's claim or part of the claim.

5. The Tribunal's award or order shall be made in writing within 21 days after the close of hearing unless extended by the Registrar.

6. Costs referred to in rules 31, 32 and 33 of these Rules may be awarded in the discretion of the Tribunal.

7. Rules 28.2, 29.1 and 29.2 of these Rules shall apply, with the necessary or appropriate changes, to a summary award made under this Article.

8. Where the application is dismissed, the Tribunal shall proceed to continue with the arbitration.

ANNEXURE E

IBA GUIDELINES REGARDING IMPARTIALITY, INDEPENDENCE AND DISCLOSURE OF ARBITRATOR

Part I:
General Standards Regarding Impartiality, Independence and Disclosure

(1) General Principle

Every arbitrator shall be impartial and independent of the parties at the time of accepting an appointment to serve and shall remain so during the entire arbitration proceeding until the final award has been rendered or the proceeding has otherwise finally terminated.

***Explanation* to General Standard 1:**

The Working Group is guided by the fundamental principle in international arbitration that each arbitrator must be impartial and independent of the parties at the time he or she accepts an appointment to act as arbitrator and must remain so during the entire course of the arbitration proceedings.

The Working Group considered whether this obligation should extend even during the period that the award may be challenged but has decided against this. The Working Group takes the view that the arbitrator's duty ends when the arbitral tribunal has rendered the final award or the proceedings have otherwise been finally terminated (*e.g.*, because of a settlement). If, after setting aside or other proceedings, the dispute is referred back to the same arbitrator, a fresh round of disclosure may be necessary.

(2) Conflicts of Interest

(a) An arbitrator shall decline to accept an appointment or, if the arbitration has already been commenced, refuse to continue to act as an arbitrator if he or she has any doubts as to his or her ability to be impartial or independent.

(b) The same principle applies if facts or circumstances exist, or have arisen since the appointment, that, from a reasonable third person's point of view having knowledge of the relevant facts, give rise to justifiable doubts as to the arbitrator's impartiality or independence, unless the parties have accepted the arbitrator in accordance with the requirements set out in General Standard (4).

(c) Doubts are justifiable if a reasonable and informed third party would reach the conclusion that there was a likelihood that the arbitrator may be influenced by factors other than the merits of the case as presented by the parties in reaching his or her decision.

(d) Justifiable doubts necessarily exist as to the arbitrator's impartiality or independence if there is an identity between a party and the arbitrator, if the arbitrator is a legal representative of a legal entity that is a party in the arbitration, or if the arbitrator has a significant financial or personal interest in the matter at stake.

***Explanation* to General Standard 2:**

(a) It is the main ethical guiding principle of every arbitrator that actual bias from the arbitrator's own point of view must lead to that arbitrator declining his or her appointment. This standard should apply regardless of the stage of the proceedings. This principle is so self-evident that many national laws do not explicitly say so. See *e.g.*, article 12, UNCITRAL Model Law. The Working Group, however, has included it in the General Standards because explicit expression in these Guidelines helps to avoid confusion and to create confidence in procedures before arbitral tribunals. In addition, the Working Group believes that the broad standard of 'any doubts as to an ability to be impartial and independent' should lead to the arbitrator declining the appointment.

(b) In order for standards to be applied as consistently as possible, the Working Group believes that the test for disqualification should be an objective one. The Working Group uses the wording 'impartiality or independence' derived from the broadly adopted article 12 of the UNCITRAL Model Law, and the use of an appearance test, based on justifiable doubts as to the impartiality or independence of the arbitrator, as provided in article 12(2) of the UNCITRAL Model Law, to be applied objectively (a 'reasonable third person test'). As described in the *Explanation* to General Standard 3(d), this standard should apply regardless of the stage of the proceedings.

(c) Most laws and rules that apply the standard of justifiable doubts do not further define that standard. The Working Group believes that this General Standard provides some context for making this determination.

(d) The Working Group supports the view that no one is allowed to be his or her own judge; *i.e.*, there cannot be identity between an arbitrator and a party. The Working Group believes that this situation cannot be waived by the parties. The same principle should apply to persons who are legal representatives of a legal entity that is a party in the arbitration, like board members, or who have a significant economic interest in the matter at stake. Because of the importance of this principle, this non-waivable situation is made a General Standard, and examples are provided in the non-waivable Red List.

The General Standard purposely uses the terms 'identity' and 'legal representatives.' In the light of comments received, the Working Group considered whether these terms should be extended or further defined, but decided against doing so. It realises that there are situations in which an employee of a party or a civil servant can be in a position similar, if not identical, to the position of an official legal representative. The Working Group decided that it should suffice to state the principle.

(3) Disclosure by the Arbitrator

(a) If facts or circumstances exist that may, in the eyes of the parties, give rise to doubts as to the arbitrator's impartiality or independence, the arbitrator shall disclose such facts or circumstances to the parties, the arbitration institution or other appointing authority (if any, and if so required by the applicable institutional rules) and to the co-arbitrators, if any, prior to accepting his or her appointment or, if thereafter, as soon as he or she learns about them.

(b) It follows from General Standards 1 and 2(a) that an arbitrator who has made a disclosure considers himself or herself to be impartial and independent of the parties despite the disclosed facts and therefore capable of performing his or her duties as arbitrator. Otherwise, he or she would have declined the nomination or appointment at the outset or resigned.

(c) Any doubt as to whether an arbitrator should disclose certain facts or circumstances should be resolved in favour of disclosure.

(d) When considering whether or not facts or circumstances exist that should be disclosed, the arbitrator shall not take into account whether the arbitration proceeding is at the beginning or at a later stage.

***Explanation* to General Standard 3:**

(a) General Standard 2(b) above sets out an objective test for disqualification of an arbitrator. However, because of varying considerations with respect to disclosure, the proper standard for disclosure may be different. A purely objective test for disclosure exists in the majority of the jurisdictions analysed and in the UNCITRAL Model Law. Nevertheless, the Working Group recognises that the parties have an interest in being fully informed about any circumstances that may be relevant in their view.

Because of the strongly held views of many arbitration institutions (as reflected in their rules and as stated to the Working Group) that the disclosure test should reflect the perspectives of the parties, the Working Group in principle accepted, after much debate, a subjective approach for disclosure. The Working Group has adapted the language of article 7(2) of the ICC rules for this standard. However, the Working Group believes that this principle should not be applied without limitations. Because some situations should never lead to disqualification under the objective test, such situations need not be disclosed, regardless of the parties' perspective. These limitations to the subjective test are reflected in the Green List, which lists some situations in which disclosure is not required.

Similarly, the Working Group emphasises that the two tests (objective test for disqualification and subjective test for disclosure) are clearly distinct from each other, and that a disclosure shall not automatically lead to disqualification, as reflected in General Standard 3(b).

In determining what facts should be disclosed, an arbitrator should take into account all circumstances known to him or her, including to the extent known the culture and the customs of the country of which the parties are domiciled or nationals.

(b) Disclosure is not an admission of a conflict of interest. An arbitrator who has made a disclosure to the parties considers himself or herself to be impartial and independent of the parties, despite the disclosed facts, or else he or she would have declined the nomination or resigned. An arbitrator making disclosure thus feels capable of performing his or her duties. It is the purpose of disclosure to allow the parties to judge whether or not they agree with the evaluation of the arbitrator and, if they so wish, to explore the situation further. The Working Group hopes that the promulgation of this General Standard will eliminate the misunderstanding that disclosure demonstrates doubts sufficient to disqualify the arbitrator. Instead, any challenge should be successful only if an objective test, as set forth above, is met.

(c) Unnecessary disclosure sometimes raises an incorrect implication in the minds of the parties that the disclosed circumstances would affect his or her impartiality or independence. Excessive disclosures thus unnecessarily undermine the parties' confidence in the process.

Nevertheless, after some debate, the Working Group believes it important to provide expressly in the General Standards that in case of doubt the arbitrator should disclose. If the arbitrator feels that he or she should disclose but that professional secrecy rules or other rules of practice prevent such disclosure, he or she should not accept the appointment or should resign.

(d) The Working Group has concluded that disclosure or disqualification (as set out in General Standard 2) should not depend on the particular stage of the arbitration. In order to determine whether the arbitrator should disclose, decline the appointment or refuse to continue to act or whether a challenge by a party should be successful, the facts and circumstances alone are relevant and not the current stage of the procedure or the consequences of the withdrawal. As a practical matter, institutions make a distinction between the commencement of an arbitration proceeding and a later stage. Also, courts tend to apply different standards.

Nevertheless, the Working Group believes it important to clarify that no distinction should be made regarding the stage of the arbitral procedure. While there are practical concerns if an arbitrator must withdraw after an arbitration has commenced, a distinction based on the stage of arbitration would be inconsistent with the General Standards.

(4) Waiver by the Parties

(a) If, within 30 days after the receipt of any disclosure by the arbitrator or after a party learns of facts or circumstances that could constitute a potential conflict of interest for an arbitrator, a party does not raise an express objection with regard to that arbitrator, subject to paragraphs (b) and (c) of this General Standard, the party is deemed to have waived any potential conflict of interest by the arbitrator based on such facts or circumstances and may not raise any objection to such facts or circumstances at a later stage.

(b) However, if facts or circumstances exist as described in General Standard 2(d), any waiver by a party or any agreement by the parties to have such a person serve as arbitrator shall be regarded as invalid.

(c) A person should not serve as an arbitrator when a conflict of interest, such as those exemplified in the waivable Red List, exists. Nevertheless, such a person may accept appointment as arbitrator or continue to act as an arbitrator, if the following conditions are met:

(i) All parties, all arbitrators and the arbitration institution or other appointing authority (if any) must have full knowledge of the conflict of interest; and

(ii) All parties must expressly agree that such person may serve as arbitrator despite the conflict of interest.

(d) An arbitrator may assist the parties in reaching a settlement of the dispute at any stage of the proceedings. However, before doing so, the arbitrator should receive an express agreement by the parties that acting in such a manner shall not disqualify the arbitrator from continuing to serve as arbitrator. Such express agreement shall be considered to be an effective waiver of any potential conflict of interest that may arise from the arbitrator's participation in such process or from information that the arbitrator may learn in the process. If the assistance by the arbitrator does not lead to final settlement of the case, the parties remain bound by their waiver. However, consistent with General Standard 2(a) and notwithstanding such agreement, the arbitrator shall resign if, as a consequence of his or her involvement in the settlement process, the arbitrator develops doubts as to his or her ability to remain impartial or independent in the future course of the arbitration proceedings.

***Explanation* to General Standard 4:**

(a) The Working Group suggests a requirement of an explicit objection by the parties within a certain time-limit. In the view of the Working Group, this time-limit should also apply to a party who refuses to be involved.

(b) This General Standard is included to make General Standard 4(a) consistent with the non-waivable provisions of General Standard 2(d). Examples of such circumstances are described in the non-waivable Red List.

(c) In a serious conflict of interest, such as those that are described by way of example in the waivable Red List, the parties may nevertheless wish to use such a person as an arbitrator. Here, party autonomy and the desire to have only impartial and independent arbitrators must be balanced. The Working Group believes persons with such a serious conflict of interests may serve as arbitrators only if the parties make fully informed, explicit waivers.

(d) The concept of the arbitral tribunal assisting the parties in reaching a settlement of their dispute in the course of the arbitration proceedings is well-established in some jurisdictions but not in others. Informed consent by the parties to such a process prior to its beginning should be regarded as effective waiver of a potential conflict of interest. Express consent is generally sufficient, as opposed to a consent made in writing which in certain jurisdictions requires signature. In practice, the requirement of an express waiver allows such consent to be made in the minutes or transcript of a hearing. In addition, in order to avoid parties using an arbitrator as mediator as a means of disqualifying the arbitrator, the General Standard makes clear that the waiver should remain effective if the mediation is unsuccessful. Thus, parties assume the risk of what the arbitrator may learn in the settlement process. In giving their express consent, the parties should realise the consequences of the arbitrator assisting the parties in a settlement process and agree on regulating this special position further where appropriate.

(5) Scope

These Guidelines apply equally to tribunal chairs, sole arbitrators and party-appointed arbitrators. These Guidelines do not apply to non-neutral arbitrators, who do not have an obligation to be independent and impartial, as may be permitted by some arbitration rules or national laws.

***Explanation* to General Standard 5:**

Because each member of an arbitral tribunal has an obligation to be impartial and independent, the General Standards should not distinguish among sole arbitrators, party-appointed arbitrators and tribunal chairs. With regard to secretaries of arbitral tribunals, the Working Group takes the view that it is the responsibility of the arbitrator to ensure that the secretary is and remains impartial and independent.

Some arbitration rules and domestic laws permit party-appointed arbitrators to be non-neutral. When an arbitrator is serving in such a role, these Guidelines should not apply to him or her, since their purpose is to protect impartiality and independence.

(6) Relationships

(a) When considering the relevance of facts or circumstances to determine whether a potential conflict of interest exists or whether disclosure should be made, the activities of an arbitrator's law firm, if any, should be reasonably considered in each individual case. Therefore, the fact that the activities of the arbitrator's firm involve one of the parties shall not automatically constitute a source of such conflict or a reason for disclosure.

(b) Similarly, if one of the parties is a legal entity which is a member of a group with which the arbitrator's firm has an involvement, such facts or circumstances should be reasonably considered in each individual case. Therefore, this fact alone shall not automatically constitute a source of a conflict of interest or a reason for disclosure.

(c) If one of the parties is a legal entity, the managers, directors and members of a supervisory board of such legal entity and any person having a similar controlling influence on the legal entity shall be considered to be the equivalent of the legal entity.

***Explanation* to General Standard 6:**

(a) The growing size of law firms should be taken into account as part of today's reality in international arbitration. There is a need to balance the interests of a party to use the arbitrator of its choice and the importance of maintaining confidence in the impartiality and independence of international arbitration. In the opinion of the Working Group, the arbitrator must in principle be considered as identical to his or her law firm, but nevertheless the activities of the arbitrator's firm should not automatically constitute a conflict of interest.

The relevance of such activities, such as the nature, timing and scope of the work by the law firm, should be reasonably considered in each individual case. The Working Group uses the term 'involvement' rather than 'acting for' because a law firm's relevant connections with a party may include activities other than representation on a legal matter.

(b) When a party to an arbitration is a member of a group of companies, special questions regarding conflict of interest arise. As in the prior paragraph, the Working Group believes that because individual corporate structure arrangements vary so widely an automatic rule is not appropriate. Instead, the particular circumstances of an affiliation with another entity within the same group of companies should be reasonably considered in each individual case.

(c) The party in international arbitration is usually a legal entity. Therefore, this General Standard clarifies which individuals should be considered effectively to be that party.

(7) Duty of Arbitrator and Parties

(a) A party shall inform an arbitrator, the arbitral tribunal, the other parties and the arbitration institution or other appointing authority (if any) about any direct or indirect relationship between it (or another company of the same group of companies) and the arbitrator. The party shall do so on its own initiative before the beginning of the proceeding or as soon as it becomes aware of such relationship.

(b) In order to comply with General Standard 7(a), a party shall provide any information already available to it and shall perform a reasonable search of publicly available information.

(c) An arbitrator is under a duty to make reasonable enquiries to investigate any potential conflict of interest, as well as any facts or circumstances that may cause his or her impartiality or independence to be questioned. Failure to disclose a potential conflict is not excused by lack of knowledge if the arbitrator makes no reasonable attempt to investigate.

***Explanation* to General Standard 7:**

To reduce the risk of abuse by unmeritorious challenge of an arbitrator's impartiality or independence, it is necessary that the parties disclose any relevant relationship with the arbitrator. In addition, any party or potential party to an arbitration is, at the outset, required to make a reasonable effort to ascertain and to disclose publicly available information that, applying the general standard, might affect the arbitrator's impartiality and independence. It is the arbitrator or putative arbitrator's obligation to make similar enquiries and to disclose any information that may cause his or her impartiality or independence to be called into question.

Part II

Practical Application of the General Standards

1. The Working Group believes that if the Guidelines are to have an important practical influence, they should reflect situations that are likely to occur in today's arbitration practice. The Guidelines should provide specific guidance to arbitrators, parties, institutions and courts as to what situations do or do not constitute conflicts of interest or should be disclosed.

For this purpose, the members of the Working Group analysed their respective case law and categorised situations that can occur in the following Application Lists. These lists obviously cannot contain every situation, but they provide guidance in many circumstances, and the Working Group has sought to make them as comprehensive as possible. In all cases, the General Standards should control.

2. The Red List consists of two parts: 'a non-waivable Red List' [*see* General Standards 2(c) and 4(b)] and 'a waivable Red List' [*see* General Standard 4(c)]. These lists are a non-exhaustive enumeration of specific situations which, depending on the facts of a given case, give rise to justifiable doubts as to the arbitrator's impartiality and independence; *i.e.*, in these circumstances an objective conflict of interest exists from the point of view of a reasonable third person having knowledge of the relevant facts [*see* General Standard 2(b)]. The non-waivable Red List includes situations deriving from the overriding principle that no person can be his or her own judge. Therefore, disclosure of such a situation cannot cure the conflict. The waivable Red List encompasses situations that are serious but not as severe. Because of their seriousness, unlike circumstances described in the Orange List, these situations should be considered waivable only if and when the parties, being aware of the conflict of interest situation, nevertheless expressly state their willingness to have such a person act as arbitrator, as set forth in General Standard 4(c).

3. The Orange List is a non-exhaustive enumeration of specific situations which (depending on the facts of a given case) in the eyes of the parties may give rise to justifiable doubts as to the arbitrator's impartiality or independence. The Orange List thus reflects situations that would fall under General Standard 3(a), so that the arbitrator has a duty to disclose such situations. In all these situations, the parties are deemed to have accepted the arbitrator if, after disclosure, no timely objection is made. [*See* General Standard 4(a)].

4. It should be stressed that, as stated above, such disclosure should not automatically result in a disqualification of the arbitrator; no presumption regarding disqualification should arise from a disclosure. The purpose of the disclosure is to inform the parties of a situation that they may wish to explore further in order to determine whether objectively—*i.e.*, from a reasonable third person's point of view having knowledge of the relevant facts—there is a justifiable doubt as to the arbitrator's impartiality or independence. If the conclusion is that there is no justifiable doubt, the arbitrator can act. He or she can also act if there is no timely objection by the parties or, in situations covered by the waivable Red List, a specific acceptance by the parties in accordance with General Standard 4(c). Of course, if a party challenges the appointment of the arbitrator, he or she can nevertheless act if the authority that has to rule on the challenge decides that the challenge does not meet the objective test for disqualification.

5. In addition, a later challenge based on the fact that an arbitrator did not disclose such facts or circumstances should not result automatically in either non-appointment, later disqualification or a successful challenge to any award. In view of the Working Group, non-disclosure cannot make an arbitrator partial or lacking independence; only the facts or circumstances that he or she did not disclose can do so.

6. The Green List contains a non-exhaustive enumeration of specific situations where no appearance of, and no actual, conflict of interest exists from the relevant objective point of view. Thus, the arbitrator has no duty to disclose situations falling within the Green List. In the opinion of the Working Group, as already expressed in the *Explanation* to General Standard 3(a), there should be a limit to disclosure, based on reasonableness; in some situations, an objective test should prevail over the purely subjective test of 'the eyes of the partie's.

7. Situations falling outside the time limit used in some of the Orange List situations should generally be considered as falling in the Green List, even though they are not specifically stated. An arbitrator may nevertheless wish to make disclosure if, under the General Standards, he or she believes it to be appropriate. While there has been much debate with respect to the time-limits used in the Lists, the Working Group has concluded that the limits indicated are appropriate and provide guidance where none exists now. For example, the three-year period in Orange List 3.1 may be too long in certain circumstances and too short in others, but the Working Group believes that the period is an appropriate general criterion, subject to the special circumstances of any case.

8. The borderline between the situations indicated is often thin. It can be debated whether a certain situation should be on one List of instead of another. Also, the Lists contain, for various situations, open norms like 'significant'. The Working Group has extensively and repeatedly discussed both of these issues, in the light of comments received. It believes that the decisions reflected in the Lists reflect international principles to the best extent possible and that further definition of the norms, which should be interpreted reasonably in light of the facts and circumstances in each case, would be counter-productive.

9. There has been much debate as to whether there should be a Green List at all and also, with respect to the Red List, whether the situations on the Non-Waivable Red List should be waivable in light of party autonomy. With respect to the first question, the Working Group has maintained its decision that the subjective test for disclosure should not be the absolute criterion but that some objective thresholds should be added. With respect to the second question, the conclusion of the Working Group was that party autonomy, in this respect, has its limits.

1. Non-Waivable Red List

1.1. There is an identity between a party and the arbitrator, or the arbitrator is a legal representative of an entity that is a party in the arbitration.

1.2. The arbitrator is a manager, director or member of the supervisory board, or has a similar controlling influence in one of the parties.

1.3. The arbitrator has a significant financial interest in one of the parties or the outcome of the case.

1.4. The arbitrator regularly advises the appointing party or an affiliate of the appointing party, and the arbitrator or his or her firm derives a significant financial income therefrom.

2. Waivable Red List

2.1. Relationship of the arbitrator to the dispute.

2.1.1 The arbitrator has given legal advice or provided an expert opinion on the dispute to a party or an affiliate of one of the parties.

2.1.2 The arbitrator has previous involvement in the case.

2.2. Arbitrator's direct or indirect interest in the dispute.

2.2.1 The arbitrator holds shares, either directly or indirectly, in one of the parties or an affiliate of one of the parties that is privately held.

2.2.2 A close family member of the arbitrator has a significant financial interest in the outcome of the dispute.

2.2.3 The arbitrator or a close family member of the arbitrator has a close relationship with a third party who may be liable to recourse on the part of the unsuccessful party in the dispute.

2.3. Arbitrator's relationship with the parties or counsel.

2.3.1 The arbitrator currently represents or advises one of the parties or an affiliate of one of the parties.

2.3.2 The arbitrator currently represents the lawyer or law firm acting as counsel for one of the parties.

2.3.3 The arbitrator is a lawyer in the same law firm as the counsel to one of the parties.

2.3.4 The arbitrator is a manager, director or member of the supervisory board, or has a similar controlling influence, in an affiliate of one of the parties if the affiliate is directly involved in the matters in dispute in the arbitration.

2.3.5 The arbitrator's law firm had a previous but terminated involvement in the case without the arbitrator being involved himself or herself.

2.3.6 The arbitrator's law firm currently has a significant commercial relationship with one of the parties or an affiliate of one of the parties.

2.3.7 The arbitrator regularly advises the appointing party or an affiliate of the appointing party, but neither the arbitrator nor his or her firm derives a significant financial income therefrom.

2.3.8 The arbitrator has a close family relationship with one of the parties or with a manager, director or member of the supervisory board or any person having a similar controlling influence in one of the parties or an affiliate of one of the parties or with a counsel representing a party.

2.3.9 A close family member of the arbitrator has a significant financial interest in one of the parties or an affiliate of one of the parties.

3. Orange List

3.1. Previous services for one of the parties or other involvement in the case

3.1.1 The arbitrator has within the past three years served as counsel for one of the parties or an affiliate of one of the parties or has previously advised or been consulted by the party or an affiliate of the party making the appointment in an unrelated matter, but the arbitrator and the party or the affiliate of the party have no ongoing relationship.

3.1.2 The arbitrator has within the past three years served as counsel against one of the parties or an affiliate of one of the parties in an unrelated matter.

3.1.3 The arbitrator has within the past three years been appointed as arbitrator on two or more occasions by one of the parties or an affiliate of one of the parties.

3.1.4 The arbitrator's law firm has within the past three years acted for one of the parties or an affiliate of one of the parties in an unrelated matter without the involvement of the arbitrator.

3.1.5 The arbitrator currently serves, or has served within the past three years, as arbitrator in another arbitration on a related issue involving one of the parties or an affiliate of one of the parties.

3.2. Current services for one of the parties.

3.2.1 The arbitrator's law firm is currently rendering services to one of the parties or to an affiliate of one of the parties without creating a significant commercial relationship and without the involvement of the arbitrator.

3.2.2 A law firm that shares revenues or fees with the arbitrator's law firm renders services to one of the parties or an affiliate of one of the parties before the arbitral tribunal.

3.2.3 The arbitrator or his or her firm represents a party or an affiliate to the arbitration on a regular basis but is not involved in the current dispute.

3.3. Relationship between an arbitrator and another arbitrator or counsel.

3.3.1 The arbitrator and another arbitrator are lawyers in the same law firm.

3.3.2 The arbitrator and another arbitrator or the counsel for one of the parties are members of the same barristers' chambers.

3.3.3 The arbitrator was within the past three years a partner of, or otherwise affiliated with, another arbitrator or any of the counsel in the same arbitration.

3.3.4 A lawyer in the arbitrator's law firm is an arbitrator in another dispute involving the same party or parties or an affiliate of one of the parties.

3.3.5 A close family member of the arbitrator is a partner or employee of the law firm representing one of the parties, but is not assisting with the dispute.

3.3.6 A close personal friendship exists between an arbitrator and a counsel of one party, as demonstrated by the fact that the arbitrator and the counsel regularly spend considerable time together unrelated to professional work commitments or the activities of professional associations or social organisations.

3.3.7 The arbitrator has within the past three years received more than three appointments by the same counsel or the same law firm.

3.4. Relationship between arbitrator and party and others involved in the arbitration.

3.4.1 The arbitrator's law firm is currently acting adverse to one of the parties or an affiliate of one of the parties.

3.4.2 The arbitrator had been associated within the past three years with a party or an affiliate of one of the parties in a professional capacity, such as a former employee or partner.

3.4.3 A close personal friendship exists between an arbitrator and a manager or director or a member of the supervisory board or any person having a similar controlling influence in one of the parties or an affiliate of one of the parties or a witness or expert, as demonstrated by the fact that the arbitrator and such director, manager, other person, witness or expert regularly spend considerable time together unrelated to professional work commitments or the activities of professional associations or social organisations.

3.4.4 If the arbitrator is a former judge, he or she has within the past three years heard a significant case involving one of the parties.

3.5. Other circumstances.

3.5.1 The arbitrator holds shares, either directly or indirectly, which by reason of number or denomination constitute a material holding in one of the parties or an affiliate of one of the parties that is publicly listed.

3.5.2 The arbitrator has publicly advocated a specific position regarding the case that is being arbitrated, whether in a published paper or speech or otherwise.

3.5.3 The arbitrator holds one position in an arbitration institution with appointing authority over the dispute.

3.5.4 The arbitrator is a manager, director or member of the supervisory board, or has a similar controlling influence, in an affiliate of one of the parties, where the affiliate is not directly involved in the matters in dispute in the arbitration.

4. Green List

4.1. Previously expressed legal opinions.

4.1.1 The arbitrator has previously published a general opinion (such as in a law review article or public lecture) concerning an issue which also arises in the arbitration (but this opinion is not focused on the case that is being arbitrated).

4.2. Previous services against one party.

4.2.1 The arbitrator's law firm has acted against one of the parties or an affiliate of one of the parties in an unrelated matter without the involvement of the arbitrator.

4.3. Current services for one of the parties.

4.3.1 A firm in association or in alliance with the arbitrator's law firm, but which does not share fees or other revenues with the arbitrator's law firm, renders services to one of the parties or an affiliate of one of the parties in an unrelated matter.

4.4. Contacts with another arbitrator or with counsel for one of the parties.

4.4.1 The arbitrator has a relationship with another arbitrator or with the counsel for one of the parties through membership in the same professional association or social organisation.

4.4.2 The arbitrator and counsel for one of the parties or another arbitrator have previously served together as arbitrators or as co-counsel.

4.5. Contacts between the arbitrator and one of the parties.

4.5.1 The arbitrator has had an initial contact with the appointing party or an affiliate of the appointing party (or the respective counsels) prior to appointment, if this contact is limited to the arbitrator's availability and qualifications to serve or to the names of possible candidates for a chairperson and did not address the merits or procedural aspects of the dispute.

4.5.2 The arbitrator holds an insignificant amount of shares in one of the parties or an affiliate of one of the parties, which is publicly listed.

4.5.3 The arbitrator and a manager, director or member of the supervisory board, or any person having a similar controlling influence, in one of the parties or an affiliate of one of the parties, have worked together as joint experts or in another professional capacity, including as arbitrators in the same case.

ANNEXURE F

IBA RULES OF EVIDENCE

Preamble

1. These IBA Rules on the Taking of Evidence in International Arbitration are intended to provide an efficient, economical and fair process for the taking of evidence in international arbitrations, particularly those between Parties from different legal traditions. They are designed to supplement the legal provisions and the institutional, *ad hoc* or other rules that apply to the conduct of the arbitration.

2. Parties and Arbitral Tribunals may adopt the IBA Rules of Evidence, in whole or in part, to govern arbitration proceedings, or they may vary them or use them as guidelines in developing their own procedures. The Rules are not intended to limit the flexibility that is inherent in, and an advantage of, international arbitration, and Parties and Arbitral Tribunals are free to adapt them to the particular circumstances of each arbitration.

3. The taking of evidence shall be conducted on the principles that each Party shall act in good faith and be entitled to know, reasonably in advance of any Evidentiary Hearing or any fact or merits determination, the evidence on which the other Parties rely.

Definitions

In the IBA Rules of Evidence:

"Arbitral Tribunal" means a sole arbitrator or a panel of arbitrators;

"Claimant" means the Party or Parties who commenced the arbitration and any Party who, through joinder or otherwise, becomes aligned with such Party or Parties;

"Document" means a writing, communication, picture, drawing, programme or data of any kind, whether recorded or maintained on paper or by electronic, audio, visual or any other means;

"Evidentiary Hearing" means any hearing, whether or not held on consecutive days, at which the Arbitral Tribunal, whether in person, by teleconference, videoconference or other method, receives oral or other evidence;

"Expert Report" means a written statement by a Tribunal-Appointed Expert or a Party-Appointed Expert;

"General Rules" mean the institutional, *ad hoc* or other rules that apply to the conduct of the arbitration;

"IBA Rules of Evidence" or 'Rules' means these IBA Rules on the Taking of Evidence in International Arbitration, as they may be revised or amended from time-to-time;

"Party" means a party to the arbitration;

"Party-Appointed Expert" means a person or organisation appointed by a Party in order to report on specific issues determined by the Party;

"Request to Produce" means a written request by a Party that another Party produce Documents;

"Respondent" means the Party or Parties against whom the Claimant made its claim, and any Party who, through joinder or otherwise, becomes aligned with such Party or Parties, and includes a Respondent making a counter-claim;

"Tribunal-Appointed Expert" means a person or organisation appointed by the Arbitral Tribunal in order to report to it on specific issues determined by the Arbitral Tribunal; and

"Witness Statement" means a written statement of testimony by a witness of fact.

Article 1: Scope of Application

1. Whenever the Parties have agreed or the Arbitral Tribunal has determined to apply the IBA Rules of Evidence, the Rules shall govern the taking of evidence, except to the extent that any specific provision of them may be found to be in conflict with any mandatory provision of law determined to be applicable to the case by the Parties or by the Arbitral Tribunal.

2. Where the Parties have agreed to apply the IBA Rules of Evidence, they shall be deemed to have agreed, in the absence of a contrary indication, to the version as current on the date of such agreement.

3. In case of conflict between any provisions of the IBA Rules of Evidence and the General Rules, the Arbitral Tribunal shall apply the IBA Rules of Evidence in the manner that it determines best in order to accomplish the purposes of both the General Rules and the IBA Rules of Evidence, unless the Parties agree to the contrary.

4. In the event of any dispute regarding the meaning of the IBA Rules of Evidence, the Arbitral Tribunal shall interpret them according to their purpose and in the manner most appropriate for the particular arbitration.

5. Insofar as the IBA Rules of Evidence and the General Rules are silent on any matter concerning the taking of evidence and the Parties have not agreed otherwise, the Arbitral Tribunal shall conduct the taking of evidence as it deems appropriate, in accordance with the general principles of the IBA Rules of Evidence.

Article 2: Consultation on Evidentiary Issues

1. The Arbitral Tribunal shall consult the Parties at the earliest appropriate time in the proceedings and invite them to consult each other with a view to agreeing on an efficient, economical and fair process for the taking of evidence.

2. The consultation on evidentiary issues may address the scope, timing and manner of the taking of evidence, including:

(a) the preparation and submission of Witness Statements and Expert Reports;

(b) the taking of oral testimony at any Evidentiary Hearing;

(c) the requirements, procedure and format applicable to the production of Documents;

(d) the level of confidentiality protection to be afforded to evidence in the arbitration; and

(e) the promotion of efficiency, economy and conservation of resources in connection with the taking of evidence.

3. The Arbitral Tribunal is encouraged to identify to the Parties, as soon as it considers it to be appropriate, any issues:

(a) that the Arbitral Tribunal may regard as relevant to the case and material to its outcome; and/or

(b) for which a preliminary determination may be appropriate.

Article 3: Documents

1. Within the time ordered by the Arbitral Tribunal, each Party shall submit to the Arbitral Tribunal and to the other Parties all Documents available to it on which it relies, including public Documents and those in the public domain, except for any Documents that have already been submitted by another Party.

2. Within the time ordered by the Arbitral Tribunal, any Party may submit to the Arbitral Tribunal and to the other Parties a Request to Produce.

3. A Request to Produce shall contain:

(a) (i) a description of each requested Document sufficient to identify it, or

(ii) a description in sufficient detail (including subject-matter) of a narrow and specific requested category of Documents that are reasonably believed to exist; in the case of Documents maintained in electronic form, the requesting Party may, or the Arbitral Tribunal may order that it shall be required to, identify specific files, search terms, individuals or other means of searching for such Documents in an efficient and economical manner;

(b) a statement as to how the Documents requested are relevant to the case and material to its outcome; and

(c) (i) a statement that the Documents requested are not in the possession, custody or control of the requesting Party or a statement of the reasons why it would be unreasonably burdensome for the requesting Party to produce such Documents, and

(ii) a statement of the reasons why the requesting Party assumes the Documents requested are in the possession, custody or control of another Party.

4. Within the time ordered by the Arbitral Tribunal, the Party to whom the Request to Produce is addressed shall produce to the other Parties and, if the Arbitral Tribunal so orders, to it, all the Documents requested in its possession, custody or control as to which it makes no objection.

5. If the Party to whom the Request to Produce is addressed has an objection to some or all of the Documents requested, it shall state the objection in writing to the Arbitral Tribunal and the other Parties within the time ordered by the Arbitral Tribunal. The reasons for such objection shall be any of those set forth in article 9.2 or a failure to satisfy any of the requirements of article 3.3.

6. Upon receipt of any such objection, the Arbitral Tribunal may invite the relevant Parties to consult with each other with a view to resolving the objection.

7. Either Party may, within the time ordered by the Arbitral Tribunal, request the Arbitral Tribunal to rule on the objection. The Arbitral Tribunal shall then, in consultation with the Parties and in timely fashion, consider the Request to Produce and the objection. The Arbitral Tribunal may order the Party to whom such Request is addressed to produce any requested Document in its possession, custody or control as to which the Arbitral Tribunal determines that (i) the issues that the requesting Party wishes to prove are relevant to the case and material to its outcome; (ii) none of the reasons for objection set forth in article 9.2 applies; and (iii) the requirements of article 3.3 have been satisfied. Any such Document shall be produced to the other Parties and, if the Arbitral Tribunal so orders, to it.

8. In exceptional circumstances, if the propriety of an objection can be determined only by review of the Document, the Arbitral Tribunal may determine that it should not review the Document. In that event, the Arbitral Tribunal may, after consultation with the Parties, appoint an independent and impartial expert, bound to confidentiality, to review any such Document and to report on the objection. To the extent that the objection is upheld by the Arbitral Tribunal, the expert shall not disclose to the Arbitral Tribunal and to the other Parties the contents of the Document reviewed.

9. If a Party wishes to obtain the production of Documents from a person or organisation who is not a Party to the arbitration and from whom the Party cannot obtain the Documents on its own, the Party may, within the time ordered by the Arbitral Tribunal, ask it to take whatever steps are legally available to obtain the requested Documents, or seek leave from the Arbitral Tribunal to take such steps itself. The Party shall submit such request to the Arbitral Tribunal and to the other Parties in writing, and the request shall contain the particulars set forth in article 3.3, as applicable. The Arbitral Tribunal shall decide on this request and shall take, authorize the requesting Party to take, or order any other Party to take, such steps as the Arbitral Tribunal considers appropriate if, in its discretion, it determines that (i) the Documents would be relevant to the case and material to its outcome, (ii) the requirements of article 3.3, as applicable, have been satisfied and (iii) none of the reasons for objection set forth in article 9.2 applies.

10. At any time before the arbitration is concluded, the Arbitral Tribunal may (i) request any Party to produce Documents, (ii) request any Party to use its best efforts to take or (iii) itself take, any step that it considers appropriate to obtain Documents from any person or organisation. A Party to whom such a request for Documents is addressed may object to the request for any of the reasons set forth in article 9.2. In such cases, article 3.4 to article 3.8 shall apply correspondingly.

11. Within the time ordered by the Arbitral Tribunal, the Parties may submit to the Arbitral Tribunal and to the other Parties any additional Documents on which they intend to rely or which they believe have become relevant to the case and material to its outcome as a consequence of the issues raised in Documents, Witness Statements or Expert Reports submitted or produced, or in other submissions of the Parties.

12. With respect to the form of submission or production of Documents:

(a) copies of Documents shall conform to the originals and, at the request of the Arbitral Tribunal, any original shall be presented for inspection;

(b) Documents that a Party maintains in electronic form shall be submitted or produced in the form most convenient or economical to it that is reasonably usable by the recipients, unless the Parties agree otherwise or, in the absence of such agreement, the Arbitral Tribunal decides otherwise;

(c) a Party is not obligated to produce multiple copies of Documents which are essentially identical unless the Arbitral Tribunal decides otherwise; and

(d) translations of Documents shall be submitted together with the originals and marked as translations with the original language identified.

13. Any Document submitted or produced by a Party or non-Party in the arbitration and not otherwise in the public domain shall be kept confidential by the Arbitral Tribunal and the other Parties, and shall be used only in connection with the arbitration. This requirement shall apply except and to the extent that disclosure may be required of a Party to fulfil a legal duty, protect or pursue a legal right, or enforce or challenge an award in *bona fide* legal proceedings before a State court or other judicial authority. The Arbitral Tribunal may issue orders to set forth the terms of this confidentiality. This requirement shall be without prejudice to all other obligations of confidentiality in the arbitration.

14. If the arbitration is organised into separate issues or phases (such as jurisdiction, preliminary determinations, liability or damages), the Arbitral Tribunal may, after consultation with the Parties, schedule the submission of Documents and Requests to Produce separately for each issue or phase. Article 4 Witnesses of Fact

1. Within the time ordered by the Arbitral Tribunal, each Party shall identify the witnesses on whose testimony it intends to rely and the subject-matter of that testimony.

2. Any person may present evidence as a witness, including a Party or a Party's officer, employee or other representative.

3. It shall not be improper for a Party, its officers, employees, legal advisors or other representatives to interview its witnesses or potential witnesses and to discuss their prospective testimony with them.

4. The Arbitral Tribunal may order each Party to submit within a specified time to the Arbitral Tribunal and to the other Parties Witness Statements by each witness on whose testimony it intends to rely, except for those witnesses whose testimony is sought pursuant to articles 4.9 or 4.10. If Evidentiary Hearings are organised into separate issues or phases (such as jurisdiction, preliminary determinations, liability or damages), the Arbitral Tribunal or the Parties by agreement may schedule the submission of Witness Statements separately for each issue or phase.

5. Each Witness Statement shall contain:

(a) the full name and address of the witness, a statement regarding his or her present and past relationship (if any) with any of the Parties, and a description of his or her background, qualifications, training and experience, if such a description may be relevant to the dispute or to the contents of the statement;

(b) a full and detailed description of the facts, and the source of the witness's information as to those facts, sufficient to serve as that witness's evidence in the matter in dispute. Documents on which the witness relies that have not already been submitted shall be provided;

(c) a statement as to the language in which the Witness Statement was originally prepared and the language in which the witness anticipates giving testimony at the Evidentiary Hearing;

(d) an affirmation of the truth of the Witness Statement; and

(e) the signature of the witness and its date and place.

6. If Witness Statements are submitted, any Party may, within the time ordered by the Arbitral Tribunal, submit to the Arbitral Tribunal and to the other Parties revised or additional Witness Statements, including statements from persons not previously named as witnesses, so long as any such revisions or additions respond only to matters contained in another Party's Witness Statements, Expert Reports or other submissions that have not been previously presented in the arbitration.

7. If a witness whose appearance has been requested pursuant to article 8.1 fails without a valid reason to appear for testimony at an Evidentiary Hearing, the Arbitral Tribunal shall disregard any Witness Statement related to that Evidentiary Hearing by that witness unless, in exceptional circumstances, the Arbitral Tribunal decides otherwise.

8. If the appearance of a witness has not been requested pursuant to article 8.1, none of the other Parties shall be deemed to have agreed to the correctness of the content of the Witness Statement.

9. If a Party wishes to present evidence from a person who will not appear voluntarily at its request, the Party may, within the time ordered by the Arbitral Tribunal, ask it to take whatever steps are legally available to obtain the testimony of that person,

or seek leave from the Arbitral Tribunal to take such steps itself. In the case of a request to the Arbitral Tribunal, the Party shall identify the intended witness, shall describe the subjects on which the witness's testimony is sought and shall state why such subjects are relevant to the case and material to its outcome. The Arbitral Tribunal shall decide on this request and shall take, authorize the requesting Party to take or order any other Party to take, such steps as the Arbitral Tribunal considers appropriate if, in its discretion, it determines that the testimony of that witness would be relevant to the case and material to its outcome.

10. At any time before the arbitration is concluded, the Arbitral Tribunal may order any Party to provide for, or to use its best efforts to provide for, the appearance for testimony at an Evidentiary Hearing of any person, including one whose testimony has not yet been offered. A Party to whom such a request is addressed may object for any of the reasons set forth in article 9.2.

Article 5: Party-Appointed Experts

1. A Party may rely on a Party-Appointed Expert as a means of evidence on specific issues. Within the time ordered by the Arbitral Tribunal, (i) each Party shall identify any Party-Appointed Expert on whose testimony it intends to rely and the subject-matter of such testimony; and (ii) the Party-Appointed Expert shall submit an Expert Report.

2. The Expert Report shall contain:

(a) the full name and address of the Party-Appointed Expert, a statement regarding his or her present and past relationship (if any) with any of the Parties, their legal advisors and the Arbitral Tribunal, and a description of his or her background, qualifications, training and experience;

(b) a description of the instructions pursuant to which he or she is providing his or her opinions and conclusions;

(c) a statement of his or her independence from the Parties, their legal advisors and the Arbitral Tribunal;

(d) a statement of the facts on which he or she is basing his or her expert opinions and conclusions;

(e) his or her expert opinions and conclusions, including a description of the methods, evidence and information used in arriving at the conclusions. Documents on which the Party-Appointed Expert relies that have not already been submitted shall be provided;

(f) if the Expert Report has been translated, a statement as to the language in which it was originally prepared, and the language in which the Party-Appointed Expert anticipates giving testimony at the Evidentiary Hearing;

(g) an affirmation of his or her genuine belief in the opinions expressed in the Expert Report;

(h) the signature of the Party-Appointed Expert and its date and place; and

(i) if the Expert Report has been signed by more than one person, an attribution of the entirety or specific parts of the Expert Report to each author.

3. If Expert Reports are submitted, any Party may, within the time ordered by the Arbitral Tribunal, submit to the Arbitral Tribunal and to the other Parties revised or additional Expert Reports, including reports or statements from persons not previously identified as Party-Appointed Experts, so long as any such revisions or additions respond only to matters contained in another Party's Witness Statements, Expert Reports or other submissions that have not been previously presented in the arbitration.

4. The Arbitral Tribunal in its discretion may order that any Party-Appointed Experts who will submit or who have submitted Expert Reports on the same or related issues meet and confer on such issues. At such meeting, the Party-Appointed Experts shall attempt to reach agreement on the issues within the scope of their Expert Reports, and they shall record in writing any such issues on which they reach agreement, any remaining areas of disagreement and the reasons therefore.

5. If a Party-Appointed Expert whose appearance has been requested pursuant to article 8.1 fails without a valid reason to appear for testimony at an Evidentiary Hearing, the Arbitral Tribunal shall disregard any Expert Report by that Party-Appointed Expert related to that Evidentiary Hearing unless, in exceptional circumstances, the Arbitral Tribunal decides otherwise.

6. If the appearance of a Party-Appointed Expert has not been requested pursuant to article 8.1, none of the other Parties shall be deemed to have agreed to the correctness of the content of the Expert Report.

Article 6: Tribunal-Appointed Experts

1. The Arbitral Tribunal, after consulting with the Parties, may appoint one or more independent Tribunal-Appointed Experts to report to it on specific issues designated by the Arbitral Tribunal. The Arbitral Tribunal shall establish the terms of reference for any Tribunal-Appointed Expert Report after consulting with the Parties. A copy of the final terms of reference shall be sent by the Arbitral Tribunal to the Parties.

2. The Tribunal-Appointed Expert shall, before accepting appointment, submit to the Arbitral Tribunal and to the Parties a description of his or her qualifications and a statement of his or her independence from the Parties, their legal advisors and the Arbitral Tribunal. Within the time ordered by the Arbitral Tribunal, the Parties shall inform the Arbitral Tribunal whether they have any objections as to the Tribunal-Appointed Expert's qualifications and independence. The Arbitral Tribunal shall decide promptly whether to accept any such objection. After the appointment of a Tribunal-Appointed Expert, a Party may object to the expert's qualifications or independence only if the objection is for reasons of which the Party becomes aware 14 after the appointment has been made. The Arbitral Tribunal shall decide promptly what, if any, action to take.

3. Subject to the provisions of article 9.2, the Tribunal-Appointed Expert may request a Party to provide any information or to provide access to any Documents, goods, samples, property, machinery, systems, processes or site for inspection, to the extent relevant to the case and material to its outcome. The authority of a Tribunal-Appointed Expert to request such information or access shall be the same as the authority of the Arbitral Tribunal. The Parties and their representatives shall have the right to receive any such information and to attend any such inspection. Any disagreement between a Tribunal-Appointed Expert and a Party as to the relevance, materiality or appropriateness of such a request shall be decided by the Arbitral Tribunal, in the manner provided in articles 3.5 through 3.8. The Tribunal-Appointed Expert shall record in the Expert Report any non-compliance by a Party with an appropriate request or decision by the Arbitral Tribunal and shall describe its effects on the determination of the specific issue.

4. The Tribunal-Appointed Expert shall report in writing to the Arbitral Tribunal in an Expert Report. The Expert Report shall contain:

(a) the full name and address of the Tribunal-Appointed Expert, and a description of his or her background, qualifications, training and experience;

(b) a statement of the facts on which he or she is basing his or her expert opinions and conclusions;

(c) his or her expert opinions and conclusions, including a description of the methods, evidence and information used in arriving at the conclusions. Documents on which the Tribunal-Appointed Expert relies that have not already been submitted shall be provided;

(d) if the Expert Report has been translated, a statement as to the language in which it was originally prepared, and the language in which the Tribunal-Appointed Expert anticipates giving testimony at the Evidentiary Hearing;

(e) an affirmation of his or her genuine belief in the opinions expressed in the Expert Report;

(f) the signature of the Tribunal-Appointed Expert and its date and place; and

(g) if the Expert Report has been signed by more than one person, an attribution of the entirety or specific parts of the Expert Report to each author.

5. The Arbitral Tribunal shall send a copy of such Expert Report to the Parties. The Parties may examine any information, Documents, goods, samples, property, machinery, systems, processes or site for inspection that the Tribunal-Appointed Expert has examined and any correspondence between the Arbitral Tribunal and the Tribunal-Appointed Expert. Within the time ordered by the Arbitral Tribunal, any Party shall have the opportunity to respond to the Expert Report in a submission by the Party or through a Witness Statement or an Expert Report by a Party-Appointed Expert. The Arbitral Tribunal shall send the submission, Witness Statement or Expert Report to the Tribunal-Appointed Expert and to the other Parties.

6. At the request of a Party or of the Arbitral Tribunal, the Tribunal-Appointed Expert shall be present at an Evidentiary Hearing. The Arbitral Tribunal may question the Tribunal-Appointed Expert, and he or she may be questioned by the Parties or by any Party-Appointed Expert on issues raised in his or her Expert Report, the Parties' submissions or Witness Statement or the Expert Reports made by the Party-Appointed Experts pursuant to article 6.5.

7. Any Expert Report made by a Tribunal-Appointed Expert and its conclusions shall be assessed by the Arbitral Tribunal with due regard to all circumstances of the case.

8. The fees and expenses of a Tribunal-Appointed Expert, to be funded in a manner determined by the Arbitral Tribunal, shall form part of the costs of the arbitration.

Article 7: Inspection

Subject to the provisions of article 9.2, the Arbitral Tribunal may, at the request of a Party or on its own motion, inspect or require the inspection by a Tribunal-Appointed Expert or a Party-Appointed Expert of any site, property, machinery or any other goods, samples, systems, processes or Documents, as it deems appropriate. The Arbitral Tribunal shall, in consultation with the Parties, determine the timing and arrangement for the inspection. The Parties and their representatives shall have the right to attend any such inspection.

Article 8: Evidentiary Hearing

1. Within the time ordered by the Arbitral Tribunal, each Party shall inform the Arbitral Tribunal and the other Parties of the witnesses whose appearance it requests. Each witness (which term includes, for the purposes of this article, witnesses of fact and any experts) shall, subject to article 8.2, appear for testimony at the Evidentiary Hearing if such person's appearance has been requested by any Party or by the Arbitral Tribunal. Each witness shall appear in person unless the Arbitral Tribunal allows the use of videoconference or similar technology with respect to a particular witness.

2. The Arbitral Tribunal shall at all times have complete control over the Evidentiary Hearing. The Arbitral Tribunal may limit or exclude any question to, answer by or

appearance of a witness, if it considers such question, answer or appearance to be irrelevant, immaterial, unreasonably burdensome, duplicative or otherwise covered by a reason for objection set forth in article 9.2. Questions to a witness during direct and re-direct testimony may not be unreasonably leading.

3. With respect to oral testimony at an Evidentiary Hearing:

(a) the Claimant shall ordinarily first present the testimony of its witnesses, followed by the Respondent presenting the testimony of its witnesses;

(b) following direct testimony, any other Party may question such witness, in an order to be determined by the Arbitral Tribunal. The Party who initially presented the witness shall subsequently have the opportunity to ask additional questions on the matters raised in the other Parties' questioning;

(c) thereafter, the Claimant shall ordinarily first present the testimony of its Party-Appointed Experts, followed by the Respondent presenting the testimony of its Party-Appointed Experts. The Party who initially presented the Party-Appointed Expert shall subsequently have the opportunity to ask additional questions on the matters raised in the other Parties' questioning;

(d) the Arbitral Tribunal may question a Tribunal-Appointed Expert, and he or she may be questioned by the Parties or by any Party-Appointed Expert, on issues raised in the Tribunal-Appointed Expert Report, in the Parties' submissions or in the Expert Reports made by the Party-Appointed Experts;

(e) if the arbitration is organised into separate issues or phases (such as jurisdiction, preliminary determinations, liability and damages), the Parties may agree or the Arbitral Tribunal may order the scheduling of testimony separately for each issue or phase;

(f) the Arbitral Tribunal, upon request of a Party or on its own motion, may vary this order of proceeding, including the arrangement of testimony by particular issues or in such a manner that witnesses be questioned at the same time and in confrontation with each other (witness conferencing);

(g) the Arbitral Tribunal may ask questions to a witness at any time.

4. A witness of fact providing testimony shall first affirm, in a manner determined appropriate by the Arbitral Tribunal, that he or she commits to tell the truth or, in the case of an expert witness, his or her genuine belief in the opinions to be expressed at the Evidentiary Hearing. If the witness has submitted a Witness Statement or an Expert Report, the witness shall confirm it. The Parties may agree or the Arbitral Tribunal may order that the Witness Statement or Expert Report shall serve as that witness's direct testimony.

5. Subject to the provisions of article 9.2, the Arbitral Tribunal may request any person to give oral or written evidence on any issue that the Arbitral Tribunal considers to be relevant to the case and material to its outcome. Any witness called and 18 questioned by the Arbitral Tribunal may also be questioned by the Parties.

Article 9: Admissibility and Assessment of Evidence

1. The Arbitral Tribunal shall determine the admissibility, relevance, materiality and weight of evidence.

2. The Arbitral Tribunal shall, at the request of a Party or on its own motion, exclude from evidence or production any Document, statement, oral testimony or inspection for any of the following reasons:

(a) lack of sufficient relevance to the case or materiality to its outcome;

(b) legal impediment or privilege under the legal or ethical rules determined by the Arbitral Tribunal to be applicable;

(c) unreasonable burden to produce the requested evidence;

(d) loss or destruction of the Document that has been shown with reasonable likelihood to have occurred;

(e) grounds of commercial or technical confidentiality that the Arbitral Tribunal determines to be compelling;

(f) grounds of special political or institutional sensitivity (including evidence that has been classified as secret by a government or a public international institution) that the Arbitral Tribunal determines to be compelling; or

(g) considerations of procedural economy, proportionality, fairness or equality of the Parties that the Arbitral Tribunal determines to be compelling.

3. In considering issues of legal impediment or privilege under article 9.2(b), and insofar as permitted by any mandatory legal or ethical rules that are determined by it to be applicable, the Arbitral Tribunal may take into account:

(a) any need to protect the confidentiality of a Document created or statement or oral communication made in connection with and for the purpose of providing or obtaining legal advice;

(b) any need to protect the confidentiality of a Document created or statement or oral communication made in connection with and for the purpose of settlement negotiations;

(c) the expectations of the Parties and their advisors at the time the legal impediment or privilege is said to have arisen;

(d) any possible waiver of any applicable legal impediment or privilege by virtue of consent, earlier disclosure, affirmative use of the Document, statement, oral communication or advice contained therein, or otherwise; and

(e) the need to maintain fairness and equality as between the Parties, particularly if they are subject to different legal or ethical rules.

4. The Arbitral Tribunal may, where appropriate, make necessary arrangements to permit evidence to be presented or considered subject to suitable confidentiality protection.

5. If a Party fails without satisfactory explanation to produce any Document requested in a Request to Produce to which it has not objected in due time or fails to produce any Document ordered to be produced by the Arbitral Tribunal, the Arbitral Tribunal may infer that such document would be adverse to the interests of that Party.

6. If a Party fails without satisfactory explanation to make available any other relevant evidence, including testimony, sought by one Party to which the Party to whom the request was addressed has not objected in due time or fails to make available any evidence, including testimony, ordered by the Arbitral Tribunal to be produced, the Arbitral Tribunal may infer that such evidence would be adverse to the interests of that Party.

7. If the Arbitral Tribunal determines that a Party has failed to conduct itself in good faith in the taking of evidence, the Arbitral Tribunal may, in addition to any other measures available under these Rules, take such failure into account in its assignment of the costs of the arbitration, including costs arising out of or in connection with the taking of evidence.

ANNEXURE G

COURT OF APPEAL, CIVIL DIVISION

MAREVA COMPANIA NAVIERA SA *vs.* INTERNATIONAL BULK CARRIERS SA

The Mareva,

[1980] 1 All ER 213

COUNSEL: Bernard Rix for the shipowners.

The charterers were not represented.

SOLICITORS: Holman, Fenwick & Willan (for the shipowners).

JUDGES: Lord Denning, MR, Roskill and Ormrod, L.JJ

DATE: 23rd June 1975

Injunction—Interlocutory—Danger that defendant may transfer assets out of jurisdiction—Injunction restraining disposition of defendant's assets within jurisdiction—Whether court having jurisdiction to grant injunction in advance of judgment—Supreme Court of Judicature (Consolidation) Act, 1925, section 45(1).

Appeal

The plaintiffs, Mareva Compania Naviera SA ("the shipowners"), issued a writ on 25th June, 1975 claiming against the defendants, International Bulk Carriers SA ("the charterers"), unpaid hire and damages for repudiation of a charterparty. On an *ex parte* application Donaldson, J granted an injunction until 17.00 hours on 23rd June restraining the charterers from removing or disposing out of the jurisdiction monies standing to the credit of the charterers' account at a London bank. The shipowners appealed against Donaldson J's refusal to extend the injunction beyond 17.00 hours on 23rd June. The facts are set out in the judgment of Lord Denning MR.

23rd June, 1975. The following judgments were delivered.

LORD DENNING M.R. This raises a very important point of practice. It follows a recent case, *Nippon Yusen Kaisha* v. *Karageorgis*, (1975) I WLR 1093 (CA). The plaintiffs are shipowners who owned the vessel **Mareva**. They let it to the defendants ("the charterers") on a time charter for a trip out to the Far East and back. The vessel was to be put at the disposal of the charterers at Rotterdam. Hire was payable half monthly in advance and the rate was $ 3,850 a day from the time of delivery. The vessel was duly delivered to the charterers on 12th May, 1975. The charterers sub-chartered it. They let it on a voyage charter to the President of India. Freight was payable under that voyage charter: 90 per cent was to be paid against the documents and the 10 per cent later.

Under that voyage charter the vessel was loaded at Bordeaux on 29th May, 1975 with a cargo of fertiliser consigned to India. The Indian High Commission, in accordance with the obligations under the voyage charter, paid 90 per cent of the freight. But paid it to a bank in London. It was paid out to the Bank of Bilbao in London to the credit of the charterers. The total sum which the Indian High Commission paid into the bank was £174,000. Out of that the charterers paid to the shipowners, the plaintiffs, the first two instalments of the half monthly hire. They paid those instalments by credit transferred to the shipowners. The third was due on 12th June, 1975, but the charterers failed to pay it. They could easily have done it, of course, by making a credit transfer in favour of the shipowners. But they did not do it. Telexes passed which make it quite plain that the charterers were unable to pay. They said they were not able to fulfil any part of their obligations under the charter, and they had no alternative but to stop trading. Their efforts to obtain further financial support had been fruitless.

Whereupon the shipowners treated the charterers' conduct as a repudiation of the charter. They issued a writ on 20th June. They claimed the unpaid hire, which comes to $30,800, and damages for the repudiation. The total will be very large. They have served the writ on agents here, and they have applied also for service out of the jurisdiction. But meanwhile they believe that there is a grave danger that these monies in the bank in London will disappear. So they have applied for an injunction to restrain the disposal of those monies which are now in the bank. They rely on the recent case of *Nippon Yusen Kaisha* v. *Karageorgis*, (1975) I WLR 1093 (CA). Donaldson, J felt some doubt about that decision because we were not referred to *Lister & Co* v. *Stubbs*, (1890) 45 Ch D 1. There are observations in that case to the effect that the court has no jurisdiction to protect a creditor before he gets judgment. Cotton LJ said [45 Ch D 1 (13): ([1886-90) All ER Rep 797 (799)]:

> "I know of no case where, because it was highly probable that if the action were brought to a hearing the plaintiff could establish that a debt was due to him from the defendant, the defendant has been ordered to give security until that has been established by the judgment or decree."

And Lindley LJ said {45 Ch D 1 (15): [1890] All ER Rep 797 (800)]: "... we should be doing what I conceive to be very great mischief if we were to stretch a sound principle to the extent to which the Appellants ask us to stretch it ... "

Donaldson J felt that he was bound by *Lister & Co.* v. *Stubbs*, (1890) 45 Ch D 1 and that he had no power to grant an injunction. But, in deference to the recent case, he did grant an injunction, but only until 17.00 hours today (23rd June, 1975), on the understanding that by that time this court would be able to reconsider the position.

Now counsel for the charterers has been very helpful. He has drawn our attention not only to *Lister & Co* v. *Stubbs* but also to section 45 of the Supreme Court of Judicature (Consolidation) Act, 1925, which repeats section 25(8) of the Judicature Act, 1873. It says:

> "A *mandamus* or an injunction may be granted or a receiver appointed by an interlocutory Order of the Court in all cases in which it shall appear to the Court to be just or convenient ... "

In *Beddow* v. *Beddow*, (1878) 9 Ch D 89 (93), Jessel MR gave a very wide interpretation to that section. He said: "I have unlimited power to grant an injunction in any case where it would be right or just to do so ....".

There is only one qualification to be made. The court will not grant an injunction to protect a person who has no legal or equitable right whatever. That appears from *North London Railway Co.* v. *Great Northern Railway Co.*, (1883) 11 QBD 30 But, subject to that qualification, the statute gives a wide general power to the courts. It is well summarised in *Halsbury's Laws of England*:

> "... now, therefore, whenever a right, which can be asserted either at law or in equity, does exist, then, whatever the previous practice may have been, the

> Court is enabled by virtue of this provision, in a proper case, to grant an injunction to protect that right."

In my opinion that principle applies to a creditor who has a right to be paid the debt owing to him, even before he has established his right by getting judgment for it. If it appears that the debt is due and owing, and there is a danger that the debtor may dispose of his assets so as to defeat it before judgment, the court has jurisdiction in a proper case to grant an interlocutory judgment so as to prevent him disposing of those assets. It seems to me that this is a proper case for the exercise of this jurisdiction. There is money in a bank in London which stands in the name of these charterers. The charterers have control of it. They may at any time dispose of it or remove it out of this country. If they do so, the shipowners may never get their charter hire. The ship is now on the high seas. It has passed Cape Town on its way to India. It will complete the voyage and the cargo will be discharged. And the shipowners may not get their charter hire at all. In face of this danger, I think this court ought to grant an injunction to restrain the charterers from disposing of these monies now in the bank in London until the trial or judgment in this action. If the charterers have any grievance about it when they hear of it, they can apply to discharge it. But meanwhile the shipowners should be protected. It is only just and right that this court should grant an injunction. I would therefore continue the injunction.

ROSKILL LJ. I agree that this injunction should be extended until judgment in the action or until further order. The application to this court is made *ex parte,* and is necessitated by the fact that the learned Judge, Donaldson J, understandingly in the circumstances, refused to extend the jurisdiction beyond 17.00 hours this afternoon (23rd June 1975). Though the admirable argument to which we have listened puts the case very fairly both for and against continuing the injunction, the fact remains that, we have only heard argument from one side and I do not think it would be right to express any opinion as to what the result would be were this matter hereafter to be argued fully. But, as at present advised, it seems reasonably clear, first, that this court has jurisdiction to continue this injunction, and, *secondly,* that the difficult question is whether on the present facts this court ought at this stage to continue it until judgment or further order. Donaldson J, in his judgment of which we have a full note, has asked a number of other questions of this court which at present it would be wrong for us to seek to answer. If the charterers were represented, it would no doubt be said on their behalf that the decision of this court in *Lister & Co.* v. *Stubbs,* (1890) 45 Ch D 1 precludes this court, not as a matter of jurisdiction but as a matter of practice, from granting this injunction.

Indeed it is right to say that, as far as my own experience in the Commercial Court is concerned, an injunction in this form has in the past from time-to-time been applied for but has been consistently refused. This court should not, therefore, on an *ex parte* interlocutory application be too ready to disturb the practice of the past save for good reasons. But on the facts of this case, there are three good reasons for granting this injunction. *First,* this ship was on time charter from the plaintiffs to the defendants on the New York Produce Form, which provided, a little unusually, for a daily rate of hire payable half-monthly in advance and only the first two half-monthly instalments have been paid; *secondly,* there has been what would seem to be a plain and unexcused default in the payment of the *third* half-monthly instalment, and indeed a repudiation of the time charter by the charterers; *thirdly,* that third instalment fell due when the ship was under voyage charter from the time charterers to the President of India as voyage charterers.

On the evidence the charterers have already received £174,000 from the voyage charterers. Yet they have sent a telex to the shipowners in London on 17th June stating that their efforts to raise further financial support have been fruitless and that they have no alternative but to stop trading. If therefore this court does not interfere by injunction, it is apparent that the shipowners will suffer a grave injustice which this court has the power to help avoid; the injustice being that the ship will have to continue on her voyage to India and perhaps, as is not unknown in Indian ports, wait a long time there for discharge without remuneration while the charterers will be able to dissipate that £174,000.

In my judgment it would be wrong to tolerate this if it can be avoided. If it is necessary to find a reason for distinguishing this case from *Lister & Co.* v. *Stubbs*, (1890) 45 Ch D 1, I would venture to suggest that it is at least arguable that the court should interfere to protect the shipowners' rights which arise under clause 18 of the time charter. The relevant part reads: "That the Owners shall have a lien upon all cargoes, and all sub-freights for any amounts due under this Charter, including General Average contributions."

There is or may be a legal or perhaps equitable right which the shipowners may be entitled to have protected by the court. The full extent and nature of that right has long been a controversial matter which may have to be resolved hereafter and I therefore say no more about it.

For those rather narrow reasons I should continue this injunction until judgment or further order. It is open to the charterers to apply to discharge the injunction or to apply for a stay under the arbitration clause at any time if they are so advised. I agree with the order proposed by Lord Denning M.R.

ORMROD LJ. I agree. In my judgment the charterers here have a very strong case on the merits. We have not heard any argument from the other side because it is an *ex parte* application. In these circumstances I would reserve my own views until I have heard argument from the other side if any such argument is put forward. But, in the absence of any such argument, in my view this injunction should be continued.

Appeal allowed. Injunction continued.

ANNEXURE H

Court of Appeal

ANTON PILLER KG vs. MANUFACTURING PROCESSES LTD. AND OTHERS

[1975 A. No. 6292]

Dec. 8, 1975.

The following judgments were delivered.

LORD DENNING M.R. During the last 18 months the judges of the Chancery Division have been making orders of a kind not known before. They have some resemblance to search warrants. Under these orders the plaintiff and his solicitors are authorised to enter the defendant's premises so as to inspect papers, provided the defendant gives permission.

Now this is the important point: The court orders the defendant to give them permission. The judges have been making these orders on *ex parte* applications without prior notice to the defendant. None of the cases have been reported except the one before Templeman J. on December 3, 1974, *E.M.I. Ltd.* v. *Pandit,* [1975] 1 WLR 302: (1975) 1 All ER 418. But in the present case Brightman J. refused to make such an order.

On appeal to us, Mr. Laddie appears for the plaintiffs. He has appeared in most of these cases, and can claim the creditor the responsibility for them. He represented to us that in this case it was in the interests of justice that the application should not be made public at the time it was made. So we heard it *in camera*. It was last Tuesday. After hearing his submissions, we made the order. We now come to give our reasons in public. But at the outset I must state the facts, for it is obvious that such an order can only be justified in the most exceptional circumstances.

Anton Piller KG ("Pillers"), the plaintiffs, are German manufacturers of high repute. They make electric motors and generators. They play an important part in the big new computer industry. They supply equipment for it. They have recently designed a frequency converter specially for supplying the computers of International Business Machines.

Since 1972 Pillers have had, as their agents in the United Kingdom, a company here called Manufacturing Processes Ltd. ("M.P.L."), which is run by Mr. A. H. S. Baker and Mr. B. P. Wallace, their two directors. These agents are dealers who get machines from Pillers in Germany and sell them to customers in England. Pillers supply M.P.L. with much confidential information about the machines, including a manual showing how they work, and drawings which are the subject of copyright.

Very recently Pillers have found out—so they say—that these English agents, M.P.L., have been in secret communication with other German companies called Ferrostaal and Lechmotoren. The object of these communications is that M.P.L. should supply these other German companies with drawings and materials and other confidential information so that they can manufacture power units like Pillers. Pillers got to know of these communications through two "defectors," if I may call them so. One was the commercial manager of M.P.L., Mr. Brian Firth; the other was the sales manager, Mr. William Raymond Knight. These two were so upset by what was going on in M.P.L. that on their own initiative, without any approach by Pillers whatever, on October 2, 1975, one or both flew to Germany. They told Pillers what they knew about the arrangements with Ferrostaal and Lechmotoren. They disclosed also that M.P.L. was negotiating with Canadian and United States firms. In making these disclosures, both Mr. Firth and Mr. Knight were putting themselves in a perilous position, but Pillers assured them that they would safeguard their future employment.

The disclosures—coming from defectors—might have been considered untrustworthy. But they were supported by documents which emanated from both Ferrostaal and Lechmotoren. They showed that M.P.L. was in regular communication with those German companies. They were sending them drawings and arranging for inspection of the Piller machine, for the express purpose that the Lechmotoren company might manufacture a prototype machine copied from Pillers. One of the most telling communications was a telex from a representative of Ferrostaal to Mr. Wallace saying:

> "It is the opinion of Mr. S. (of Lechmotoren) that the best way to find a final solution for the prototype is to send Mr. Beck (also of Lechmotoren) to you as soon as the latest design of P. (Piller) has arrived in your factory. In this case it is guaranteed that the Lech prototype will have exactly the same features as the P-type. We hope you will agree to this proposal and we ask you to let us have your telex in order to arrange Mr. Beck's visit accordingly."

On getting this information, Pillers were extremely worried. They were about to produce a fine new frequency converter called the "Silent Block". They feared that M.P.L., in co-operation with the German manufacturers, would make a copy of their "Silent Block" and ruin their market. They determined to apply to the court for an injunction to restrain M.P.L. and their directors, the defendants, from infringing their copyright or using confidential information or making copies of their machines. But they were fearful that if the defendants were given notice of this application, they would take steps to destroy documents or send them to Germany or elsewhere, so that there would be none in existence by the time that discovery was had in the action.

So, on Wednesday, November 26, 1975, Pillers' solicitors prepared a draft writ of summons and, with an affidavit, they went before Brightman J. and asked, first, for an interim injunction to restrain infringement, etc., and, *secondly*, for an order that they might be permitted to enter the defendants' premises so as to inspect the documents of the plaintiffs and remove them, or copies of them. Brightman J. granted an interim injunction, but refused to order inspection or removal of the documents. He said:

> "There is strong *prima facie* evidence that the defendant company is now engaged in seeking to copy the plaintiffs' components for its own financial profit to the great detriment of the plaintiffs and in breach of the plaintiffs' rights."

He realised that the defendants might suppress evidence or misuse documentary material, but he thought that that was a risk which must be accepted in civil matters save in extreme cases.

"Otherwise," he said, "it seems to me that an order on the lines sought might become an instrument of oppression, particularly in a case where a plaintiff of big standing and deep pocket is ranged against a small man who is alleged on the evidence of one side only to have infringed the plaintiffs' rights."

Let me say at once that no court in this land has any power to issue a search warrant to enter a man's house so as to see if there are papers or documents there which are of an incriminating nature, whether libels or infringements of copyright or anything else of the kind. No constable or bailiff can knock at the door and demand entry so as to inspect papers or documents. The householder can shut the door in his face and say "Get out." That was established in the leading case of *Entick* v. *Carrington,* (1765) 2 Wils 275. None of us would wish to whittle down that principle in the slightest. But the order sought in this case is not a search warrant. It does not authorise the plaintiffs' solicitors or anyone else to enter the defendants' premises against their will. It does not authorise the breaking down of any doors, nor the slipping in by a back door, nor getting in by an open door or window. It only authorises entry and inspection by the permission of the defendants. The plaintiffs must get the defendants' permission. But it does do this: It brings pressure on the defendants to give permission. It does more. It actually orders them to give permission with, I suppose, the result that if they do not give permission, they are guilty of contempt of court.

This may seem to be a search warrant in disguise. But it was fully considered in the House of Lords 150 years ago and held to be legitimate. The case is *United Company of Merchants of England, Trading to the East Indies* v. *Kynaston,* (1821) 3 Bli (O.S.) 153. Lord Redesdale said (163-164):

> "The arguments urged for the appellants at the Bar are founded upon the supposition that the court has directed a forcible inspection. This is an erroneous view of the case. The order is to permit; and if the East India Company should refuse to permit inspection, they will be guilty of a contempt of the court.... It is an order operating on the person requiring the defendants to permit inspection, not giving authority of force, or to break open the doors of their warehouse."

That case was not, however, concerned with papers or things. It was only as to the value of a warehouse; and that could not be obtained without an inspection. But the distinction drawn by Lord Redesdale affords ground for thinking that there is jurisdiction to make an. order that the defendant "do permit" when it is necessary in the interests of justice.

Accepting such to be the case, the question is in what circumstances ought such an order be made., If the defendant is given notice beforehand and is able to argue the *pros* and *cons,* it is warranted by that case in the House of Lords and by R.S.C., Order 29, rules 2(1) and (5). But it is a far stronger thing to make such an order *ex parte* without giving him notice. This is not covered by the rules of the Supreme Court and must be based on the inherent jurisdiction of the court. There are one or two old precedents which give some colour for it, *Hennessy* v. *Rohmann, Osborne & Co.,* [1877] WN 14: (1877) 36 LT 51, and *Morris* v. *Howell,* (1888) 22 LR IR 77, an Irish case. But they do not go very far. So it falls to us to consider it on principle. It seems to me that such an order can be made by a judge *ex parte,* but it should only be made where it is essential that the plaintiff should have inspection so that justice can be done between the parties: and when, if the defendant were forewarned, there is a grave danger that vital evidence will be destroyed, that papers will be burnt or lost or hidden, or taken beyond the jurisdiction, and so the ends of justice be defeated: and when the inspection would do no real harm to the defendant or his case.

Nevertheless, in the enforcement of this order, the plaintiffs must act with due circumspection. On the service of it, the plaintiffs should be attended by their solicitor, who is an officer of the court. They should give the defendants an opportunity of considering it and of consulting their own solicitor. If the defendants wish to apply to discharge the order as having been improperly obtained, they must be allowed to do so.

If the defendants refuse permission to enter or to inspect, the plaintiffs must not force their way in. They must accept the refusal, and bring it to the notice of the court afterwards, if need be on an application to commit.

You might think that with all these safeguards against abuse, it would be of little use to make such an order. But it can be effective in this way: It serves to tell the defendants that, on the evidence put before it, the court is of opinion that they ought to permit inspection-nay, it orders them to permit-and that they refuse at their peril. It puts them in peril not only of proceedings for contempt, but also of adverse inferences being drawn against them; so much so that their own solicitor may often advise them to comply. We are told that in two at least of the cases such an order has been effective. We are prepared, therefore, to sanction its continuance, but only in an extreme case where there is grave danger of property being smuggled away or of vital evidence being destroyed.

On the evidence in this case, we decided last tuesday that there was sufficient justification to make an order. We did it on the precedent framed by Templeman J. It contains an undertaking in damages which is to be supported (as the plaintiffs are overseas) by a bond for £10,000. It gives an interim injunction to restraint the infringement of copyright and breach of confidential information, etc. It orders that the defendants do permit one or two of the plaintiffs and one or two of their solicitors to enter the defendants' premises for the purpose of inspecting documents, files or things, and removing those which belong to the plaintiffs. This was, of course, only an interim order pending the return of the summons. It is to be heard, we believe, tomorrow by the judge.

ORMROD L.J. I agree with all that Lord Denning M.R. has said. The proposed order is at the extremity of this court's powers. Such order, therefore, will rarely be made, and only when there is no alternative way of ensuring that justice is done to the applicant.

There are three essential pre-conditions for the making of such an order, in my judgment. *Firstly,* there must be an extremely strong *prima facie* case. *Secondly,* the damage, potential or actual, must be very serious for the applicant. Thirdly, there must be clear evidence that the defendants have in their possession incriminating documents or things, and that there is a real possibility that they may destroy such material before any application *inter-partes* can be made.

The form of the order makes it plain that the court is not ordering or granting anything equivalent to a search warrant. The order is an order on the defendant in personam to permit inspection. It is therefore open to him to refuse to comply with such an order, but at his peril either of further proceedings for contempt of court—in which case, of course, the court will have the widest discretion as to how to deal with it, and if it turns out that the order was made improperly in the first place, the contempt will be dealt with accordingly—but more important, of course, the refusal to comply may be the most damning evidence against the defendant at the subsequent trial. Great responsibility clearly rests on the solicitors for the applicant to ensure that the carrying out of such an order is meticulously carefully done with the fullest respect for the defendant's rights, as Lord Denning M.R. has said, of applying to the court, should he feel it necessary to do so, before permitting the inspection.

In the circumstances of the present case, all those conditions to my mind are satisfied, and this order is essential in the interests of justice.

I agree, therefore, that the appeal should be allowed.

SHAW L.J. I agree with both judgments. The overriding consideration in the exercise of this salutary jurisdiction is that it is to be resorted to only in circumstances where the normal processes of the law would be rendered nugatory if some immediate and effective measure was not available. When such an order is made, the party who has procured the court to make it must act with prudence and caution in pursuance of it.

Interim order allowing appeal affirmed.

Solicitors: *Collyer-Bristow & Co. for Band, Hatton & Co., Coventry.*

ANNEXURE I

EXTRACTS FROM

CONSULTATION PAPER ON PROPOSED AMENDMENTS TO THE ARBITRATION AND CONCILIATION ACT, 1996

Issued by

MINISTRY OF LAW AND JUSTICE
GOVERNMENT OF INDIA

Introduction:

1. The Arbitration and Conciliation Act, 1996 enacted in 1996 is an Act to consolidate and amend the law relating to domestic arbitration, international commercial arbitration and enforcement of foreign arbitral awards. Copy of the Act is annexed as Annexure-I. The Act is based on the Model Law adopted by the United Nations Commission on International Trade Law (UNCITRAL) in 1985. The objects and basis of the said Act is to speedy disposal with least court intervention. Some of the objects, as mentioned in the Statement of Objects and Reasons for the Arbitration and Conciliation Bill, 1995 are as follows:

(a) to comprehensively cover international commercial arbitration and conciliation as also domestic arbitration and conciliation;

(b) to minimise the supervisory role of courts in the arbitral process;

(c) to provide that every final arbitral award is enforced in the same manner as if it were a decree of court.

2. In the year 2001, the Law Commission of India undertook a comprehensive review of the working of the said Act and recommended many amendments to the Act in its 176th Report submitted to the Government. Summary of recommendations made in the report is annexed as Annexure-II.

The Government after considering the recommendations of the Report and after consulting the State Governments and certain institutions, decided to accept almost all the recommendations. Accordingly the Arbitration and Conciliation (Amendment) Bill, 2003 was introduced in Rajya Sabha on 22nd December, 2003. A copy of the Bill is annexed herewith as Annexure-III.

It may be stated that in July, 2004, Government constituted a Committee under the Chairmanship of Justice Dr. B.P. Saraf to make in-depth study of the implications of the recommendations of the Law Commission made in its 176th Report and all aspects relating to the Arbitration and Conciliation (Amendment) Bill, 2003. The report submitted by the said Committee is annexed as Annexure-IV.

3. The Bill was then referred to the Departmental Related Standing Committee on Personnel, Public Grievances, Law and Justice for examination and report. The said Committee after taking oral evidence of eminent advocates and the representatives from trade and industry, Public Sector Undertakings, representatives of this Department, submitted its report to the Houses of Parliament on 4th August, 2005. The Committee was of the view that the provisions of the Bill gave room for excessive intervention by the Courts in the arbitration proceedings and emphasised upon the need for establishing an institution in India which would measure up to international standards and for popularising institutionalised arbitration. The Committee further expressed the view that since many provisions of the Bill were contentious, the Bill may be withdrawn and a fresh legislation may be brought after considering the recommendations of the Committee. Copy of the report is annexed as Annexure-V.

4. In view of the large number of amendments recommended by the Committee and because many provisions of the Bill were contentious, the said Bill was withdrawn from the Rajya Sabha. At that time it was decided that a new legislation will be brought in Parliament after undertaking an in depth examination of the various recommendations of the Committee.

5. As we know that main purpose of the 1996 Act is to encourage an ADR method for resolving disputes speedy and without much interference of the Courts. In fact section 5 of the Act provides, "Notwithstanding anything contained in any other law for the time being in force, in matters covered by this Part (*i.e.*, Part I), no judicial authority shall intervene except where so provided in this Part." However, with the passage of time, some difficulties in its applicability of the Act have been noticed. The Supreme Court and High Courts have interpreted many provisions of the Act and while doing so they have also realised some *lacunas* in the Act which leads to conflicting views. Further, in some cases, courts have interpreted the provisions of the Act in such a way which defeats the main object of such a legislation. Therefore, it becomes necessary to remove the difficulties and *lacunas* in the Act so that ADR method may become more popular and object of enacting arbitration law may be achieved.

6. The following sections of the Act and interpretation by courts have given rise to difficulties which require to be addressed:

(A) Application of Part I-Section 2(2)—

(i) The 1996 Act covers both domestic arbitration (where both parties are Indian national) as well as international commercial arbitration where at least one party is not an Indian national. The Act of 1996 has been divided in three Parts. Part I entitled, "ARBITRATION" and there are 10 Chapters containing sections 2 to 43. Part II entitled, "Enforcement of certain Foreign Awards" and contains Chapter I and II containing sections 44 to 60. Chapter I of Part II deals with "New York Convention Awards" and Chapter II deals with 'Geneva Convention Awards". Part III (sections 61 to 81) deals with 'Conciliation'. Part IV (sections 82 to 86) provides for Supplementary Provisions.

Section 2(2) provides for applicability of Part I. Existing section 2(2) reads as follows:

"Section 2(2): This Part shall apply where the place of arbitration is in India."

(ii) There are conflicting views of the Courts in India about applicability of Part I in respect of International Commercial Arbitration where seat of arbitration is not in India. In a case before the Delhi High Court [*Dominant Offset Pvt. Ltd.* v. *Adamovske Strojirny AS*, (1997) 68 DLT 157: 1997 (2) Arb LR 335 (Delhi)] the petitioners entered into two agreements with a foreign concern for technology transfer and for purchase of certain machines. The agreement carried an arbitration clause which provided that the place of arbitration would be London and the arbitration tribunal would be International Chamber of Commerce in Paris. The parties having developed a dispute, a petition was filed in the High Court of Delhi with a prayer for reference to arbitration in terms of the arbitration clause for enforcement of the agreement. The Court extensively studied the provisions of the Act so as to see whether it was a matter coming under Part I of the Act. The Court held that Part I of the Act applies to International Commercial arbitration conducted outside India. The Court opined that section 2(2) which states that "Part I shall apply where the place of arbitration is in India" is "an inclusive definition and does not exclude the applicability of Part I to those arbitrations which are not being held in India". The Court also held that the application under section 11 for the appointment of arbitrators could be treated as a petition under section 8 for reference of the parties to arbitration. This decision was followed in *Olex Focas Pvt. Ltd.* v. *Skoda Export Company Ltd.*, AIR 2000 Del 161: 1999 (37) Arb LR 533. In this case the High Court allowed relief under section 9 (interim measure by Court) and ruled—

> "A careful reading and scrutiny of the provisions of 1996 Act leads to the clear conclusion that sub-section (2) of section 2 is an inclusive definition and it does not exclude the applicability of Part I to this arbitration which is not being held in India. The other clauses of section 2 clarify the position beyond any doubt that this Court in an appropriate case can grant interim relief or interim injunction."

However, Court added that courts should be extremely cautious in granting interim relief in cases where the venue of arbitration is outside India and both parties are foreigners.

(iii) The Calcutta High Court in *East Coast Shipping Ltd.* v. *M.J. Scrap Pvt. Ltd.*, (1997) 1 Cal HN 444: 1997 (101) Cal WN 336, took a different view and held that Part I of the Act would apply only to arbitrations where the place of arbitration is in India. In a subsequent decision of Division Bench of the Delhi High Court in *Marriott International Inc.* v. *Ansal Hotels Ltd.*, AIR 2000 Del 377 (DB): 2000 (3) Arb LR 369: 2000 (86) DLT 873, Delhi High Court endorsed the view expressed by the Calcutta High Court. The Division Bench referred the another decision reported as *Kitechnology N.V.* v. *Union GmbH Plastmaschinen*, (1998) 47 Del RJ 397, in which the Single Judge of Delhi High Court held that where none of the parties to the agreement was an Indian and the agreement was to be covered by German Law which provided arbitration to be held at Frankfurt, section 9 of the Act will have no applicability and the Court will have no jurisdiction to pass an interim order in that matter.

(iv) A Division Bench of the Calcutta High Court in *White Industries, Australia Ltd* v. *Coal India Ltd.* held that an award published and rendered in accordance with ICC rules in Paris (though the proceedings were held, for the convenience of the parties, in London) could be challenged in a proceeding initiated in a Court in India under section 34 of the Act since the contract between the parties stipulated that the "agreement shall be subject to and governed by the laws in force in India except that the Indian Arbitration Act of 1940 shall not apply". A Division Bench speaking through the Chief Justice A.K. Patnaik of Chhattishgarh High Court in *Bharat Aluminium Company Limited* v. *Kaiser Aluminium Technical Services Inc.*, AIR 2005 Chh 21, however took a contrary view.

(v) However, Supreme Court in the case of *Bhatia International* v. *Bulk Trading*, (2002) 4 SCC 105: AIR 2002 SC 1432: 2002 AIR SCW 1285: 2002 (1) Arb LR 675: JT 2002 (3) SC 150: 2002 (2) SCJ 420: (2002) 2 SCALE 612: 2002 (2) Supreme 395, has held that in absence of the word 'only' in section 2(2), part I of the Act would apply to arbitration held outside India, so long as the law of India governed the contract. The decision in Bhatia International though was not concerned with enforcement of arbitral award, certain principles laid down therein with regard to application of the provisions contained in Part I of the Act in respect of arbitration proceedings that are held in Paris in accordance with the rules of the International Chamber of Commerce (ICC), have far reaching consequences.

(vi) In *Bhatia International* the question was whether an application filed under section 9 of the Act in the Court of the third Additional District Judge, Indore by the foreign party against the appellant praying for interim injunction restraining the appellant from alienating transferring and/or creating third party rights, disposing of, dealing with and/or selling their business assets and properties, was maintainable. The Additional District Judge held that the application was maintainable, which view was affirmed by the High Court. The Supreme Court, reaffirming the decision of the High Court, held that an application for interim measure could be made to the courts of India, whether or not the arbitration takes place in India or abroad. The Court went on to hold that "the arbitration not having taken place in India, all or some of the provisions of Part I may also get excluded by an express or implied agreement of parties. But if not so excluded the provisions of Part I will also apply to 'foreign awards'. The opening words of sections 45 and 54, which are in Part II, read 'notwithstanding anything contained in Part I'. Such a *non-obstante* clause had to be put in because the provisions of Part I apply to Part II". Supreme Court referred to similar provision in UNCITRAL Model law. Article 1(2) of the UNCITRAL Model Law reads as follows:

> "(2) The provisions of this law, except articles 8, 9, 35 and 36, apply only if the place of arbitration is in the territory of this State."

Supreme Court highlighted the word 'only' and observed as follows:

> 'Thus, article 1(2) of the UNCITRAL Model Law uses the word "only" to emphasise that the provisions of that law are to apply if the place of arbitration is in the territory of that State. Significantly, in section 2(2) the word "only" has been omitted. The omission of this word changes the whole complexion of the sentence. The omission of the word "only" in section 2(2) indicates that this sub-section is only an inclusive and clarificatory provision. As stated above, it is not providing that provisions of Part I do not apply to arbitrations which take place outside India."

(vii) The Supreme Court observed that if the Part I of the Act is not made applicable to arbitration held outside India it would have serious consequences such as (a) amount to holding that the Legislature has left a lacunae in the said Act. There would be lacunae as neither Part I or Part II would apply to arbitrations held in a country which is not a signatory to the New York Convention or the Geneva Convention. It would mean that there is no law, in India, governing such arbitrations; (b) leave a party remediless in as much as in international commercial arbitrations which take place out of India the party would not be able to apply for interim relief in India even though the properties and assets are in India. Thus, a party may not be able to get any interim relief at all.

(viii) The Supreme Court made certain observations in respect of International commercial arbitration which take place in a non-convention country. The Court observed that international commercial arbitration may be held in a non-convention country. Part II only applies to arbitrations which take place in a convention country. The Supreme Court referred to the definition of international commercial arbitration which is defined in section 2(f) of the Act and held that the definition makes no distinction between international commercial arbitration which takes place in India or those take place outside India. The Supreme Court also observed that sections 44 and 53 define foreign award as being award covered by arbitrations under the New York Convention and the Geneva Convention, respectively. Special provisions for enforcement of these foreign awards are made in Part II of the Act. To the extent Part II provides a separate definition of an arbitral award and separate provision for enforcement of foreign awards, the provision in Part I dealing with these aspects will not apply to such foreign awards.

(ix) The court finally concluded that "the provisions of Part I would apply to all arbitrations and to all proceedings relating thereto. Where such arbitration is held in India the provisions of Part I would compulsorily apply and parties are free to deviate only to the extent permitted by the derogable provisions of Part I. In cases of international commercial arbitrations held out of India provisions of Part I would apply unless the parties by agreement, express or implied, exclude all or any of its provisions. In that case the laws or rules chosen by the parties would prevail. Any provision, in Part I, which is contrary to or excluded by that law or rules will not apply".

(x) Supreme Court also stated in their judgment that 1996 Act does not appear to be a well-drafted legislation. In view of this Supreme Court observed that the High Courts of Orissa, Bombay, Madras, Delhi and Calcutta cannot be faulted for interpreting the provisions in the different manner.

(xi) It may be mentioned that Supreme Court in the case of *Shreejee Traco (I) Pvt. Ltd.* v. *Paper Line International Inc.*, (2003) 9 SCC 79 considered the scope of Part I of the Act in respect of appointment of an arbitrator under section 11(4) in a case where the agreement provided that any disputes or claims would be submitted to arbitration in New York. The Supreme Court after referring section 2(2) held, "on a plane reading of this provision it is clear that Parliament intended the provisions of Part I to be applicable where the place of arbitration is in India." The Supreme Court also held as follows:

> "So far as the language employed by Parliament in drafting sub-section (2) of section 2 of the Act is concerned, suffice it to say that the language is clear and unambiguous. Saying that this Part would apply where the place of arbitration is in India tantamounts to saying that it will not apply where the place of arbitration is not in India. For the foregoing reasons it is held that the petition under section 11(4) of the Act is not maintainable before the Chief Justice of India or his designate."

(xii) A two-judge Bench of the Supreme Court[1], reiterating its decision in Bhatia International held that a award made in England through a arbitral process conducted by the London Court of International Arbitration, though a foreign award, Part I of 1996 Act would be applicable to such award and hence the courts in India would have jurisdiction both under section 9 and section 34 of the Act and entertain a challenge to its validity. It is of some significance that both in *Bhatia International* as well as in *Venture Global Engineering* case, the provisions under the Arbitration Act invoking the provisions contained in Part I thereof had been initiated by foreign parties against the Indian parties, though the proceedings of the arbitration were held abroad and the culmination of which undoubtedly are foreign awards.

(xiii) The factual background of the case was thus: *Venture Global Engineering* (VGE, a company incorporated in USA had entered into a joint venture with Satyam Computer Services (Satyam) to constitute an Indian Company—Satyam Venture Engineering Company Limited (SVES). The two companies had equal shares *i.e.*, 50-50 in the joint venture (SVES). They had also entered into shareholder's agreement, which *inter alia* provided that "the share holders shall at all times act in accordance with the Company Act and other applicable Act/Rules being enforced in Indian at any time". In February,

1. *Venture Global Engineering* v. *Satyam Computers Services Ltd.*, 2008 (1) SCALE 214: AIR 2008 SC 1061: 2008 AIR SCW 667: 2008 (1) Arb LR 137: (2008) 4 SCC 190.

2005, disputes arose between the parties, which were referred to sole arbitration of Mr. Paul Hannon, appointed by the London Court of International Arbitration and the award made in England, directed Venture to transfer its 50 per cent shares in SVES to Satyam. Satyam filed a petition before the US District Court, Eastern District Court of Michigan for recognition and enforcement of the award, which was contested by Venture. Venture filed a Civil Suit in the Court of the First Additional Chief Judge, City Civil Court, Secunderabad, seeking a declaration for setting-aside the award and for a permanent injunction on the transfer of shares under the award. The City Civil Court, though initially, granted an order of injunction, at the intervention of Satyam, finally rejected the plaint. An appeal was preferred by the Venture before the High Court of Andhra Pradesh, was also unsuccessful. Venture, therefore, approached the Supreme Court. Relying upon the decision in *Bhatia International*[1], contending, *inter alia,* that in terms of the declaration of law by Supreme Court, Part I of the Act would also apply to foreign awards and hence the courts in India had jurisdiction to entertain a challenge to the validity of the award and that in view or the over-riding provision contained in the Share-Holder's Agreement, Satyam cannot approach the US Courts for enforcement of the award. On behalf of the Satyam, it was contended that since, the award made in England thus was a foreign award, no suit or other proceedings can lie against such award in view of section 44 of the Act and that an application for setting-aside such an award under section 34 of the Act could not lie in any event. A two-judge bench, which heard the case, felt that *Bhatia International* decided the principal issue namely that since the parties did not, by agreement, exclude the provision of Part I of the Act from being made applicable to arbitration proceedings in England, the provisions of the Part I would apply even to foreign award and hence the courts in India can entertain a challenge to the validity of such an award. Accepting the contentions of Venture, the court held:

> "That the provisions of Part I of the Act would apply to all arbitrations including international commercial arbitrations and to hold that where such arbitration is held in India, the provisions of Part I would compulsorily extent permitted by the provisions of Part I. It is also clear that even in the case of international commercial arbitration held out of India provisions of Part I would apply unless the parties by agreement, express or implied, exclude all or any of its provisions. We are also of the view that such an interpretation does not lead to any conflict between any of the provisions of the Act an there is no *lacuna* as such."

(xiv) The reason, which persuaded the court that a challenge to foreign award can lay in India, was the fact that an award, which is otherwise opposed to Public Policy of India and thus not enforceable even under the New York Convention, can be enforced, by a party by seeking its enforcement of such an award in another country. It is in view of such apprehension, the court observed:

> "In any event, to apply section 34 to foreign international awards would not be inconsistent with section 48 of the Act, or any other provision of Part II as a situation may arise, where, even in respect of properties situate in India and where an award would be invalid if opposed to the public policy of India, merely because the judgment-debtor resides abroad, the award can be enforced against properties in Indian through personal compliance of the judgment-debtor and by holding out the threat of contempt as its being sought to be done in the present case. In such an event, the judgment-debtor cannot be deprived of his right under section 34 to invoke the public policy of India, to set aside the award. As observed earlier,

1. *Bhatia International* v. *Bulk Trading S.A.,* (2002) 4 SCC 105: AIR 2002 SC 1432: 2002 AIR SCW 1285: 2002 (1) Arb LR 675: JT 2002 (3) SC 150: 2002 (2) SCJ 420: (2002) 2 SCALE 612: 2002 (2) Supreme 395.

the public policy of India includes—(a) the fundamental policy of India; or (b) the interests of India; or (c) justice or morality; or (d) in addition, it, it is patently illegal. This extended definition of public policy can be by-passed by taking the award to a foreign country for enforcement.

(xv) The Supreme Court in *Indtel Technical Services (P) Ltd.* v. *W.S. Atkins Rail Ltd.*, (2008) 10 SCC 308: AIR 2009 SC 1132: 2009 AIR SCW 343: 2008 (3) Arb LR 391: (2008) 11 SCALE 735, while referring *Bhatia International* observed as follows:

> 37. The decision in *Bhatia International* case 1 it has been rendered by a Bench of three judges and governs the scope of the application under consideration, as it clearly lays down that the provisions of Part I of the Arbitration and Conciliation Act, 1996, would be equally applicable to international commercial arbitrations held outside India, unless any of the said provisions are excluded by agreement between the parties expressly or by implication, which is not so in the instant case.

(xvi) It is evident from the above discussion that there is no uniformity in judicial decisions in respect of applicability of Part I of the Act in respect of cases where the seat of arbitration is not in India. As per *Bhatia International* (Supra) and *(sic) Satyam Computors,* in cases of international commercial arbitrations held out of India provisions of Part I would apply unless the parties by agreement, exclude all or any of its provisions. The result is that all the provisions of Part I including provisions relating to appointment of arbitrator (section 11), challenge of arbitration award (section 34) would also be applicable to International Commercial Arbitration where seat of arbitration is not in India. However, in view of the observations made by the Supreme Court in *Shreejee Traco (I) Pvt. Ltd.* v. *Paper Line International Inc.*, (2003) 9 SCC 79, no provisions of Part I would apply to cases where the place of arbitration is not in India.

(xvii) It may be stated that it is the broad principle in International Commercial Arbitration that a law of the country where it is held, namely, the Seat or forum or laws of the arbitration, governs the arbitration. However, if all the provisions of Part I are not made applicable to International Commercial Arbitration where the seat of arbitration is not in India, some practical problems are arising. There may be cases where the properties and assets of a party to Arbitration may be in India. Section 9 of the Act which falls in Part I provide for interim measures by the Court. As per section 9, a party may, apply to a court for certain interim measures of protection including for preservation, interim custody or sale of goods, securing the amount in disputes, detention, preservation or inspection of any property, interim injunction, etc. If provision of section 9 is not made applicable to International Commercial Arbitration where seat of arbitration is not in India, a party may be out of remedy if the assets and property are in India. In cases of International Arbitration where the seat of arbitration is outside India, a serious controversy has arisen in the Indian courts. These are cases where interim measures could not be granted by Indian courts under section 9 to an Indian national before commencement of arbitration (or after the award) against property of a foreign party. By the time the Indian party takes steps to move the courts in the country in which the seat of arbitration is located, the property may have been removed or transferred.

(xviii) There is another aspect which relates to enforcement of arbitration award rendered in a non-convention country *i.e.*, a country which is not signatory either to New York Convention or to the Geneva Convention. In *Bhatia International* Supreme Court referred to definition of International Commercial Arbitration provided in sections 2(1)(f) and 11 held that the definition makes no distinction between Iinternational Commercial Arbitrations held in India or outside India. An International Commercial Arbitration may be held in a country which is a signatory to either the New York Convention or the Geneva Convention (hereinafter called "the convention country"). An International

Commercial Arbitration may be held in a non-convention country. The said Act nowhere provides that its provisions are not to apply to International Commercial Arbitrations which take place in a non-convention country. Part II only applies to arbitrations which take place in a convention country.

(xix) In this regard we may point out that an award to be a 'foreign award' has to be made in the territory of a foreign State notified by the Central Government as having made a reciprocal provision for enforcement of New York Convention or Geneva Convention. The Supreme Court in *Badat & Co.* v. *East India Trading Co.*, (1964) 4 SCR 19: AIR 1964 SC 538: 1965 (1) SCJ 747 was dealing with a case that arose before the Foreign Awards (Recognition and Enforcement) Act, 1961 became applicable. The court held as follows:

> "Before we do so, it would be desirable to examine the position regarding the enforcement of foreign awards and foreign judgments based upon awards. Under the Arbitration Protocol and Convention Act, 1937 (6 of 1937), certain commercial awards made in foreign countries are enforceable in India as if they were made on reference to arbitration in India. The provisions of this Act, however, apply only to countries which are parties to the Protocol set forth in the First Schedule to the Act or to awards between persons of whom one is subject to the jurisdiction of some one of such powers as the Central Government being satisfied that the reciprocal provisions have been made, may, by notification declare to be parties to the Convention, set forth in the Second Schedule to the Act. It is common ground that these provisions are not applicable to the awards in question. Apart from the provisions of the aforesaid statute, foreign awards and foreign judgments based upon awards are enforceable in India on the same grounds and in the same circumstances in which they are enforceable in England under the common law on grounds of justice, equity and good conscience. It will thus be seen that there is a conflict of opinion on a number of points concerning the enforcement of foreign awards or judgments, based upon foreign awards. However, certain propositions appear to be clear. One is that where the award is followed by a judgment in a proceeding which is not merely formal but which permits of objections being taken to the validity of the award by the party against whom judgment is sought, the judgment will be enforceable in England. Even in that case, however, the plaintiff will have the right to sue on the original cause of action. The second principle is that even a foreign award will be enforced in England provided it satisfies *mutatis mutandis* the tests applicable for the enforcement of foreign judgments on the ground that it creates a contractual obligation arising out of submission to arbitration. On two matters connected with this there is difference of opinion. One is whether an award which is followed by a judgment can be enforced as an award in England or whether the judgment alone can be enforced. The other is whether an award which is not enforceable in the country in which it was made without obtaining an enforcement order or a judgment can be enforced in England or whether in such a case the only remedy is to sue on the original cause of action. The third principle is that a foreign judgment or a foreign award may be sued upon in England as giving good cause of action provided certain conditions are fulfilled one of which is that it has become final."

(xx) Thus, it is well-established that the awards rendered in countries with which India does not have reciprocal arrangements cannot be enforced in India as if it were a decree. Perhaps *Badat's* case was not brought to the notice of the court in *Bhatia International* v. *Bulk Traders SA* case, which is why observations pertaining to non-convention countries came to be made. As stated above provisions of Part II which deals with enforcement of foreign award, is not and cannot be made applicable to an International Commercial arbitration which takes place in non-convention country and where there is no reciprocal agreement between that country and Central Government. Not only this, foreign award must be given in one of those territories in respect of which reciprocal arrangement has been made. Section 44 of the Arbitration and Conciliation Act, 1996 defines the term 'foreign award". According to section 44, an arbitral award is a foreign award if it is made in pursuance of an agreement to which New York Convention [reproduced in First Schedule to the Act] applies and made in a territory to which the New York Convention applies on the basis of reciprocity.

(xxi) Section 44 reads as follows:

> "44. *Definition.*—In this Chapter, unless the context otherwise requires, 'foreign award' means an award of differences between persons arising out of legal relationships, whether contractual or not, considered as commercial under the law in force in India, made on or after the 11th day of October, 1960 — after the 11th day of October, 1960—
>
> (a) in pursuance of an agreement in writing for arbitration to which the Convention set forth in the First Schedule applied, and
>
> (b) in one of such territories as the Central Government, being satisfied that reciprocal provisions have been made, may, by notification in the Official Gazette, declare to be territories to which the said Convention applies."

(xxii) It may also be pointed out that clause (3) of article 1 of New York Convention on the Recognition and Enforcement of Arbitral Awards permits the signing, ratifying or acceding State to declare on the basis of reciprocity that it will apply the convention made only in the territory of another contracting State. India has made reservation and declared that convention will apply only on the basis of reciprocity.

(xxiii) Therefore, when an international arbitral award is made in a country or territory in respect of which there is no reciprocal arrangement between Central Government and Government of that country, it cannot be enforced under the Arbitration and Conciliation Act, 1996. For the purpose of enforcement of such an arbitral award party has to file a civil suit in India.

(xxiv) It is part of the law of arbitration in several countries to allow a few provisions of their arbitration statutes to apply to international arbitrations held outside their countries. Sections 2(1) and (2) of the English Arbitration Act, 1996 reads as follows:

> "2. *Scope of application of provisions.*—(1) The provisions of this Part apply where the seat of arbitration is in England and Wales or Northern Ireland.
>
> (2) The following sections apply even if the seat of the arbitration is outside England and Wales or Northern Ireland or no seat has been designated or determined, (a) sections 9 to 11 (Stay of legal proceedings, & (c); and (b) section 66 (enforcement of arbitral award".

(xviii) In order to remove the difficulties stated above, it is proposed to amend section 2(2) of the Arbitration and Conciliation Act, 1996 as follows:

> "(2) This Part shall apply only where the place of arbitration is in India:
>
> Provided that provisions of sections 9 and 27 shall also apply to International Commercial Arbitration where the place of arbitration is not in India if an award made in such place is enforceable and recognised under Part II of this Act."

(B) Amendment in section 11

(i) Section 11 of the Act provides for appointment of arbitrators. Sub-sections (4) to (12) deal with appointment of arbitrator by the Chief Justice or any person or institution designated by him when the parties fail to appoint an arbitrator or where the arbitration is to be held with three arbitrators, and the two appointed arbitrators fail to agree on the third arbitrator within the stipulated time.

(ii) The scope and effect of these provisions had been the subject-matter of several decisions rendered by the Supreme Court. In *Ador Samia (P) Ltd.* v. *Peekay Holdings Ltd.*, (1999) 8 SCC 572: AIR 1999 SC 3246: 1999 AIR SCW 3220: 1999 (3) Arb LR 185: JT 1999 (6) SC 194: (1999) 5 SCALE 157: 1999 (7) Supreme 309, a Bench of two learned Judges of the Supreme Court held that the Chief Justice or any person or institution designated by him acts in administrative capacity under section 11 of the Act and hence an order passed in exercise of such power, does not attract the provisions of the article 136 of the Constitution.

(iii) A two-Judge Bench referred the case in *Adur Samia (P) Ltd.* v. *Peekay Holdings Ltd.* for reconsideration to the Bench of three learned Judges. A three-judges Bench in *Konkan Railway Corp. Ltd.* v. *Mehul Construction Co.*, (2000) 7 SCC 201: AIR 2000 SC 2821: 2000 AIR SCW 2960: 2000 (3) Arb LR 162: JT 2000 (9) SC 362: 2000 (3) SCJ 265: (2000) 6 SCALE 71: 2000 (5) Supreme 657 affirmed the view taken by the two-Judge Bench in *Adur Samia (P) Ltd.* v. *Peekay Holdings Ltd.*, holding that the order passed by the Chief Justice or his designate under section 11 of the Act was an administrative order not amenable to the jurisdiction of the court under article 136.

(iv) Subsequently, a Bench of two Judges in *Konkan Railway Corp. Ltd.* v. *Rani Construction (P) Ltd.*, (2000) 8 SCC 159: 2000 AIR SCW 3908: 2000 CLC 2147 referred to a Larger Bench of the said decision of three-Judge Bench for reconsideration. Thereafter, a Constitution Bench consisting of five learned Judges in *Konkan Railway Corp. Ltd.* v. *Rani Construction (P) Ltd.*, (2002) 2 SCC 388: AIR 2002 SC 778: 2002 AIR SCW 426: 2002 (1) Arb LR 326: JT 2002 (1) SC 587: 2002 (1) SCJ 556: (2002) 1 SCALE 465: 2002 (1) Supreme 419 affirmed the decision of the three-Judge Bench in *Konkan Railway Corp. Ltd.* v. *Mehul Construction Co.* holding, *inter alia*, that the order of the Chief Justice or his designate under section 11 nominating an Arbitrator is not a adjudicatory order and that neither the Chief Justice nor his designate acts as a Tribunal and hence any order passed by them cannot be a subject-matter of appeal by Special Leave under article 136. The Constitution Bench also held that since the Chief Justice or his designate is not required to perform any adjudicatory function and that, the order nominating an Arbitrator would be amenable to challenge under section 12 read with section 13 of the Act. Since the exercise of the power is purely administrative in nature, it does not contemplate a response from the other party and hence a notice to the opposite party is not necessary. Constitution Bench also held that since the Chief Justice or his designate is not required to perform any adjudicatory function and that, the order nominating an Arbitrator would be amenable to challenge under section 12 read with section 13 of the Act. Since the exercise of the power is purely administrative in nature, it does not contemplate a response from the other party and hence a notice to the opposite party is not necessary.

(v) Subsequently, the decision of the Constitution Bench has been reconsidered by the Larger Bench consisting of seven-Judges in *SBP Co.* v. *Patel Engineering Ltd.*, (2005) 8 SCC 618: AIR 2006 SC 450: 2005 AIR SCW 5932: 2005 (3) Arb LR 285: JT 2005 (9) SC 219: 2005 (7) SCJ 461: (2005) 9 SCALE 1: 2005 (7) Supreme 610. The Court overruled the decision in *Konkan Railway Corp. Ltd.* v. *Rani Construction (P) Ltd.*, (2002) 2 SCC 388: AIR 2002 SC 778: 2002 AIR SCW 426: 2002 (1) Arb LR 326: JT 2002 (1) SC 587: 2002 (1) SCJ 556: (2002) 1 SCALE 465: 2002 (1) Supreme 419 rendered by five learned Judges and held that the power exercised by the Chief Justice of the High Courts or the Chief Justice of India under section 11(6) of the Act is judicial power and not an administrative power and that such power, in its entirety, could be delegated only to another Judge of that Court. The Supreme Court concluded as follows:

(a) The power exercised by the Chief Justice of the High Court or the Chief Justice of India under section 11(6) of the Act is not an administrative power. It is a judicial power.

(b) The power under section 11(6) of the Act, in its entirety, could be delegated, by the Chief Justice of the High Court only to another Judge of that Court and by the Chief Justice of India to another Judge of the Supreme Court.

(c) In case of designation of a Judge of the High Court or of the Supreme Court, the power that is exercised by the designated Judge would be that of the Chief Justice as conferred by the statute.

(d) The Chief Justice or the designated Judge will have the right to decide the preliminary aspects as indicated in the earlier part of this judgment. These will be his own jurisdiction to entertain the request, the existence of a valid arbitration agreement, the existence or otherwise of a live claim, the existence of the condition for the exercise of his power and on the qualifications of the arbitrator or arbitrators. The Chief Justice or the designated Judge would be entitled to seek the opinion of an institution in the matter of nominating an arbitrator qualified in terms of section 11(8) of the Act if the need arises but the order appointing the arbitrator could only be that of the Chief Justice or the designated Judge.

(e) Once the matter reaches the Arbitral Tribunal or the sole arbitrator, the High Court would not interfere with the orders passed by the arbitrator or the Arbitral Tribunal during the course of the arbitration proceedings and the parties could approach the Court only in terms of section 37 of the Act or in terms of section 34 of the Act.

(f) Since an order passed by the Chief Justice of the High Court or by the designated Judge of that Court is a judicial order, an appeal will lie against that order only under article 136 of the Constitution to the Supreme Court.

(g) There can be no appeal against an order of the Chief Justice of India or a Judge of the Supreme Court designated by him while entertaining an application under section 11(6) of the Act.

(h) In a case where an Arbitral Tribunal has been constituted by the parties without having recourse to section 11(6) of the Act, the Arbitral Tribunal will have the jurisdiction to decide all matters as contemplated by section 16 of the Act.

(vi) The Supreme Court held that the Chief Justice or the designated Judge will have the right to decide preliminary aspects as regards his own jurisdiction to entertain the request, existence of a valid arbitral agreement, the existence or otherwise of a live claim, the existence of the conditions for the exercise of the power and on the qualifications of the Arbitrator. The Chief Justice or the designated Judge would be entitled to seek the opinion of an institution in the matter nominating an Arbitrator but the order appointing an Arbitrator could be passed only by the Chief Justice or the designated Judge. Even designation of a District Judge as the authority under section 11(6) of the Act was not warranted under the scheme of the Act. The order passed by the Chief Justice of the High Courts or by the designated Judge of that Court being a judicial order, is appealable under article 136 of the Constitution to the Supreme Court but no such appeal would lie against the order made by the Chief Justice of India or a Judge of the Supreme Court designated by him. Where the Arbitral Tribunal is constituted by the parties without taking recourse to section 11 of the Act, the Arbitral Tribunal will have the jurisdiction to decide all the matters as contemplated by section 16 of the Act.

(vii) The decision of the Supreme Court has rendered the provisions contained in sub-sections (4), (5), (7), (8) and (9) of section 11 with regard to appointment of Arbitrators by any person or institution designated by the Chief Justice of India and totally ineffective. It may be pointed out that question of appointment of arbitrator by the Chief Justice arises only when a party fails to appoint an arbitrator or where the two appointed arbitrators fail to agree on the third arbitrators.

(viii) This is clearly contrary to the objective of the Act that is, to encourage litigants to take recourse to the alternative dispute resolution mechanism by Arbitration. Institutional Arbitration, throughout the world, is recognised as the primary mode of resolution of international commercial disputes. Institutional arbitration is an arbitration administered by an arbitral institution. The parties may stipulate in the arbitration agreement to refer an arbitral dispute between them for resolution to a particular institution. When party have not named any institution or when they fail to an agreement on the name of any Institution, the Chief Justice instead of choosing an arbitrator may choose an institute and the said institute shall refer the matter to one or more arbitrator from their panel. The Indian institutions include the Indian Council of Arbitration and the International Centre for Alternative Dispute Resolution. International institutions include the International Court of Arbitration, the London Court of International Arbitration and the American Arbitration Association. All these institutions have rules expressly formulated for conducting arbitration. These rules are formulated on the basis of experience and hence, they address all possible situations that may arise in the course of arbitration. The following advantages accrue in the case of institutional arbitration in comparison with *ad hoc* arbitration:

(1) In *ad hoc* arbitration, procedures will have to be agreed to by the parties and the arbitrator. This needs co-operation between the parties. When a dispute is in existence, it is difficult to expect such co-operation. In institutional arbitration, the rules are already there. There is no need to worry about formulating rules or spend time on making rules.

(2) In *ad hoc* arbitration, infrastructure facilities for conducting arbitration is a problem, so there is temptation to hire facilities of expensive hotels. In the process, arbitration costs increase. Getting trained staff is difficult. Library facilities are another problem. In institutional arbitration, the arbitral institution will have infrastructure facilities for conduct of arbitration; they will have trained secretarial and administrative staff. There will also be library facilities. There will be professionalism in conducting arbitration. The costs of arbitration also are cheaper in institutional arbitration.

(3) In institutional arbitration, the institution will maintain a panel of arbitrators along with their profiles. The parties can choose from the panel. It also provides for specialised arbitrators. While in *ad hoc* arbitration, these advantages are not available.

(4) In institutional arbitration, many arbitral institutions have an experienced committee to scrutinise the arbitral awards. Before the award is finalised and given to the parties, it is scrutinised by the experienced panel. So the possibility of the court setting aside the award is minimum. This facility is not available in *ad hoc* arbitration. Hence, there is higher risk of court interference.

(5) In institutional arbitration, the arbitrator's fee is fixed by the arbitral institution. The parties know beforehand what the cost of arbitration will be. In *ad hoc* arbitration, the arbitrator's fee is negotiated and agreed to. The Indian experience shows that it is quite expensive.

(6) In institutional arbitration, the arbitrators are governed by the rules of the institution and they may be removed from the panel for not conducting the arbitration properly, whereas in *ad hoc* arbitration, there is no such fear.

(7) In case, for any reason, the arbitrator becomes incapable of continuing as arbitrator in institutional arbitration, it will not take much time to find substitutes. When a substitute is found, the procedure for arbitration remains the same. The proceedings can continue from where they were stopped, whereas these facilities are not available in *ad hoc* arbitration.

(8) In institutional arbitration, as the secretarial and administrative staff is subject to the discipline of the institution, it is easy to maintain confidentiality of the proceedings. In *ad hoc* arbitration, it is difficult to expect professionalism from the secretarial staff. Institutional arbitration is an arbitration administered by an arbitral institution. The parties may stipulate in the arbitration agreement to refer an arbitral dispute between them for resolution to a particular institution. The Indian institutions include the Indian Council of Arbitration and the International Centre for Alternative Dispute Resolution. International institutions include the International Court of Arbitration, the London Court of International Arbitration and the American Arbitration Association. All these institutions have rules expressly formulated for conducting arbitration. These rules are formulated on the basis of experience and hence, they address all possible situations that may arise in the course of arbitration.

(ix) Institutions of international repute not only provide a time and cost effective mechanism but also enable the parties to resolve their disputes in a cordial and informal atmosphere of arbitration and continue their relationship even after such disputes have arisen. It has, therefore, become imperative to amend the law so as to bring it in conformity with the desired objectives underlying the statute. This proposal also fully accords with the recommendations made by the Parliamentary Committee.

(x) It is, therefore, proposed that section 11 of the Arbitration and Conciliation Act, 1996 may be amended to the limited extent as follows:

(a) In sub-section (4) in clause (b) for the words, "by the Chief Justice or any person or institution designated by him" the words "by the High Court or any person or institution designated by it" shall be substituted.

(b) In sub-section (5) for the words, "by the Chief Justice or any person or institution designated by him" the words "by the High Court or any person or institution designated by it" shall be substituted.

(c) In sub-section (6) for the words, "by the Chief Justice or any person or institution designated by him" the words "by the High Court or any person or institution designated by it" shall be substituted.

(d) For sub-section (7), following sub-section shall be substituted, namely:—

(e) "A decision on a matter entrusted by sub-section (4) or sub-section (5) or sub-section (6) to the High Court or the person or institution designated by it shall be final and no appeal including a letter patent appeal shall lie against such decision."

(f) In sub-section (8) for the words, "by the Chief Justice or any person or institution designated by him" the words "by the High Court or any person or institution designated by it" shall be substituted.

(g) In sub-section (9) for the words, "the Chief Justice of India or any person or institution designated by him" the words "the Supreme Court or any person or institution designated by it" shall be substituted.

(h) In sub-section (10) for the words, "The Chief Justice", the words, "High Court" shall be substituted.

(i) In sub-section (11), for the words, "the Chief Justice of different High Courts or their designates, the Chief Justice or his designate to whom the request has been first made under the relevant sub-section shall alone be", the words, "different High Courts or their designates, the High Court or its designate to which the request has been first made under the relevant sub-section shall alone be" shall be substituted.

(j) For sub-section (12) following sub-section shall be substituted, namely:—

"12(a) Where the matters referred to in sub-sections (4), (5), (6), (7), (8) and (10) arise in an international commercial arbitration, the reference to "High Court" in those sub-sections shall be construed as a reference to the "Supreme Court".

'(b) Where the matters referred to in sub-sections (4), (5), (6), (7), (8) and (10) arise in any other arbitration, the reference to "High Court" in those sub-sections shall be construed as a reference to the "High Court" within whose local limits the principal civil court referred in clause (e) of sub-section (1) of section 2 is situate and, where the High Court itself is the Court referred to in that clause, to that High Court.'

(l) After sub-section (12), following sub-sections shall be inserted, namely:—

"(13) Notwithstanding anything contained in the foregoing provisions in this sections, where an application under this section is made to the Supreme Court, or High Court as the case may be, for appointment of arbitrator in respect of 'Commercial Dispute of specified value', the Supreme Court or the High Court or their designate, as the case may be, shall authorise any arbitration institution to make appointment for the arbitrator.

Explanation.—For the purpose the of this sub-section, expression 'Commercial Dispute" and "specified value" shall have same meaning assigned to them in the Commercial Division of High Court Act, 2009."

(14) An application made under this section for appointment of arbitrator shall be disposed of by the Supreme Court or the High Court or their designate, as the case may be, as expeditiously as possible, and endeavour shall be made to dispose of the matter within sixty days from the date of service of notice on the opposite party."

(C) Amendment in section 12

(i) Section 12 deals with grounds of challenge to the appointment of an arbitrator while section 13 deals with the challenge procedure. Section 12(1) provides that a person who is approached in connection with his possible appointment as an arbitrator, he shall disclose in writing "any circumstances likely to give rise to justifiable doubts as to his independence or impartiality". Sub-section (2) of section 12 lays this responsibility on the arbitrator even during the course of arbitration proceedings. Sub-section (3) of section 12 enables a party to challenge the arbitrator only if (a) circumstances exist that give rise to justifiable doubts as to his independence or impartiality, or (b) he does not possess the qualifications agreed to by the parties. Sub-section (4) refers to one's own appointed arbitrator and he can be challenged only for reasons of which he becomes aware after the appointment is made.

(ii) Section 12 reads as follows:

> "12. *Grounds for challenge.*—(1) When a person is approached in connection with his possible appointment as an arbitrator, he shall disclose in writing any circumstances likely to give rise to justifiable doubts as to his independence or impartiality.
>
> (2) An arbitrator, from the time of his appointment and throughout the arbitral proceedings, shall, without delay, disclose to the parties in writing any circumstances referred to in sub-section (1) unless they have already been informed of them by him."
>
> (3) An arbitrator may be challenged only if—
>
> (a) circumstances exist that give rise to justifiable doubts as to his independence or impartiality, or
>
> (b) he does not possess the qualifications agreed to by the parties.
>
> (4) A party may challenge an arbitrator appointed by him, or in whose appointment he has participated, only for reason of which he becomes aware after the appointment has been made."

(iii) So far as section 12(1) is concerned, it is said that the "circumstances" which the arbitrator is to disclose are those which he considers relevant so as to raise a justifiable doubt as to his independence or impartiality. After all, the circumstances are mostly within his personal knowledge and unless there is an obligation to disclose all relevant facts, without limiting them to those which, in his view, can raise justifiable doubts, there is likelihood of an unfair adjudication.

(iv) The earlier ICC rules required the arbitrator to disclose:

> "Whether there exists any past or present relationship, direct or indirect, with any of the parties or any of their counsel, whether financial, professional, social or other kind."

Business or professional relationship or connection with subject-matter of arbitration or its outcome or prior connection with some dispute have been treated as important matter to be disclosed by the arbitrators. It is a matter of propriety of Arbitrator. International Bar Association has approved guidelines on conflict of interest in International Arbitration. Copy of these guidelines are annexed as Annexure-VI. The Law Commission in its 176th Report recommended substitution of section 12(1) as follows:

> "(1) When a person is approached in connection with his possible appointment as an arbitrator, he shall disclose in writing any circumstances, such as the existence of any past or present relationship, either direct or indirect, with any of the parties or any of their counsel, whether financial, business, professional, social or other kind or in relation to the subject-matter in dispute, which are likely to give rise to justifiable doubts as to his independence or impartiality" justifiable doubts as to his independence or impartiality." In view of this it is proposed to empower the Central Government to prescribe by rules, guidelines on conflict of interest on the lines of IBA guidelines."

Sub-section (1) of section 12 is proposed to be substituted as following, namely:—

"(1) When a person is approached in connection with his possible appointment as an arbitrator, he shall disclose in writing any circumstances—

(i) such as the existence of any past or present relationship, either direct or indirect, with any of the parties or any of their counsel, whether financial, business, professional, social or other kind or in relation to the subject-matter in dispute, which are likely to give rise to justifiable doubts as to his independence or impartiality; and

(ii) such other circumstances as may be provided in the rules made by the Central Government in this behalf."

(D) Amendment in section 28

Section 28 deals with rules applicable to substance of the dispute. It reads as follows:

"28. *Rules applicable to substance of dispute.*—(1) Where the place of arbitration is situated in India,—

(a) in an arbitration other than an international commercial arbitration, the Arbitral Tribunal shall decide the dispute submitted to arbitration in accordance with the substantive law for the time being in force in India;

(b) in international commercial arbitration,—

(i) the Arbitral Tribunal shall decide the dispute in accordance with the rules of law designated by the parties as applicable to the substance of the dispute;

(ii) any designation by the parties of the law or legal system of a given country shall be construed, unless otherwise expressed, as directly referring to the substantive law of that country and not to its conflict of laws and rules;

(iii) failing any designation of the law under sub-clause (ii) by the parties, the Arbitral Tribunal shall apply the rules of law it considers to be appropriate given all the circumstances surrounding the dispute.

(2) The Arbitral Tribunal shall decide *ex æquo et bono* or as *amiable compositeur* only if the parties have expressly authorised it to do so.

(3) In all cases, the Arbitral Tribunal shall decide in accordance with the terms of the contract and shall take into account the usages of the trade applicable to the transaction."

Supreme Court in *Oil & Natural Gas Corpn. Ltd.* v. *SAW Pipes Ltd.*, (2003) 5 SCC 705: AIR 2003 SC 2629: 2003 AIR SCW 3041: 2003 (2) Arb LR 5: JT 2003 (4) SC 171: (2003) 4 SCALE 92: 2003 (3) Supreme 449, considered a question whether the award could be set-aside, if the Arbitral Tribunal has not followed the mandatory procedure prescribed under sections 28, which affects the rights of the parties. Under sub-section (1)(a) of section 28 there is a mandate to the Arbitral Tribunal to decide the dispute in accordance with the substantive law for the time being in force in India. Admittedly, substantive law would include the Indian Contract Act, the Transfer of Property Act and other such laws in force. Suppose, if the award is passed in violation of the provisions of the Transfer of Property Act or in violation of the Indian Contract Act, the question would be—whether such award could be set-aside.

Similarly, under sub-section (3), the Arbitral Tribunal is directed to decide the dispute in accordance with the terms of the contract and also after taking into account the usage of the trade applicable to the transaction. If the Arbitral Tribunal ignores the terms of the contract or usage of the trade applicable to the transaction, whether the said award could be interfered. Supreme Court opined that reading section 34 conjointly with other provisions of the Act, it appears that the legislative intent could not be that if the award is in contravention of the provisions of the Act, still, however, it couldn't be set-aside by the court. If it is held that such award could not be interfered, it would be contrary to the basic concept of justice. If the Arbitral Tribunal has not followed the mandatory procedure prescribed under the Act, it would mean that it has acted beyond its jurisdiction and thereby the award would be patently illegal which could be set-aside under section 34. The Supreme Court finally held that if the award is contrary to the substantive provisions of law or the provisions of the Act or against the terms of the contract, it would be patently illegal, which could be interfered under section 34.

It may be pointed out that European Convention on Commercial, Arbitration that entered into force on April 21, 1961, in article VII it is stated that, "the arbitrators shall into account of the terms of the contract and trade usages".

In order to overcome the situation arises due to Supreme Court decision in *ONGC* case, it is proposed to substitute sub-section (3) of section 28 as follows:—

> "(3) In all cases, the arbitral tribunal shall take into account the terms of the contract and trade usage applicable to the transaction."

(E) Amendment in section 31(7)(b) regarding rate of interest

There are three stages of grant of interest in the arbitral proceedings under the Act—(i) pre-reference; (ii) *pendent lite* and (iii) post award. Clause (a) of sub-section (7) of section 31 empowers the arbitral tribunal to include in the sum for which award is made interest at such rate as it deems reasonable on the whole or any part of the money, for whole or any part of the period between the date on which the cause arose and the date on which award is made, provided (a) there is no agreement between the parties prohibiting the award of such interest by the arbitral tribunal; and (b) the arbitral award is for the payment of money. As provided in clause (b) of sub-section (7) of section 31, unless the arbitral award otherwise directs, the rate of interest shall be 18 per cent. per annum from the date of award to the date of payment. This is a salutary provision in the statute which is intended to deter parties from raising frivolous disputes by putting them on notice that interest on the amount directed to be paid is payable.

However, the interest at the rate of 18 per cent. per annum in the present economic scenario appears to be too harsh. It would be reasonable to prescribe rate of interest 1 per cent. higher than current rate of interest rate fixed by the Reserve Bank of India. Therefore, it is proposed to substitute clause (b) of sub-section (7) of section 31 as follows:—

> '(b) A sum directed to be paid by arbitral award shall carry interest at the rate of one per cent. higher then the current rate of interest from the date of award to the date of payment.
>
> *Explanation.*—The expression "Current rate of interest" shall have same meaning as assigned to it under clause (b) of section 2 of the Interest Act, 1978.'

(F) Amendment in section 34 for providing meaning of "public policy of India" and for harmonising it with sections 13 and 16

Public Policy

(i) As per existing section 34(2)(b)(ii) an arbitral award may be set aside by the Court if the arbitral award is in conflict with the public policy of India, section 34 provides that an arbitral award may be set-aside by a court on certain grounds specified therein. The grounds mentioned in clause (a) to sub-section (2) of section 34 entitles the court to set-aside an award only if the parties seeking such relief furnishes proof as regards the existence of the grounds mentioned therein. The grounds are: (1) incapacity of a party; (2) arbitration agreement being not valid; (3) the party making the application not being given proper notice of appointment of arbitrator or of the proceedings or otherwise unable to present his case; (4) the arbitral award dealing with the dispute not falling within the terms of submission to arbitration; and (5) composition of the tribunal or the arbitral procedure being not in accordance with the agreement of the parties.

(ii) Clause (b) of sub-section (2) of section 34 mentions two grounds which are, however, left to be found out by the court itself. The grounds are: (1) the subject-matter of the dispute not capable of settlement by arbitration that is to say, the disputes are not arbitrable; and (2) that the award is in conflict with the public policy of India. All these ground are common to both domestic as well as international arbitral awards.

(iii) The Supreme Court in the case of *Oil & Natural Gas Corpn. Ltd.* v. *SAW Pipes Ltd.*, (2003) 5 SCC 705: AIR 2003 SC 2629: 2003 AIR SCW 3041: 2003 (2) Arb LR 5: JT 2003 (4) SC 171: (2003) 4 SCALE 92: 2003 (3) Supreme 449 examined the scope and ambit of jurisdiction of the Court under section 34 of the Act. It was held that if the award is (a) contrary to the substantive provision of law, or (b) the provisions of the Act, or (c) against the terms of the contract, it would be patently illegal which could be interfered under section 34. Supreme Court further held that phrase "public policy of India" used in section 34 is required to be given a wider meaning and stated that the concept of public policy connotes some matter which concerns public good and the public interest. The award which is on face of it, patently in violation of statutory provisions cannot be said to be in public interest.

(iv) In *Oil & Natural Gas Corpn. Ltd.* v. *SAW Pipes Ltd.*. reiterating several principles of construction of contract and referring to the contractual provisions which were the subject-matter of the arbitral award, the court ruled that "in the facts of the case, it cannot be disputed that if contractual term, as it is, is to be taken into consideration, the award is, on the face of it, erroneous and in violation of the terms of the contract and thereby it violates section 28(3) of the Act". Culling out the ratio from the decisions rendered under the 1940 Act, the court held:

> "It is true that if the Arbitral Tribunal has committed mere error of fact or law in reaching its conclusion on the disputed question submitted to it for adjudication then the court would have no jurisdiction to interfere with the award. But, this would depend upon reference made to the arbitrator: (a) if there is a general reference for deciding the contractual dispute between the parties and if the award is based on erroneous legal proposition, the court could interfere; (b) it is also settled law that in a case of reasoned award, the court can set-aside the same if it is, on the face of it, erroneous on the proposition of law or its application; (c) if a specific question of law is submitted to the arbitrator, erroneous decision in point of law does not make the award bad, so as to permit its being set-aside, unless the court is satisfied that the arbitrator had proceeded illegally".

(v) The decision in *ONGC* case, though rendered by a Bench of two Hon'ble Judges, has far-reaching consequences. *Firstly*, the decision construes the new Act, as, in its entirety (sections 2 to 43), laying down only rules of procedures (*vide* para 8 of the judgment). It rules that "power and procedure are synonymous" and that "there is no distinction between jurisdiction/power and the procedure". Referring to sections 24, 28 and 31 of the Act and construing the words "arbitral procedure" in section 34(2)(v) (and after observing that all the provisions appearing in Part I of the Act lay down arbitral procedure) it concludes that "the jurisdiction or the power of the arbitral tribunal is prescribed under the Act and if the award is *de hors* the said provisions, it would be, on the face of it, illegal".

(vi) Construing the phrase "public policy of India" appearing in section 34(2)(b)(ii), the court held that in a case where the validity of the award is challenged on the ground of being opposed to "public policy of India", an wider meaning ought to be given to the said phrase so that "patently illegal awards" could be set-aside. The court distinguished the earlier decision in *Renu Sagar* case on the ground that in the said case the phrase "public policy of India" appearing in section 7(1)(b)(ii) of the Foreign Awards (Recognition and Enforcement) Act, 1961 was construed which necessarily related to enforcement of foreign award after it became final. Though the court accedes that "it is for the Parliament to provide for limited or wider jurisdiction of the court in case where award is challenged", it still holds that, in its view, a wider meaning is required to be given to the phrase "public policy of India" so as to "prevent frustration of legislation and justice". Stating the reasons in support of its view the court held that "giving limited jurisdiction to the court for having finality to the award and resolving the dispute by speedier method would be much more frustrated by permitting patently illegal award to operate. Patently illegal award is required to be set at naught, otherwise it would promote injustice".

(vii) This decision had been the subject-matter of public debate and criticism in various fora. The Law Commission of India also suggested an amendment to the Act by insertion of *Explanation II* to section 34 of the Act.

Accordingly in order to nullify the effect of above decision of the Supreme Court, it is proposed that the existing *Explanation* in section 34 be renumbered as *Explanation 1* and after that *Explanation* as so renumbered the following *Explanation* shall be inserted.

> "*Explanation II.*—For the purposes of this section "an award is in conflict with the public policy of India" only in the following circumstances, namely:—
>
> When the award is contrary to the—
>
> (i) fundamental policy of India; or
>
> (ii) interests of India; or
>
> (iii) justice or morality."

Harmonising section 34 with sections 13 and 16—

It may be pointed out that section 13 deals with the procedure for challenging an arbitrator. Sub-section (1) recognises the freedom of the parties to agree on a procedure for challenging an arbitrator. Sub-section (2) provides a supplementary procedure for challenging an arbitrator. The reasons for such a challenge are exhaustively laid down in section 12. As provided in sub-section (3), unless the arbitrator challenged under sub-section (2) withdraws from office or the other party agrees to the challenge, the arbitral tribunal shall decide on challenge. Sub-section (4) provides that if a challenge under any procedure agreed upon by the parties or under procedure under sub-section (2) is not successful, the arbitral tribunal shall continue the arbitral proceedings and make an arbitral award. However, as provided in sub-section (5) the party which challenges the appointment of the arbitrator may file an application for setting aside such an arbitral award in accordance with section 34. Hence, until the arbitral award is made after the challenge to the appointment of arbitrator being unsuccessful, the party challenging the appointment of arbitrator cannot make any application to the Court in connection with challenge to the appointment of the arbitrator nor the court can entertain any such application. However in section 34 there is no specific mention of such a ground for setting-aside an arbitral award.

Similarly as provided in section 16, the arbitral tribunal may rule on its own jurisdiction. A plea that the arbitral tribunal does not have jurisdiction can be raised as per sub-section (2) and a plea that the arbitral tribunal is exceeding the scope of its authority can be raised in terms of sub-section (3). As provided in sub-section (5), the arbitral tribunal can decide on these pleas and where the tribunal takes a decision rejecting the plea, continue with the arbitral proceedings and make an arbitral award. However, as per sub-section (6) a party aggrieved by such an arbitral award may make an application for setting-aside such an arbitral award in accordance with section 34. An appeal lies under section 37 against the order of the arbitral tribunal accepting the plea under sub-section (2) and (3) of section 16. However, no appeal is provided against an order rejecting such plea. The only right that the petitioner has in such a case is to challenge the award under section 34 after it is made.

The Law Commission in 176th Report considered the question whether it was desirable to provide for an appeal under section 37 to court against decision of the arbitral tribunal rejecting the plea of bias or disqualification under section 13. After due deliberation, the Law Commission was of the view that there should not be an immediate right of appeal under section 37 against the decision of the tribunal rejecting the plea of bias or disqualification under section 13.

The Law Commission in its 176th Report also considered the request from certain quarters for a right of appeal to the Court against an order of the arbitral tribunal rejecting the objections in regard to the existence or validity of the arbitration agreement under sub-sections (2) and (3) of section 16.

The Law Commission rejected the request for providing appeal against an order refusing a plea of want of jurisdiction.

Section 34 does not enable the parties to question the decision of the arbitral tribunal made under section 13(2) rejecting a plea of bias or to question the decision of the said tribunal made under section 16(2) or (3) rejecting a plea of want of jurisdiction on the part of the arbitral tribunal. Though the existence of these remedies was referred to in sections 13(5) and 16(6), these remedies were not included in section 34 and further the use of the word 'only' in section 34(1) contradicted what was stated in sections 13 and 16. Therefore, the Law Commission, recommended insertion of a clarification in section 34 by way of an *explanation* that an applicant, while seeking to set-aside the award, can attack the interlocutory order of the arbitral tribunal rejecting a plea of want of jurisdiction, as permitted by section 16(6).

Instead of insertion of another *Explanation* as proposed by the Law Commission, it would be appropriate to have a substantive provision in section 34 for providing separate ground for challenging the arbitral award. Therefore, it is proposed to add following sub-clause (iii) in clause (b) of sub-section (2) of section 34—

> "(iii) the application contains a plea questioning the decision of the arbitral tribunal rejecting—
>
> (a) a challenge made by the applicant under sub-section (2) of section 13; or
>
> (b) a plea made under sub-section (2) or sub-section (3) of section 16;".

(G) Insertion of new section 34A

Law Commission while suggesting amendment in section 34 also recommended that in case of domestic arbitration, new ground for challenges, *viz.*, mistake appearing on face of award may be made available. Accordingly, it recommended for inserting a new section 34A.

It is desirable to provide some recourse to a party aggrieved by a patent and serious illegality in the award which has caused substantial injustice and irreparable harm to the applicant. It is a delicate task to strike a balance between two equally important but conflicting considerations, namely giving finality to the arbitral award and redressing substantial injustice caused by some patent and serious illegality in the award. As no tribunal is infallible, it is desirable to provide some recourse to a party who has suffered substantial injustice due to patent and serious illegality committed by the arbitral tribunal. It is true that whatever expression is used in the grounds of recourse to take care of such situation, the possibility of abuse thereof by a disgruntled party cannot be ruled out. However, one cannot lose sight of the ground realties.

There is no denying the fact that the overall scenario in the field of arbitration is not as ideal as it should be. As pointed by Lord Mustill, arbitration has become a business, often involving very large sums, and bringing in its train substantial monetary earnings for all concerned and there has been a concurrent decline in the standards of at least some of those who take part in it. It is no good wringing hands about this, for it is a fact to be faced, and part of facing is to recognise that some means must be found of protecting this voluntary process from those who will not act as they have agreed or as is expected of them. Here lies the need for providing some ground of recourse in case of patent and serious illegality causing substantial injustice.

In this context it may be necessary to refer to the case of *Sikkim Subba Associates* v. *State of Sikkim*, (2001) 5 SCC 629: AIR 2001 SC 2062: 2001 AIR SCW 1868: 2001 (2) Arb LR 17: JT 2001 (5) SC 186: (2001) 3 SCALE 721, wherein the arbitrator awarded an astronomical sum as damages without any basis or proof of such damages as required by law in total disregard to the basic and fundamental principles, is a glaring example of misuse of power by the arbitrator and the need for some recourse at least in such extreme cases. In that case, the arbitrator made an award determining a sum of over Rs. 33 crores with proportionate costs and future interest at the rate of 12 per cent p.a. on the said amount as the amount payable by the State of Sikkim to the organising agents of the lottery. The Supreme Court set-aside the award on the ground of gross illegality. The grave nature of the illegality in the award in that case is evident from the following observations of the Supreme Court:

> "The arbitrator who is obliged to apply law and adjudicate claims according to law, is found to have thrown to the winds all such basic and fundamental principles and chosen to award an astronomical sum as damages without any basis or concrete proof of such damages, as required in law".
>
> * * *
>
> "Though the entire award bristles with numerous infirmities and errors of very serious nature undermining the very credibility and objectivity of the reasoning as well as the ultimate conclusions arrived at by the arbitrator, it would suffice to point out a few of them with necessary and relevant materials on record in support thereof to warrant and justify the interference of this Court with the award allowing damages of such a fabulous sum, as a windfall in favour of the appellants, more as a premium for their own defaults and breaches."
>
> * * *
>
> "The manner in which the arbitrator has chosen to arrive at the quantum of damages alleged to have been sustained by the appellants not only demonstrates perversity of approach, but *per se* proves flagrant violation of the principles of law governing the very award of damages. The principles enshrined in section 54 in adjudicating the question of breach and section 73 of the Contract Act incorporating the principles for the determination of the damages, are found to have been observed more in their breach."

It is therefore proposed that an additional ground of challenge, namely, "patent and serious illegality, which has caused or is likely to cause substantial injustice to the applicant" may be added as a ground for recourse in case of purely domestic awards.

Accordingly, it is proposed to insert a new section 34A as suggested by the Law Commission with some changes:

> "*34A. Application for setting aside arbitral award on additional ground of patent and serious illegality.*—(1) Recourse to a Court against an arbitral award made in an arbitration other than an international commercial arbitration, can also be made by a party under sub-section (1) of section 34 on the additional ground that there is a patent and serious illegality, which has caused or is likely to cause substantial injustice to the applicant.
>
> (2) Where the ground referred to in sub-section (1) is invoked in an application filed under sub-section (1) of section 34, while considering such ground, the Court must be satisfied that the illegality identified by the applicant is patent and serious and has caused or is likely to cause substantial injustice to the applicant."

(H) Substitution of section 36

Existing section 36 deals with enforcement of an arbitral award. It reads:

> "*36. Enforcement.*—Where the time for making an application to set-aside the, arbitral award under section 34 has expired or such application having been made, it has been refused, the award shall be enforced under the Code of Civil Procedure, 1908 (5 of 1908) in the same manner as if it were a decree of the Court."

Section 36, as it stands now, provides that the enforcement of the award will come to a stop upon the filing of an application under sub-section (1) of section 34 to set-aside the award to a stop upon the filing of an application under sub-section (1) of section 34 to set-aside the award.

The Law Commission in their Report had observed that parties are filing applications to set-aside the award even though there is no substance whatsoever in such applications and, to put a stop to this practice, proposed the amendment of section 36 by deleting the words which say that the award will not be enforced once an application is filed under sub-section (1) of section 34.

To give effect to the above recommendation of the Law Commission, the Amendment Bill of 2003 sought to substitute the existing section 36. That was a very good provision. It will have a salutary effect on the expeditious execution of the awards.

It provided that an award will be enforceable after the period fixed for filing applications under section 34 has expired, unless the court stays its enforcement. The court is vested with powers to refuse stay or grant stay subject to conditions. While granting stay, the court can impose conditions, keeping the scope of interference in applications under sub-section (1) of section 34 in mind. The manner of imposing conditions and interim measures has also been specified. Therefore, it is proposed to substitute section 36 as follows:

> "*36. Enforcement of award.*—(1) Where the time for making an application to set-aside the arbitral award under sub-section (1) of section 34 has expired, then, subject to the provisions of sub-sections (2) to (4), the award shall be enforced under the Code of Civil Procedure, 1908 in the same manner as if it were a decree of the Court.
>
> (2) Where an application is filed in the Court under sub-section (1) of section 34 to set-aside an arbitral award, the filing of such an application shall not

by itself operate as a stay of the award unless, upon a separate application made for that purpose, the Court grants stay of the operation of the award in accordance with the provisions of sub-section (3).

(3) Upon filing of the separate application under sub-section (2) for stay of the operation of the award, the Court may, subject to such conditions as it may deem fit to impose, grant stay of the operation of the arbitral award for reasons in brief to be recorded in writing:

Provided that the Court shall, while considering the grant of stay, keep in mind the grounds for setting-aside the award.

(4) The power to impose conditions referred to in sub-section (3) includes the power to grant interim measures not only against the parties to the award or in respect of the property which is the subject-matter of the award but also to issue *ad interim* measures against third parties or in respect of property which is not the subject-matter of the award, insofar as it is necessary to protect the interests of the party in whose favour the award is passed.

(5) The *ad interim* measures granted under sub-section (4) may be confirmed, modified, or vacated, as the case may be, by the Court subject to such conditions, if any, as it may, after hearing the affected parties, deem fit."

(I) Arbitration relates to Commercial Disputes of specified value

In the Amendment Bill of 2003 it was proposed to insert a new Chapter IXA, comprising sections 37A to 37F, to provide that every High Court shall, constitute an Arbitration Division in the High Court to deal, irrespective of pecuniary value, with the applications under sub-section (1) of section 34 to set-aside awards under the principal Act, new and pending, and enforcement of awards under the principal Act, new and pending.

The object of that amendment was to avoid the present procedure at two levels, one in the subordinate courts (or original side of High Court) and another by way of appeal to or in he High Court. Now, by a separate law it is proposed to constitute Commercial Division in the High Court. In the said law it is also proposed that the said Commercial Division will also entertain applications under sections 34 and 36 and appeals under section 37 of the Arbitration and Conciliation Act, 1996 where the arbitration relates to "Commercial Disputes" of specified value. For this purpose, consequential amendment for amending definition of "Court" in section 2 of the Arbitration Act is also being amended. As the application under section 34 would be filed before the Commercial Division of the High Court, appeal against order passed by the Commercial Division under section 37 would lie before the Supreme Court. For this purpose, the Lok Sabha has passed the Commercial Division of High Courts Bill, 2009. Copy of the Bill is annexed as Annexure-VII.

(J) Suggestion for Insertion of provision for implied arbitration agreement in commercial contract of high consideration value—

We have received a suggestion from certain quarters that after the judgment delivered by Seven-Judge Bench of Supreme Court in the case of *S.B.P. Company* v. *Patel Engineering Ltd.*, (2005) 8 SCC 618, a situation has arisen to the effect that in the matter of appointment of arbitrator, the role of arbitration institution has become almost nil. As held by the Supreme Court in aforesaid case, the Chief Justice or the designated Judge would be entitled to seek only the opinion of an institution in the matter of nominating an arbitrator if need arises, but the order appointing arbitrator could only be that of the Chief Justice or the designated Judge. Supreme Court has further held that before appointing an arbitrator the Chief Justice or the designated Judge will have a right to decide certain preliminary issues including the issue of existence of a valid arbitration agreement.

Standing Committee of the Parliament in its report on the Arbitration and Conciliation (Amendment) Bill, 2003 has recommended to promote institutional arbitration.

In order to avoid raising of an issue of existence of a valid arbitration agreement and also to promote institutional arbitration, it has been suggested by certain persons that in respect of commercial contract of high threshold value, there should be a deemed arbitration clause in every such contract, unless the parties expressly and in writing agree otherwise. To achieve this object, insertion of following clause in the Arbitration and Conciliation Act, 1996 has been suggested:

(i) Unless parties expressly and in writing agree otherwise, every commercial contract with a consideration of specified value (Rs. 5 crore or more) shall deemed to have in writing specified arbitration agreement.

(ii) Specified Arbitration Agreement as referred in clause (i) shall contain following clause:

"All disputes except (here specify the excepted disputes, if any) arising out of or in connection with the present contract shall be finally settled under the rules of Arbitration of (here specify the name of the approved arbitral institution) by one or more of the arbitrators appointed in accordance with the said rules."

(iii) Any arbitration agreement that differs from the said clause will stand modified along the lines of the specified arbitration agreement.

SUBJECT INDEX

•••